THE DYNAMICS OF
INDUSTRIAL CLUSTERING

THE DYNAMICS
OF INDUSTRIAL
CLUSTERING

*International Comparisons in Computing
and Biotechnology*

Edited by

G. M. PETER SWANN, MARTHA PREVEZER,
AND DAVID STOUT

OXFORD UNIVERSITY PRESS
1998

338
D997

Oxford University Press, Great Clarendon Street, Oxford OX2 6DP
Oxford New York
Athens Auckland Bangkok Bogota Bombay
Buenos Aires Calcutta Cape Town Dar es Salaam
Delhi Florence Hong Hong Istanbul Karachi
Kuala Lumpur Madras Madrid Melbourne
Mexico City Nairobi Paris Singapore
Taipei Tokyo Toronto Warsaw
and associated companies in
Berlin Ibadan

Oxford is a trade mark of Oxford University Press

Published in the United States
by Oxford University Press Inc., New York

ſl

British Library Cataloguing in Publication Data
Data available

Library of Congress Cataloging in Publication Data
The dynamics of industrial clustering: international comparisons in
computing and biotechnology / edited by G. M. Peter Swann, Martha
Prevezer, and David Stout
p. cm.
Includes bibliographical references and index.
1. High technology industries—Location—Great Britain. 2. High
technology industries—Location—United States. 3. Computer
industry—location—Great Britain. 4. Computer industry—Location—
United States. 5. Biotechnology industries—Location—Great
Britain. 6. Biotechnology industries—Location—United States.
I. Swann, G. M. P. II. Prevezer, Martha. III. Stout, David.
HC260.H53D96 1998
338.'—DC21   97-27476
                                                        CIP

ISBN 0–19–828959–6

1 3 5 7 9 10 8 6 4 2

Typeset by Best-set Typesetter Ltd., Hong Kong
Printed in Great Britain
on acid-free paper by
Biddles Ltd, Guildford & King's Lynn

Preface and Acknowledgements

THE aim of this book is to develop a new perspective on the dynamics of industrial clustering. Of course, the theme of industrial clustering is not new, and indeed it has been the object of attention from a wide variety of social scientists for much of this century. However, it has in the last five years attracted renewed attention from economists, who have become aware of its central importance in industrial economics—and indeed in economics more generally. We consider that some recent developments in the economic analysis of path dependence offer some exciting new insights into the dynamics of the clustering process.

This book has been written for the general audience. The main aim is to work through the broad implications of the clustering analysis developed here. While some quite technical models underline much of our argument, these are not discussed in detail in the text. Some details are presented in appendices, while others are developed in other papers.

The book may at times seem more assertive and speculative than is justified by the analysis and empirical results presented here, and perhaps a little light on scholarly detail. We make no apology for that. The book is opening up a strand of analysis which is interesting and suggestive, and has fresh implications for industrial policy. It leaves many unanswered questions, and some of the empirical inquiries need further work. But it is written in the hope that the perspectives presented here are interesting and novel enough to encourage others to invest the time and effort required to measure some of the most important magnitudes here, and thus deepen our understanding of the clustering process.

The book is the work of several researchers currently, or formerly, in the Centre for Business Strategy at London Business School. It could not have been written without the generous financial support of the Gatsby Foundation, to which we express our gratitude. The authors of each chapter have been identified, but we would also like to express our thanks to other CBS colleagues, notably: Saadet Toker for help with the data collection for the UK computing study and the econometric analysis in the US biotechnology study; Chris Walters for invaluable econometric work in the US and UK biotechnology studies; Paul Geroski, for helpful discussions over several parts of the book; and Romano Dyerson and Beverley Aston for discussion about clustering in other industries.

We have benefited from useful comments (in response to this and related work) by Zoltan Acs, Cristiano Antonelli, David Audretsch, Patrick Barwise, Robin Cowan, Felix Fitzroy, Ove Granstrand, Alessandro Lomi, David Mowery, Keith Pavitt, and by participants in the following conferences and seminars: ESRC Industrial Economics Study Group, LBS (May 1993); University of St Andrews (Mar. 1994); Royal Economic Society Conference, Exeter (Mar. 1994); International Telecommunications Society Conference, Sydney (July 1994); Conference of Industry Economics, Canberra (July 1994); Telecommunications Research Workshop: Canberra (July 1994); International J. A. Schumpeter Society Conference, Münster (Aug. 1994); British Academy of Management Conference, Lancaster (Sept. 1994); EUNETICS Conference on Evolutionary Economics of Technological Change, Strasbourg (Oct. 1994); LBS Research Briefing (Nov. 1994); EMOT Conference, Reading (May 1995); Society of Business Economists (June 1995); EARIE, Sophia Antipolis (Sept. 1995); 10e École d'Été Méditerranéenne d'Économie Industrielle, Cargese (Sept. 1995). We would also like to acknowledge helpful comment and discussions from students on the following courses at LBS: Ph.D. Courses in Industrial Organization (1993/4) and Advanced Topics in Economics (1994/5); MBA Elective on Creating Comparative National Advantage (1993/4 and 1994/5). None of these is responsible for any remaining errors.

Contents

Contributors

RUI BAPTISTA was a member of the Centre for Business Strategy, the London Business School. He is now a Visiting Fellow at Carnegie Mellon University, USA.

MARTHA PREVEZER is a Senior Lecturer at South Bank University, London, and was formerly a Research Fellow at the Centre for Business Strategy, the London Business School.

PAUL TEMPLE is a Lecturer at Surrey University and was previously at the Centre for Business Strategy, the London Business School.

SIMON SHOHET is a Research Fellow at the Centre for Business Strategy, the London Business School.

DAVID STOUT was the Director of the Centre for Business Strategy, the London Business School until his retirement in 1997.

G. M. PETER SWANN is Professor of Economics and Management of Innovation at Manchester Business School and PREST, University of Manchester.

1

Introduction

G. M. PETER SWANN AND MARTHA PREVEZER

1.1 WHAT IS A CLUSTER?

This book aims to provide an analysis of the dynamics of industrial clustering in high-technology industries. This analysis is illustrated by reference to the emergence of clusters in the cases of computing and biotechnology, in the USA and the UK. We use the word cluster in both a geographical and technological sense: In what follows, a *cluster* means a large group of firms in related industries at a particular location.

We should emphasize from the outset that our focus is on *high-technology* industry and *dynamics*. Clustering is not exclusively the preserve of high-technology industries, nor is it even a new phenomenon. Clusters are found in a wide variety of traditional industries (textiles in northern Italy, shipbuilding in Glasgow, steel in Pittsburgh, car manufacture in Detroit). Moreover, from the beginning of the industrial revolution powerful clustering was observed—for example in the British cotton industry. And indeed, powerful examples of clustering are found in earlier economies (wool in medieval England, the financial centre in the City of London). Nevertheless, we choose to concentrate on clustering in high-technology industries because some of the most powerful motives for clustering arise in that context. It could also be argued that, in computing, and in the information industries more generally, the motives for clustering are being eroded by the ever increasing power and bandwidth of information and communication networks. But while many observers have taken this viewpoint, clustering still remains a potent force in at least some parts of the computer industry. We suggest in the book why this should be, and why in fact such technological developments may further increase—rather than reduce—the geographical concentration of activity.

The book concentrates upon the *dynamics* of the clustering process because we believe that these dynamics are imperfectly understood in existing analysis. We assert that a cluster has in effect a life cycle, conceptually distinct from but related to the life cycle of the technologies produced at the cluster. This makes the dynamics particularly interesting. The forces that influence the growth and entry of firms in clusters are not simply related to the stage of each technology: they depend also on the stage of the cluster in its own life cycle.

In the conventional analysis of clustering, positive feedback plays a central part. Clusters that are strong in a particular technology will tend to enjoy faster growth and higher entry than other areas. But we argue that this account is incomplete for two important reasons. First, positive feedback does not continue indefinitely. Large clusters start to get congested, which may slow down both growth and particularly entry. New entrants will tend to go elsewhere. Moreover, larger and older clusters will tend to be composed of firms producing the older technologies, and as the technology passes through its life cycle, these older technologies reach their peak earlier than the newer technologies in the newer clusters. Second, the *strength* of a cluster is a multifaceted concept. A particular cluster may be strong in some parts of an industry and not in others. If we are looking at the capacity of a cluster to promote growth and entry, it may depend critically on where this strength lies and what sort of entry we are concerned with. In the book, we develop the concepts of *entry attractor* and *growth promoter*: these describe, respectively, how strength in one sector can attract entry into (promote growth in) another sector. Our results in the computing and biotechnology context suggest that some of these can be reasonably large while others are negligible.

These two properties give a rich range of possible cluster life cycles. Some of these are illustrated in the analysis of the computing industry. In biotechnology, not surprisingly, few clusters seem to have reached maturity. But these features also enable us to pose some interesting questions about longevity in clusters. And, when used in conjunction with a concept of technological convergence, they also provide us with the building blocks to analyse a related topic—the revival of old industrial clusters—though we cannot do justice to this very important topic in the present book.

1.2 A FAMOUS EXAMPLE

To understand what a cluster is, it is easiest to start with an—or perhaps *the*—example. California's Santa Clara Valley (or Silicon Valley as it is often called) is one of the classic examples of how an industrial cluster can emerge rapidly out of nothing.[1] In the 1940s, this was a predominantly agricultural valley, and in the early 1950s it boasted no more than a few fledgling electronics companies (Saxenian 1994: 20). Then a number of well-established companies moved operations to Santa Clara Valley to take advantage of the proximity to aircraft, missile, and aerospace markets. Some large firms also started to locate their R & D laboratories in the newly established Stanford Industrial Park. By the mid-1950s, Santa Clara had become one of the best locations in the country for the formation of new computer and semiconductor companies (Saxenian 1994: 24–5). The wave of entrants during the 1960s into the computer industry in California was followed by a huge surge of entry between 1977 and 1983. Indeed, by 1988 over a third of all computer companies in the USA were located in California (see Chapter 4).

A geographical cluster, then, is a collection of related companies located in a small geographical area, perhaps centred around a strong part of the science base. Firms group together to take advantage of strong demand in the location, a large supply of scientific manpower, and the network of complementary strengths in neighbouring firms. Indeed such a setting makes it possible to create a *network firm*, possibly quite small and with little vertical integration, but which thrives on this rich network by subcontracting. We give a striking example of this in the next section.

In high-technology industries geographical proximity can be vital because in the early stages of the life cycle of a product or

---

[1] Some other interesting case studies of clustering in high technology industry are described in the edited volume by Hall and Markusen (1985), and Dorfman (1985).

technology, use and transfer of *tacit* knowledge is the key to successful development. While codified knowledge can be written down in manuals, blueprints, patents, and the like—and hence transmitted over large distances—tacit knowledge is particularly difficult to transfer, and relies for the most part on informal personal contact, and hence geographical proximity (Pavitt 1987). As Maclean and Rowland (1985: 82) put it, for one semiconductor firm it was vital that manufacturing and design teams were able to meet in the pub after work to discuss progress!

Some would argue, however, that with the growth of international communications networks of ever greater bandwidth, with the growth in international travel, and the globalization of firms, it is no longer necessary for firms to be located close together in order to operate in a network. *Virtual clusters* could start to emerge, involving firms that were geographically separated. This raises some interesting questions about what sort of communications network is required to sustain a *virtual* cluster, but these issues lie beyond the scope of this book.

1.3 EXPLOITING CLUSTERS FOR COMPETITIVE ADVANTAGE

The introduction in 1977 of the Apple II microcomputer was in many ways a landmark for the computer industry. It was not the first microcomputer to be sold, but it was one of the first to give the microcomputer (or PC) industry a serious momentum. Indeed it was largely in response to the success of the Apple II that IBM entered the PC market in 1981 (Langlois 1992). The interest of this case is that Apple were successful even though they enjoyed very little vertical integration at that early stage. The product was designed to be an open system so that it could draw on the large crop of add-on boards, software, and peripherals that started to appear from third party suppliers (Langlois 1992). In the early days Apple depended on external suppliers for many components. Apple saw their business as designing, educating, and marketing, and the hardware production and assembly could be done by subcontractors (Langlois 1992). This strategy succeeded because Apple were well located in Silicon Valley—the major computer industry cluster.

Not only did this *network firm* strategy succeed for Apple, it also became a strategy that IBM chose to emulate in order to enter the PC market. By 1980, IBM had recognized that they would have to break into the market for personal computers. They recognized that their traditional computer divisions would be resistant, and considered that the best way for IBM to enter the market was to set up (in effect) a start-up company, with IBM as the venture capitalist. This start-up company did not depend exclusively on the IBM superstructure but made much use of external capabilities (Langlois 1992). First, fabrication of many components of the actual computer were put up for competitive tender to outside suppliers, and although some IBM divisions won contracts, much of the IBM PC was made externally—at least in the early days. Second, in marketing the PC, this start-up company made use of external retail outlets as well as IBM's own sales agents (Langlois 1992).

In short, not only could the network firm compete effectively against the most vertically integrated structures, but these vertically integrated structures chose to mimic the network firm by using external capabilities.

1.4 THE MAIN FEATURES OF OUR ANALYSIS

It is useful to have a foretaste of the main features of our analysis. These will be developed in more detail in subsequent chapters (especially Chapter 3). First, there is positive feedback from cluster strength to growth and entry, though, as we have just argued, diminishing returns set in as the cluster gets large. Second, there are various effects that make one cluster more attractive as an entry location, which are in the first instance (at least) independent of cluster strength. In terms of our econometric models, these are usually called *fixed effects*, but intuitively speaking they represent such things as climate, infrastructure, cultural capital, and so on. Third, especially in our analysis of biotechnology, the strength of the science base in a particular cluster can play an important role in attracting entry and promoting growth in a cluster.

The character of the analysis we use in the book could be called *path dependent*. That is to say, the evolution of competing clusters may at certain stages be heavily influenced by what would ordinarily be considered minor historical events. Thus, for example, some commentators argue that the success of Santa Clara Valley as an industrial cluster was in no small measure due to the decision of one Stanford University professor (later vice-president) to join Stanford rather than an east-coast university. This decision, it is said, was made on health grounds: the agreeable west-coast climate being preferable to the inclement north-east coast.

As noted above, the concepts of entry attractor and growth promoter play a central role throughout the book. Entry attractors are those aspects of cluster strength that attract new entrants to the cluster, while growth promoters are those that promote growth of incumbent firms. These vary between industries and technologies, between subsectors, and probably over time as well.

The final group of features which play a central role in our analysis are the concepts used to describe the position of a cluster in its life cycle. These are: *critical mass* and *take-off*, *peak entry*, and *saturation*. In analysing entry to computer industry clusters over the life cycle of the cluster, we can identify a *critical mass* at which entry starts to increase (or *take off*) rapidly, a cluster size at which *entry* reaches a *peak*, and a cluster size at which the cluster is *saturated* and entry more or less stops. The rationale and under-pinning for these features of our analysis is set out in more detail in Chapter 3. For now, however, we should focus our attention on one question of overriding importance for our analysis. *Why does geography matter?* Or indeed, *does geography matter?* Why should growth and entry into a particular area be influenced by the strength of the industry in that particular area?

As we shall see in Chapters 2 and 3, the benefits from clustering can be organized into two groups: those that operate on the *demand side* (demand is healthier in a cluster than in isolation), and those that operate on the *supply side* (supply conditions are better in a cluster). One supply-side benefit of clustering has attracted particular attention in the context of high-technology industries. In such industries, it is argued, much of the technological knowl-edge required to produce *state of the art* products is *tacit* rather than *codified*. It is easiest to define tacit knowledge by saying what it is *not*: it is not the sort of knowledge that can be written down in textbooks, manuals, and the like, and then easily assimilated by the reader. This would count as *codified* knowledge. In an era of wide area networks with high bandwidth and near-zero transmission costs, *geography simply does not matter* for the transmission of codified knowledge. Much tacit knowledge, however, is the cumulative output of long periods of learning, specific to a particular production setting, and cannot easily (if at all) be written down in a codified form. Transmission of tacit knowledge is much easier, indeed may only be possible, with face-to-face contact.

So geography clearly does matter for the transmission and sharing of tacit knowledge. And this is one of the important incentives for clustering in high-technology industries—though not, as we said already, the only one. To the extent that tacit knowledge spills over between firms in the same cluster—because of staff mobility and informal contact between employees of different organizations—the firm locating in a cluster is best placed to absorb such spillovers. Of course, if an individual firm chooses to locate its various divisions in the same cluster, then the motivation may be less to do with absorbing spillovers *from other firms* than co-ordinating tacit knowledge transfer *within the firm*.[2]

Some observers have suggested that there is a trend for more and more knowledge to become codified, and hence the importance of geography in location decisions will decline. If this is so, it would suggest a gradual decline in the incentives to cluster—but not necessarily an end to clustering. On the other hand, it seems likely that even if some tacit knowledge becomes codified, there will always be competitive incentives to develop and exploit some new tacit and private knowledge. From this perspective tacit knowledge will always be critical, and so this motive for clustering will always persist. We return to this theme in Chapter 10. Some would take a less extreme line, and simply observe that *over the life cycle of a particular technology*, there is a tendency for some tacit knowledge to become codified, so that it is easier to subcontract a part of the production chain to low-wage settings.

---

[2] We are grateful to Keith Pavitt for this point.

Indeed such trends are commonly observed in the development
of the electronics and computer industries. The implication of this
is that the leading-edge clusters will be the locus for the state
of the art developments, while standard technologies will increasingly be produced in newer, low-cost clusters.

1.5 THE MAIN THESIS

The main thesis in the book is that clusters exhibit a life cycle, not
dissimilar to the product life cycle. Clusters grow because of a
positive feedback mechanism, known technically as *agglomeration
economies*. In the early stages of a new technology, it is not unusual
for new single-technology clusters to emerge, and for these
focused clusters to grow faster than the more diffuse, multi-
technology cluster. But ultimately as clusters grow, and especially
as the technology located in the clusters approaches maturity, the
costs of locating in large mature clusters can start to outweigh
the benefits. Then the most innovative entry activity may start to
shift away from the largest clusters to new dynamic clusters, as
the former start to get congested. (This sequence is well documented in computing.) At this stage, the *diversified* mature cluster
often shows greater capacity to revive itself by attracting entry
into new industries than does the mature *single-technology* cluster.
The single-technology clusters tend to be populated by large
mechanistic firms who generate relatively few spillovers, and
hence do not attract entry. So there appears to be an important
trade-off here: specialized clusters grow fastest in the formative
stages of a new industry; diversified clusters, however, tend to
survive longer.

There are important policy issues here. In designing the membership of a science park, for example, how diversified should the
members be? Ideal members should generate positive spillovers,
but these should also be the sorts of spillovers that would be
beneficial to current incumbents or prospective entrants. Moreover, this observation suggests that we need to examine carefully
the cluster's population ecology of firms (or should we say its
industrial archaeology?) to assess its future prospects.

The book finds evidence of important cross-sectoral effects on
entry. Thus for example, we find that clusters with strong compu-

ter hardware, components, and systems sectors are more successful at attracting entry into software, peripherals, and services.
These effects play an important role in the development of
computer industry clusters, though they appear to be less important in biotechnology—at least at this stage. The science
base also plays an important role in attracting new entrants in
biotechnology. On the other hand, a cluster that is already strong
in one particular subsector of the industry is slightly less likely
to attract further entrants to that subsector. The pattern of effects
on growth, however, is essentially the reverse of this. Firms
located in a cluster that is strong in that same subsector tend
to grow faster than isolated firms. Firms located in clusters that
are strong in other subsectors tend to grow more slowly. The
science base, moreover, seems to play a much more modest
role in promoting the growth of incumbent firms than in attracting entry.

This contrast between entry attraction and growth promotion
may at first seem surprising, but we argue in later chapters that
it need not be. The basic argument is this. The incumbent is well
placed to absorb the spillovers from similar firms (in its own
sector) because these will be spillovers of knowledge that do not
fall far outside its current domain of competence. Such technological knowledge is often called *competence enhancing*. That is
why firms grow faster when located in a strong cluster of like
firms. And because these opportunities are absorbed by incumbents, there are no opportunities for entrants. In contrast the
incumbent is not well placed to absorb spillovers from firms in
different sectors, because this lies some way from its domain of
competence. Implementing changes based on such technological
knowledge would be, in contrast, *competence destroying*. As the
incumbent fails to exploit such spillovers, there is a clear opportunity for the entrant. We shall argue in Chapter 8 that strong cross-
sectoral effects play an important role in the growth of the cluster,
and may go some way towards explaining why computing (with
10–18 per cent per annum) has grown more spectacularly than
biotechnology (7–10 per cent per annum growth).

The other comparison made in the book is between the USA
and the UK. Despite some important differences in data sources,
which make for some difficulties in interpretation, we can compare the relative strength of entry attractor and growth promoter

10 G. M. Peter Swann and Martha Prevezer

effects in the computer industries of the two countries. Our starting prejudice was that clustering effects would be weaker in the
UK than in the USA, probably because the entrepreneurial capacity to absorb spillovers in the UK is thought to be less than in the
USA. To our surprise, however, there is no systematic tendency
for entry attractor and growth promoter effects to be weaker
in the UK than in the USA (Chapter 5). UK computing firms do
appear to have a slower trend growth rate than their US counterparts, but this does not appear to be attributable to a lack of
clustering synergy. However, clustering in biotechnology in the
UK does appear to be significantly weaker than in the USA, with
much less effect of the bioscience base on new entry in the UK and
less cross-sectoral feedback than even that which occurs in the
USA (which in turn is more limited than cross-sectoral feedback
in computing).

What is clear, however, is that the average UK cluster is of
course much smaller. As shown in Chapter 4, clusters have to
reach a certain size before they achieve take-off. For the USA,
Chapter 4 estimates this as a state computing employment level of
about 5,000 to 10,000, and we also estimate that a cluster reaches
its peak effectiveness (*peak entry*) at around 50,000 to 100,000.
While about 23 clusters in the US computer industry have reached
take-off and 7 have reached *peak entry*, the figures for the UK are
inevitably much smaller. Swann (1998) estimates that 3 UK clusters have reached these *take-off* sizes, while only one could be said
to be approaching *peak entry* size. On grounds of size alone, it is
hardly surprising that the UK can support far fewer clusters, but
it is salutary to keep these magnitudes in mind when assessing
the scope for UK (as opposed to European) competition in the
world computer industry.

1.6 THE PLAN OF THE BOOK

Chapter 2 offers a review of some of the existing literature related
to the theme of clustering. As the review emphasizes, important
contributions to this literature come from economic geography,
economic history, regional and urban economics, traditional economics of location, and the new economics of growth and path
dependence. The analysis presented in the book can be seen as

stemming most of all from the economics of path dependence. Chapter 3 then describes the model of clustering in high-technology industries used throughout the rest of the book. As indicated in the preface, this is kept at a non-technical (and slightly impressionistic) level. This is done to make the arguments here accessible to a wide audience, even if it is done at the expense of technical rigour.

Chapter 4 is the first of four (Chapters 4–7) looking at the experience of clustering in two industries (computing and biotechnology) and two countries (USA and UK). The main focus of each chapter is an informal summary of our econometric models of entry and growth in clusters. Again, the emphasis is on drawing out as many implications as possible from the results presented rather than on setting out the empirical analysis in the greatest detail. Chapter 5 compares clustering in UK computing with the pattern observed in the USA. Differences in data and models are laid out so that the basis for comparison is clear. Although the UK industry is if anything more concentrated geo-graphically than the US industry, its composition is different, with less core manufacturing and more activity in peripherals. This may have implications for the dynamics of clustering, we argue. Chapter 6 is the first of two chapters looking at the biotechnology industry. This chapter constructs similar models to those used for computing but with the inclusion of the science base which has been of central importance to the creation of this industry. Again differences in data and models are laid out. The second part of this chapter traces the history of the industry, its relationship with the science base, and the internal structure of the industry, looking at relationships between entrants and in-cumbents. These differ in structure significantly from those in the computing industry. We also examine the role of policy in US biotechnology in affecting the migration of clusters. Chapter 7 examines biotechnology in the UK and brings out the contrasts with the US industry. As with the US biotechnology industry, the relationship to the incumbent user industries has been significant but not as positive to the clustering momentum in the UK as in the USA, due to markedly different attitudes by UK incumbents to-wards new entrants. A comparison using the models also brings out a much weaker attraction to the local bioscience base in the UK than in the USA and a more marked regional specialization in the UK between industrial sectors. We examine the source of these differences.

Chapter 8 compares the operation of the clustering process in computing and biotechnology. The chapter suggests that some of the contrasts between the two industries are attributable to differences in their basic structure and forms of specialization. But other differences are a result of the two technologies being at different stages of their life cycles, and of the fact that while several computing industry clusters could be said to be mature, this is barely true of any biotechnology clusters. The chapter also explores to what extent the pattern of clustering in biotechnology is a result of the pre-existing pattern of clusters in computing.

Chapter 9 introduces a slightly wider perspective—the idea of development of knowledge as a resource—to examine the clustering process from a policy perspective. By looking more closely at the reasons that influence the strength of the feedback process— and especially the degree of entrepreneurial dynamism—it shows that cluster performance is dependent upon a number of public goods which policy can help to establish. In particular it may be possible for science, technology, and regional policies to help the development of coherent technological communities which promote flows of knowledge and assist in the coordination of investment activity. The more specific problems of the UK are then discussed in greater detail. Appropriately managed, technology foresight exercises may be important not only in creating coordination and trust among the relevant communities, but also in the creation of powerful locational magnets. However, institutional reform, aimed at strengthening mechanisms of technology transfer and the concentration of ideas and resources, may be essential.

Chapter 10 offers some conclusions. As we have emphasized before, some of the arguments advanced here appear a bit speculative given the evidence currently available. This last chapter risks some tentative conclusions on the ways in which the UK differs from the USA in its ability to create and foster clusters and what needs to be done to speed the process.

2

Clusters, Innovation, and Growth: A Survey of the Literature

RUI BAPTISTA

INTRODUCTION

This chapter reviews some of the literature relevant to this study of the dynamics of clustering. This study has taken an economic perspective on the dynamics of clustering, and much of the literature surveyed here comes from that tradition. But while the work of Porter (1990) and Krugman (1991a) has done much to remind economists that geography matters, and to revive interest in the economics of industrial clusters, it must be remembered that work on this theme has a long and distinguished history.

Marshall was one of the first economists to write about clusters. Indeed, from observing industrial districts, he developed the concept of external economies. In a famous passage, Marshall (1920: 271–2) observes, 'When an industry has chosen a locality for itself it is likely to stay there long: so great are the advantages which people following the same skilled trade get from near neighbourhood to one another . . . And presently subsidiary trade grows up in the neighbourhood.'

The benefits of locating in a cluster (or industrial district) are related to the availability of skilled labour and intermediate goods suppliers, and also to the easy transmission and discussion of new ideas. While economic analysis of clusters is perhaps 100 years old, the phenomenon of clustering is much older, and especially well recognized by historians of the industrial revolution. Mathias (1983: 119–20) gives a fascinating summary of how the

British cotton industry, though initially dispersed, was drawn into a cluster around Manchester: 'The factory system was pioneered on water power . . . which often forced industrialists away from the centres of population . . . [But] once steam power had been harnessed to a cotton mill, other forces slowly took charge of location . . . The mills concentrated in the more populated regions . . . where communications were easier and cheaper . . . Once a pool of skilled labour grew up in a mill town that added to the inertia of location.' While such early clusters grew very fast, they eventually became congested, and this, coupled with the onset of maturity in the industries located in these clusters, led to decline. The relative decline of many major industrial cities of the nineteenth and early twentieth centuries is testimony to that. But in an era of information and communication technologies of ever increasing bandwidths, does the geographical location of production matter any more? In short, do these information and communications technologies make clustering irrelevant? Ultimately this is an empirical matter, which will be assessed in Chapters 4–7. But there is one reason at least why geography may continue to matter, and why clustering effects are still observed.

Pavitt (1987) has noted how some economic analysis made the assumption that technological knowledge can be completely codified in the form of patents, blueprints, operating manuals, and so on. If this were true, then all such codified information could be transmitted worldwide at very low cost, and geography would not matter. But as Pavitt (1987) observes, in reality 'most technology is specific, complex, often tacit, and cumulative in its development'. Such tacit knowledge is much harder, or even impossible, to transfer by wire: it requires geographical proximity and face-to-face contact to maximize knowledge transfer of this sort.

For our purposes the main point is this: if there are any supply-side spillovers to be gained from a strong core computer manufacturing sector by computer service, software, or peripherals companies, then they may be easiest to exploit if these companies are located close to the core. And if this is so, we expect to observe important clustering effects in that industry.

Subsequent studies of these phenomena emanate from five distinct traditions. The first is the important subdiscipline of Urban and Regional Economics. This derives from the pioneering work on location theory by Weber (1928) and Lösch (1954), and the related theory of *poles de croissance* due to Perroux (1950). We could perhaps also add to this the tradition of locational models within industrial economics deriving from Hotelling's (1929) study of ice-cream sellers on a beach. The second tradition is that of geography. Economic geographers have long been concerned with the phenomenon of clustering, both at an empirical level and at a theoretical level. I cannot do justice to this literature here, so I refer simply to two reviews—Amin and Goddard (1986) and Conti et al. (1995)—which summarize some of the most important current issues from the geographers' perspective. The third tradition is history. The magnificent studies of the city by historians and economic historians such as Mumford (1961), Jacobs (1961, 1969), Briggs (1968), Bairoch (1988), and others capture some of the richness that is sometimes lost in economic analysis. The fourth tradition can be seen as a development of this historical tradition in that it emphasizes how 'history matters' while it is analytical in style. It might be called the path dependent approach to economics, including the work of Arthur (1990), David and Rosenbloom (1990), Krugman (1991a), Brezis and Krugman (1993). The fifth tradition is within mainstream economics itself, in what is commonly called *new growth theory*—Romer (1986, 1990) and Grossman and Helpman (1992)—and in the empirical study of regional spillovers—notably by Jaffe (1986) amongst others.

There are, moreover, a large number of empirical industry or technology studies that have made a substantial contribution to our understanding of clustering as a phenomenon. Some of these will be cited in what follows. While we recognize that the most comprehensive survey of these issues would seek to cover all these traditions, we have found that too daunting a task for this book. As indicated above, much of the literature surveyed here comes from the first, fourth, and fifth traditions, though we also cover some of the key studies in the other traditions.

Porter (1990: 29) noted that successful firms are usually concentrated in particular cities or states within a nation, and something about these locations provides a fertile environment. There seems to be a clear connection between geographical clustering, company growth, and innovative success, particularly in high-technology industries. The US experience in particular has been that new clusters often emerge around a relevant part of the science base.

The work to be surveyed here concentrates on the determinants of a cluster's success and on the specific reasons that lead firms to cluster together. Some other work focuses on the related questions of how local and regional networking and rivalry between competitors affect entry, growth rates, and the production and diffusion of innovations. If spillovers from manufacturing and R & D activities are highly localized in a geographical sense, then firms will find it easiest to exploit these spillovers if they are located close to the manufacturing and R & D activities.

Section 2.1 surveys literature on the factors that influence location decisions, placing special emphasis on technology and innovative activity. Section 2.2 surveys some of the main studies that have examined clustering as a phenomenon. Section 2.3 discusses the concepts of agglomeration externalities and knowledge spillovers, both of which play a key role in the clustering process. Then Section 2.4 gives a brief overview of how clusters have emerged in Europe and the USA, placing special emphasis on high-technology industries. Section 2.5 looks at the connections between clustering, performance, and innovation. Section 2.6 concludes.

2.1 THE LOCATION OF PRODUCTION ACTIVITIES

The basic arguments underpinning the location of production and innovation activities stem from several different streams of literature. These span the range from simple models of firm location decisions to much wider debates on corporate strategy and industrial policy.

Industrial-spatial organization: theory and history

Since Marshall's work (1920, 1927), the geographical concentration of production has been noted as a distinctive characteristic of industrial organization. And as noted before, it was by observing industry localization that Marshall derived the concept of external economies. These positive economies provide a strong incentive for firms to locate close together. The location benefits identified by Marshall stem from the availability of skilled workers and intermediate goods, and the easy transmission and discussion of new ideas or improvements, whether in products, technologies, or organization. Marshall's works also predicted an important shift in the focus of industrial growth that took place between the beginning of the century and the Second World War.

The industrial revolution had generated a new production system where activities were located close to sources of materials and energy—coalfields or rivers. From the first decades of the nineteenth century, industry workshops and small vertically disintegrated factories started to accumulate around large urban areas, providing pools of labour. From the 1920s onwards, increasing competition and scale economies led to the Fordist system of production, followed by capital accumulation and mass production, and further growth of these urban centres (Hudson 1992). Much production was now located in large, vertically integrated plants that characterized the overgrown industrial regions of the American 'manufacturing belt'.

This spatial division of labour was to change, however, because of diseconomies resulting from congestion, excessive growth, and the development of multi-regional and multinational companies (Massey 1984). The production processes within companies were split into independent stages, scattered through separate areas, often located in different countries with appropriate labour market and other conditions. This resulted in a 'core–periphery' contrast in the international division of labour and income (Fröbel et al. 1980). And, eventually, it led to regional and urban problems such as deindustrialization and localized unemployment.

From the 1960s onwards, however, there has been a trend towards greater geographical concentration in industries such as chemicals and steel. This trend has been reinforced from the 1970s onwards by the growth of high-technology industrial complexes concentrated in specific regions. Some have seen this trend as a result of deliberate industrial and regional strategies, and the adoption of new technologies and operations management techniques such as *Just in Time* (Hudson 1992). Others have seen the re-emergence of locally agglomerated production as a revival of the Marshallian concept of 'industrial districts' (Marshall 1927). This latter interpretation stresses the reappearance of a spatial division of labour centred around self-contained, product-specialized regional economies (Amin and Thrift 1991).

Piore and Sabel (1984) argued that the growth of consumer sophistication, along with market volatility and shorter product life cycles, called for greater flexibility in production. Rigidity caused by hierarchical control, vertical integration, and mass production would make it difficult to meet consumer demand for differentiation and quality. Their solution was to decentralize coordination and to horizontally divide labour between linked producers so as to foster greater skills and flexibility in the workforce. This transformation would lead to a concentration of small and large producers in a re-emerging Marshallian industrial district, in order to maximize the benefits from local external economies: 'These regions were both flexible and specialised. They constantly varied their products to satisfy changing tastes and extended their markets by defining new wants. They developed general-purpose technologies and a highly-skilled work force to cut production costs without inhibiting flexibility. . . . Even the strongest firms in these systems of flexible specialization depended on extensive cooperation with their competitors' (Sabel 1989: 17).

This view is consistent with Perroux's (1950) perspective on 'growth poles'. In his theory of *economic space*, the firm is located in a space consisting of poles. Each firm releases forces that interact with the forces released by *other* firms at the same pole. Each pole would then have a zone of influence, interacting with the zones of influence of other poles, and making an international network of markets. It is then pointless to talk of bounded national economies, since economic activity would be defined by spaces and forces that do not have national limits.

The *industrial districts* approach is often criticized for giving inadequate attention to scale economies, and to the advantages of vertical integration in some industries (see Robertson and Langlois 1995). According to Lazonick (1993), a small innovative firm may be unable to pursue investment strategies that would adapt it to the innovative environment, simply on the grounds of size. The dichotomy between vertical integration and horizontal division of labour through local networking is at the centre of this debate. Transaction cost theory (Williamson 1985, 1993) attempts to construct a more systematic theoretical account of the relation between industrial structure, spatial organization, and local linkages. It can be used to organize production to recognize and exploit the interdependencies between separate phases, and hence to coordinate the economic structure of the firm. In particular, should firms seek to trade in markets and/or networks or should they integrate in a hierarchical manner?

The problem with the transaction cost calculus on its own is that it ignores technological, informational, and social interdependencies that can lead to the internalization or externalization of activities, as Gordon (1991) points out. Geographical proximity not only reduces the cost of inter-industrial exchange, but also enhances the circulation of capital and information. Moreover, geographical proximity eases all the social transactions and solidarity that underpin regional business cultures (A. J. Scott 1994).

We believe that most of Marshall's original arguments are still valid—and that they continue to provide a foundation for a theory of geographical clustering of firms, and also for the relationship between clustering and innovative performance. As Scott (1988) argues, there will always be a tendency for at least some of the producers tied together in this manner to converge on a common location. This tendency is almost inevitable since the core elements of the western industrial system are usually organized as networks of producers bound together in a web of relationships.

The contribution of urban economics

Scholars of urban economics consider that urban agglomerations exist as a response to the need for manufacturing, trade, and administrative centres. But spatial concentration is costly: it increases the demand for space in the city, and therefore raises the cost of urban space. When urban agglomeration expands the geographical area of the city, it also increases transportation time and costs. Spatial concentration also increases negative externalities such as congestion and pollution. In some circumstances, however, firms will bear these costs, through increased wages and taxes.

Concentration is costly, and in principle avoidable. In consequence there have to be strong reasons for the continued concentration of economic activity in cities. The literature suggests three generic reasons: (1) the desire to minimize transport costs by proximity; (2) the existence of positive external economies from agglomeration; and (3) the opportunity to serve the market created by firms and employees located in the city.

Traditional location theory

Location theory has its foundations in the works of Weber (1928) and Lösch (1954), and was further developed by Isard (1956) and Smith (1971), *inter alia*. The main feature of location theory is this: the firm's location strategy is determined by the location of output markets and resources. In its original form, this theory proposed that location followed from the choice of a single source of inputs and a single output market. The Weberian partial equilibrium analysis shows that the minimum cost location will then be either at the source of the inputs or where the market is. This result follows because the loading and unloading of goods incurs costs. Some of these costs can be avoided by locating either at the source or at the market. In fact, the cost *per mile* tends to be lower, the longer is the distance; and this makes it worthwhile only to transport inputs over a long distance.

The analysis can be refined further either by introducing several markets or sources of inputs, or by considering transport breaks due to the need for trans-shipment of goods. Relaxing the assumption of fixed prices for both inputs and outputs leads to a general equilibrium problem. Lösch (1954) was the first to develop a general equilibrium analysis for networks of producers and consumers, allowing for variations both in demand and in cost parameters.

The problem remains one of cost minimization where particular local factors are seldom considered (see Beckmann and Thisse 1986 and Stahl 1987 for reviews of more complex models). These models usually predict a concentration of firms or even of related industries, since some industries' output will be used as a resource by others. This concentration can be even more pronounced when there are economies of scale in manufacturing. It seems clear, however, that transport costs are not the sole determinant of a firm's location decision, and a fuller analysis must examine the intrinsic characteristics of each location.

The concept of agglomeration externalities

In the urban economics literature, agglomeration externalities are defined as any economies or cost reductions which obtain if several firms locate near to each other (Evans 1985). Such effects are discussed at length by Lösch (1954) and Isard (1956). Their work identified two different kinds of externalities: *location externalities* are those economies enjoyed by firms from the same industry that locate close to each other; *urbanization externalities* are those economies enjoyed by firms from different industries that locate in the same area. These external economies are found when there is some kind of service or benefit from co-locating which would not be available (or is more expensive) elsewhere. The concept of agglomeration economies can easily encompass the transmission of technological knowledge. The effects of externalities on location have been studied extensively by many urban economists (notably Henderson 1974, 1986, 1994). Fewer studies have examined the *nature* and *sources* of externalities (though see Goldstein and Gronenberg 1984; Helsley and Strange 1990).

Henderson (1986: 48) lists four sources of location externalities recognized in the urban economics literature:

1. *economies of intra-industry specialization*, where greater industry size permits firms to pursue greater specialization;
2. *labour market economies*, where industry size reduces search costs for firms looking for workers with specific training relevant to that industry;
3. *enhanced communication* among firms, which can accelerate the adoption of innovations;
4. *public intermediate inputs* tailored to the particular need of local industries.

Henderson's classification is not far removed from Marshall's (1920) original account of the forces sustaining industrial districts. As more firms locate in the same region, these external effects become more pronounced, thus making the region even more attractive, and attracting further firms to locate there. Eventually, increasing costs from concentration and congestion would slow down the entry of firms, and the agglomeration would stop short of *excessive* concentration.

Market demand effects

Lichtenberg (1960) demonstrates that some industries derive particular benefit from being located in or near the centres of large cities. This is particularly relevant when there is a high variability of demand, and a resulting need for rapid changes in the characteristics of the products. Printing and publishing of periodicals and fashion clothes are commonly quoted as examples of this sort. Proximity to demand is important not just to enable more rapid marketing, but also to ease the gathering of information from consumers and rivals.

Even in the industries of this type, however, only a small proportion of companies locate in the inner cities, so this effect does not dominate all other influences on location. Besides, most changes in fashion or preferences do not develop within one inner city alone, but evolve at the national level. Nevertheless, proximity to the main market can be a powerful locational factor, particularly for firms in small and specialized industries. Whenever the bulk of the demand is located in the city centre, it is likely that this city centre will also attract a strong concentration of suppliers.

Industrial location and public infrastructure

One other influence on firm location decisions discussed in the literature is the existence of a public infrastructure (Evans 1985). Public infrastructure can be defined as any facility or institution provided through public funds which facilitates the exchange between production and consumption. This definition would include physical infrastructure such as ports, railways, or motorways, as well as legal, administrative, and educational systems. The quality of the infrastructure usually has a bearing on the cost of transport and training.

Martin and Rogers (1994) examine the impact of infrastructure on industrial location. They conclude that firms in sectors with significant economies of scale will locate in regions with the best infrastructure, especially if there is strong trade between them. Firms concentrate in places with better infrastructure because this allows them to take advantage of scale economies, and hence gain a competitive advantage.

The contribution of economic geography

Economic geographers have made a major contribution to the study of location of production and innovative activities, and especially the location of high-technology industry and the dynamics of regional complexes and networks. The work of geographers on production and R & D location started with the detailed mapping of production and research activities. It has moved on from this to supply more detailed analyses of both the internal characteristics of the organization and the intrinsic capacity of regions to promote and attract industry. It is no surprise then that many of the theoretical works and case studies on clusters and innovative networks come from (or draw heavily on) economic geography.

The geography of innovation has been examined by, among others, Malecki (1980), Hall and Markusen (1985), and Glasmeier (1985) for the USA and by Thwaites (1982), Howells (1984), and Keeble (1988) for the UK. Amin and Goddard (1986), Camagni (1991a), and Conti et al. (1995) provide excellent accounts of contemporary issues in the economic geography of the industrial enterprise. It seems clear that the globalization of markets and economies has become an increasingly dominant tendency that shapes the pattern of production and innovation. But at the same time, globalization heightens the importance of differences in the ability, endowments and milieux of different locations.

While the possible combinations of choices of location, processes, and products seem wider than ever, the specific local environment continues to have powerful implications for competitiveness and innovative success. Globalization seems to be leading to increased spatial differentiation in regional development rather than homogenization (Hudson 1992).

Economic geographers have recently shifted their attention to studying the growing internationalization of R & D at the multinational level (Howells 1990). Companies are establishing an internationally integrated system of R & D, where their overseas R & D laboratories specialize in those scientific and technical areas where the foreign country has particular strengths.

Multinationals often set up R & D units abroad in centres where the technological infrastructure is very strong, with the aim of reaping the positive externalities from networking. The case for geographic concentration of innovative activity and output remains, but at a global level.

Some studies of the geography of R & D place the location decision within the context of other corporate functions: headquarters, sales, marketing, and production. According to Howells (1990), sustaining the flow of information in knowledge networks, whether intra- or inter-organizational, plays a fundamental role in the location of R & D activities. The regional concentration of R & D laboratories and the rigidity of location are well documented for both the USA (Malecki 1980) and the United Kingdom (Howells 1984). Hall and Markusen (1985) also demonstrate the regional specialization and concentration of R & D activities in the computer industry. Howells and Wood (1993) argue that the location and organization of industrial R & D is dependent on: the evolution of the company's overall structure; the evolution of the R & D function itself and its locational rigidity; the type of R & D activities being considered; and the relative merits of centralized and decentralized frameworks for R & D activity.

The evolution of the modern company towards diversified, multi-divisional organizations has had important implications for the organization of R & D. R & D has ceased to be a company-wide activity, but has become more specialized to the needs of different product divisions. This has increased the complexity of locational patterns. As noted above, existing research units have been rigid in their location, and have experienced very low mortality rates. On the other hand, new research units are usually located close to existing establishments. Some of the factors that lie behind this locational rigidity are: the high cost of moving research units; the need to maintain good research communication flows; and the need to retain research staff who might join another company if research operations were moved elsewhere.

Location also depends on the type of research to be carried out. It is common to distinguish three broad categories of industrial R & D: basic research, applied research, and development work. These different R & D activities have different task environments because of their different orientation. Applied research tends to be more widely scattered, away from central research laboratories and dispersed in smaller units attached to production facilities. Development work is usually the most dispersed R & D operation, found primarily attached to manufacturing plants. But basic research tends to be concentrated in core metropolitan regions, and commonly located near to key strategic functions (Howells 1984). Indeed, Howells (1984) found that basic research in the UK tends to concentrate in a small number of establishments near to corporate headquarters, commonly in the south-east of England. Thwaites (1982) found that, even in peripheral development areas, much of the innovation was done by branch sites controlled from headquarters. The spatial pattern of R & D in the United States is somewhat different. The importance of corporate centres is not so pronounced. Malecki (1980) and Glasmeier (1985) found that much industrial innovative activity was located at federal-supported centres in the sunbelt region, close to universities and major research laboratories. This difference between the UK and USA probably reflects the relative scale of the American economy and also differences in regional public policy.

The benefits of centralization in R & D derive from economies of scale and scope, including indivisibilities that lead to a minimum efficient size, and good internal communications to key strategic functions. Centralization also reduces the risk of results 'leaking' to competitors, allows researchers to focus their attention on original ideas rather than operational problems, and makes it easier to network with related industries, academics, and government-funded R & D activities located close to the firm's R & D sites. In contrast, the benefits of decentralization of R & D derive from improved communication between R & D and functions such as sales and marketing, greater focus on operational problems and greater ability to monitor specific market needs.

One of the most important factors driving the location of innovative activity is the opportunity to establish direct contact with other organizations that can produce spillovers beneficial for the firm's research effort. This is related to the growth of inter-organizational research contacts and networking. Inter-firm links, formal or informal, seem in some respects to be an even more important factor in such location decisions than good intra-firm communications.

2.2 CLUSTER THEORY IN ECONOMICS

The core of the modern economic literature on clustering is provided by the works of Porter (1990), Krugman (1991*a*, 1991*b*), and
Arthur (1989, 1990). Porter and Krugman were perhaps the first
modern economists to regard geography as a central issue in the
analysis of markets and competition. Their work has generated a
new branch of literature in the economics of industry and international trade. Arthur's work focuses on the workings of the clustering process itself, and stems from a novel approach to the analysis
of increasing returns and positive feedback, sometimes called
'path dependence'.

Clusters and competitive advantage

One of the most widely cited works on the subject of clusters is
Michael Porter's *Competitive Advantage of Nations* (1990). In this
work, Porter develops a framework to analyse the competitive
success of different national economies. His framework (the
diamond) has four components: factor conditions; firm strategy,
structure, and rivalry; demand conditions; and related or
supporting industries. Porter argues that two specific elements—
domestic rivalry and geographical industry concentration—are
responsible for the dynamics of the system. Domestic rivalry
promotes the dynamism of the entire system, while spatial
concentration increases the intensity of interactions within the
system.

A nation's competitive advantage is boosted by its endowment
of skilled human resources, market-specific knowledge, and specialized infrastructure. Rivalry between firms provides an incentive for investment in such factors. According to Porter, these
effects would be most pronounced when rivals are located in the
same city or region. A cluster of firms that draws on common
specialized inputs and infrastructure will upgrade local factor
quality and increase its supply.

In a similar way, intense rivalry and geographical concentration have favourable effects on the composition and strength
of local demand. They also have a favourable effect on the development of related and supporting industries, for example specialized suppliers and users, because a nation's competitive

industries are usually linked through vertical or horizontal relationships. A study by Fagerberg (1995) using data for sixteen OECD countries found that advanced integration between domestic users and suppliers had a strong effect on competitiveness. Unlike Piore and Sabel (1984), however, Porter does not focus on small size as a factor in success. While national rivalry is a key factor in competitiveness, economies of scale also play a vital role. Porter (1990: 156) points out that entire clusters of industries are usually concentrated in the same city or region: 'Concentrations of domestic rivals are frequently surrounded by suppliers, and located in areas with concentrations of particularly sophisticated and significant customers. The city or region becomes a unique environment for competing in the industry.'

Geographical concentration is of foremost importance for organizational improvement and technological innovation. Concentration facilitates interchange and cooperation between universities and other research centres, customers and suppliers within a region, and industrial research. Moreover, a concentration of specific knowledge can expect to attract more specialized human capital. On the other hand, since information exchange tends to be more informal, the spread of information outside the region becomes limited.

It is important to recognize that the development of communications and the reduction in transport costs and other barriers to trade do not remove locational advantages. Instead, they can actually make them more significant, because firms that develop competitive advantage in one nation or region will now be more likely to penetrate other markets. While classical factors of production become more accessible due to globalization, specialized factors and skills remain differentiated between regions. Globalization makes the home base *more* important, rather than less important.

Increasing returns and economic geography

The work of Krugman (1991a, 1991b) focuses on the interaction between market structure and economic geography. He regards concentration as 'the most striking feature of the geography of economic activity' (Krugman 1991a: 5), and considers that spatial differences in the distribution of production are the result of increasing returns. He analyses geographical location within a country through a simple 'core-periphery' model. In this model, location is determined by the interaction of scale economies and transportation costs (Krugman 1991*b*). In *Geography and Trade* (1991*a*), Krugman restates Marshall's (1920) original thoughts on the geographical concentration of economic activity. He recasts Marshall's arguments, stating that the forces for industrial localization stem from three sources. These are supply-side externalities, since they are related to the use of primary factors, intermediate inputs, and technology.

The first source is labour market pooling. The concentration of a large number of firms belonging to one industry in the same place creates a pool of workers with similar skills. This pooled market benefits both workers and firms, making it easier to cope with uncertainty related to business cycles through the effects of increasing numbers. Increasing returns play a part in the process as well, since concentration of activities in one place (or a few) is encouraged by scale economies. Krugman demonstrates that pooling becomes advantageous whatever way the labour market is organized.

The second source has to do with the provision of intermediate inputs. A localized industry can support a greater number of specialized local suppliers of specific inputs and services, and this provides a greater variety at lower cost. Once again, the existence of economies of scale and scope means that larger centres of production can expect to have more diverse and efficient suppliers than small ones. This effect is independent of transportation costs.

The third source is the existence of technological externalities, or spillovers. If information about new technologies, goods, and processes flows more easily in the local area than over great distances, then firms located in an industrial centre enjoy positive externalities that are not so readily available to remote firms. Krugman remains sceptical about the generalization of this last argument. For although technological spillovers seem to be an important feature of many high-technology industries, it is also an empirical fact that many clusters exist in traditional industries, where such knowledge spillovers are less important. Besides, since such externalities are of a non-pecuniary nature, they are hard to trace and leave no specific trail. Krugman suggests that economists should concentrate on other effects that can be more readily measured. Nevertheless, at the very least, for industries and technologies in their formative stages, the existence of such spillovers and the fact that they are easier to absorb when located close to the source of the spillovers is a potent force for clustering.

Marshallian externalities related to factor markets and intermediate input markets have received extensive discussion in the literature, both theoretically and empirically—see, for instance, David and Rosenbloom (1990), and Hagen and Hammond (1994).

Positive feedback and lock-in by historical events

Krugman's approach assumes that increasing returns, in the form of both scale economies and positive externalities, are a key part of the industrial clustering process. Brian Arthur's work focuses more specifically on the process by which agglomeration externalities lead to the geographical concentration of firms. Positive feedback mechanisms resulting from the increasing returns act at many levels in an economy. It is often argued that the presence of increasing returns, or *network externalities*, implies that one product or technology must come to dominate a market (David 1985; Arthur 1989). For many network products or technologies, such as computer hardware and software, the value of the product is as much what it can be connected to as what it can do on its own. This makes the issue of compatibility a vital one. When one particular model gains a significant market share and installed base, people have a strong incentive to buy that same model, in order to enjoy the network externalities. As a result, a de facto standard is generated in the market (Katz and Shapiro 1985).

The same kind of reasoning can be applied to firms' location decisions. Agglomeration externalities happen when net benefits from locating in a certain region increase with the number of firms in the region. Arthur (1990) argues that if these agglomeration economies are strong enough, so that firms benefit from the presence of other firms, a predominant share of the industry may cluster in a single region, district, or location. If this is the outcome, it would not necessarily imply any intrinsic advantage of that particular location. Even if the establishment of early firms at this location is as much a matter of 'historical accident' as anything else, the attraction of subsequent firms consolidates the location as industry cluster.

The process can be described in a little more detail. Suppose, to simplify matters, that firms enter an industry one by one, choosing their location so as to maximize their benefits. If these benefits increase as they locate near other firms, then the accumulation of historical events leads to *lock-in*: the first few firms may decide based on some random geographical preference. The next entrants, however, choose on preferences modified by the benefit of locating near the first ones. Geographical concentration results then exclusively from the nature of the positive feedback process, given a certain level of agglomeration economies.

If the initial historic events are purely random, many increasing returns problems turn out to fit general non-linear probability schemes. Arthur et al. (1987) proved that most of these processes settle down to one fixed point of the probability function or, at most, a few points. The possible solutions can be obtained by finding these sets of fixed points. The precise character of increasing returns will determine the process by which a solution is reached.

Arthur (1990) built a model of industry location where firms choosing among different regions are attracted by agglomeration externalities, and where 'historical accident' is a determinant because firms are heterogeneous and enter the industry in random order. His results showed that when no upper bound to the positive feedback process was considered, a single dominant region would effectively monopolize the industry. Which region this is would depend on the factors influencing the decisions of the first entrants and on the random order of firm entry.

On the other hand, if an upper bound is imposed to increasing returns, possibly due to congestion effects of excessive agglomeration, the results will depend on the detailed (albeit random) sequence of firm entry. Some sequences might produce dominance by one region, while others lead to solutions in which several regions share the industry, and there is no tendency towards dominance—even in the long run. It seems reasonable to admit that this second solution is the most plausible from an empirical point of view. Regions do not enjoy increasing returns indefinitely. If the attractiveness resulting from the presence of others steadily increased as the cluster grew, some region should always dominate and shut out the others. In fact, what is usually observed is an outcome in which a few regions share the industry—presumably because there is an upper bound to the increasing returns.

Traditionally, economists have steered clear of models in which there are multiple equilibria, and in which the equilibrium point selected can depend on small events occurring in the initial stages of the process. Economists have preferred to focus their attention on economic problems that are not *path dependent* in this way. On the other hand, it is now being recognized that a very large number of economic problems may have this character. Even if analysis of such questions requires a change in the economist's toolkit, with less emphasis on analytical solutions and more emphasis on simulation, this is a challenge that the economics profession must face.

Demand sources of the clustering process

Most of the clustering sources discussed above are, in nature, supply-side benefits. But as Swann (1993*b*) demonstrates when classifying the forces that encourage clustering, some of the forces leading to clustering derive from the demand side. There are important demand-side benefits arising from the agglomeration of firms. These effects are not confined to the demand effects cited above in the section on urban economics. These reasons for clustering are set out in Chapter 3.

Congestion effects and excessive agglomeration

The circular relationship created by positive feedback within clusters can be a deeply conservative force. Krugman (1991*a*) points out that the geographical distribution of production that existed in the early days of the railway and industrialization remains little changed nearly a century later. It is clear, however, that not even the strongest clusters can enjoy positive feedback forever and, sooner or later, some upper bound will arise. This means that there is a non-monotonic relationship between the attractiveness of a cluster and the size of the cluster. Up to a certain point, the attractions of locating in a cluster may be increasing; beyond that point they are decreasing, as the costs of congestion outweigh the benefits of clustering. Swann (1993*b*) suggests that the costs of clustering can arise from congestion and competition effects both in input and in output markets. On the supply side, agglomeration will tend to raise the cost of real estate, as well as the cost of specialized labour. On the demand side, congestion and increased competition in the output markets will have a negative effect on firms' performance, through lower sales, profits, and growth.

While the growth of urban industrial agglomerations results from a circular, self-reinforcing process, decline will usually come rapidly and abruptly (Krugman 1991*a*) and will be influenced by people's expectations. At some point, industrial development will shift to new urban centres, rather than old ones. Brezis and Krugman (1993) suggest that as the technology underpinning a certain industry undergoes normal progress, established centres will preserve their leadership. However, with the arrival of new ideas that represent a discontinuity from the established knowledge base, the experience accumulated in these centres may be of little value to the new technological trajectory. The positive externality that arises from accumulated specialized knowledge is weakened, and agglomeration benefits can be outweighed by congestion costs, giving rise to a relocation of the industry. Technological variety within the cluster should also influence its chances of survival, as we shall see in Chapter 4 below.

2.3 THE NATURE OF AGGLOMERATION EXTERNALITIES

We have seen that most works on clusters and industrial location consider the existence of agglomeration externalities as the key force behind clustering. Externalities would involve diversity of suppliers and information spillovers about market conditions and technology. Models of dynamic externalities argue that clusters grow because they allow people to interact and learn from each other. The frequency of the interaction is ensured by proximity.

As noted before, urban economists have made important

contributions to the classification of agglomeration externalities. Isard presented a typology that identified two kinds of externality and location externalities resulted from geographical agglomeration within the same industry; urbanization externalities would arise from agglomeration of firms in different industries. Jacobs (1969, 1984) viewed this second type of externality, relating to industry diversity in a city or region, as the main factor behind growth: 'People who think of cities simply as towns that have kept growing larger are believers in a *preformation* theory of city growth, an enlargement of what is essentially already there. I am arguing, rather, an *epigenesis* theory of cities: the idea that a city grows by a process of gradual diversification and differentiation of its economy' (1969: 126). Later work by Bairoch (1988) supports Jacobs's arguments, particularly about the effects of diversity on innovation and diffusion of technologies. Jacobs's conclusions were also reiterated by Lucas (1988) in the context of *new growth* economics. Lucas argued that cities play the role of *external human capital* for economic activity and the growth of knowledge.

The other type of externality arises from industry specialization, and its origins lie in traditional economic theory. Romer (1986, 1990) and Krugman (1991*a*) develop the arguments about specialization set out in Marshall (1920). This development, coupled with Arrow's (1962*a*) analysis of the nature of invention and technological advance, has yielded a new theory of innovation and growth. The Marshall–Arrow–Romer theory argues that common-industry externalities, deriving from the proximity of firms in the same industry, have an important influence on firm growth. This happens because knowledge accumulated by one firm tends to help other firms' technological development. Industries that are regionally specialized benefit most from within-industry transmission of knowledge and should, therefore, grow faster than those that are regionally dispersed.

Empirical studies on the pervasiveness of agglomeration externalities are few, concentrating mainly on the implications for productivity and firm growth. Henderson (1986) found strong evidence that industry concentration in a particular location raises factor productivity. This is supported by Ciccone and Hall (1993), who found a positive elasticity between geographical density of employment and productivity. Glaeser et al. (1992) do not detect a positive relation between industry concentration and city employment growth, but find evidence that industry diversity and competition have a positive effect on growth. Henderson (1994) concludes that in order to maintain high levels of growth in a particular industry, a region needs concentrations of employment in that industry, but also needs a diversified industrial base, since this tends to raise labour productivity. The empirical studies later in this book (Chapters 4–7) offer some further evidence on these important questions.

R & D spillovers as agglomeration externalities

Central to the arguments about geographical clustering of successful innovators is a particular kind of agglomeration externality: the knowledge externality, or spillover. It is sometimes forgotten, however, that spillovers resulting from contact with other firms or institutions do not simply enhance technological innovation and productivity. They may also alter the financing, marketing, and general managerial and organizational practices of the beneficiaries and, by affecting firm growth, can change the nature and evolution of concentration and market structure. Moreover, while networking, geographical proximity, and everyday contact are important spillover mechanisms, there are other kinds of strategic arrangements, such as joint ventures and foreign direct investment, which can also act as efficient mechanisms for managing spillovers (see Blomström 1992). In short, spillovers are a broader concept than agglomeration externalities, particularly because the spillover is not necessarily spatially bounded.

Theory

It is widely accepted that technological change lies at the heart of economic growth (Romer 1986, 1990). The *new growth* theories find that, unless there are significant externalities arising from technology, or other sources of social increasing returns, it is unlikely that economic growth can proceed at an undiminished rate (Griliches 1991). It is also recognized that technological innovation, far from being a purely random and exogenous process, is guided by market forces (Grossman and Helpman 1992). Technological change arises because of conscious, intentional investments and explicit decisions taken by many different economic units who respond to market incentives, translating new scientific knowledge into goods and processes, and thereby creating new technologies.

Dosi (1988a), in his survey of sources, procedures, and effects of innovation, concludes that technical change reflects an interplay between technological opportunities created by scientific discovery and inducements emerging from market opportunities. This means that technology can be seen as an output of knowledge, research, industrial development, and innovation.

New Growth Theory considers that technological progress has two special properties: non-rivalry and partial excludability (Romer 1990). A non-rival good is one for which the use by one firm or person does not preclude or limit its use by another. To the extent that technology is knowledge—though note again the comments by Pavitt, cited in the introduction to this chapter—it appears to be non-rival because the cost of replicating knowledge seems to be small when compared with the cost of creating it in the first place. Excludability reflects both legal and technological conditions. Property rights can be assigned by law to the creators of new ideas through mechanisms such as patents. Nevertheless, technological information can still spill over to other firms, and as a result technological knowledge is only partially excludable. Of course, as Pavitt (1987) argues, much technology is, in practice, specific to the firm that originates it, complex, often tacit, and cumulative in its development. This means that in practice the leakage of technological information does not necessarily imply the transfer of technology.

As Arrow (1962b) points out in his seminal contribution, intangibles such as information and knowledge can never be thought of as completely appropriable commodities, since the very use of the information in a productive way is bound to reveal it, at least in part. The very essence of a patent or any other form of proprietary knowledge forces the inventor to disclose the results of his research activity, in order to limit their use by others. Spillovers occur whenever a firm acquires knowledge from another firm, a university, or a government institution without having to pay for that information in a market transaction. They represent the impact of discovered ideas or compounds in the research endeavours of others (Griliches 1991).

Spence (1984) found that an increase in spillovers reduces the
incentive to invest in R & D, but also reduces the level of R & D
investment required to achieve a given level of cost reduction.
Cohen and Levinthal (1989) showed that firms might have an
additional private incentive to invest in R & D since this spending
also develops their ability to identify and explore the pool
of knowledge generated by other firms and available in the
environment.

Empirical evidence

Several different approaches have been used to assess the existence of R & D spillovers and their contribution to productivity
growth. Terleckyj (1980) used input-output data on each industry's purchases of materials and capital as indicators of the
amount of 'borrowed' knowledge. He reported higher rates of
return for 'borrowed' knowledge than for own R & D. His
approach, however, considered only knowledge which is embodied in goods or services, and did not cover the actual transfer of
ideas between research teams in different industries. Scherer
(1982, 1984) found that 'used' R & D—that is, internal process
R & D plus embodied knowledge 'borrowed' from outside—
showed considerably higher returns than own product R & D,
confirming Terleckyj's results.

Jaffe (1986) used data on the distribution of firms' patents
by technological class to determine the distance between them
in technological space. Assuming that firms are more likely
to absorb spillovers from other firms which are close in technological space, he constructed a measure of technological opportunity, weighting the R & D of other firms according to their
technological proximity. Jaffe reported positive effects of technological opportunity on patenting activity and own R & D. He also
found that productivity growth increases with both own R & D
and R & D of neighbouring firms in the technological space, as do
the returns to R & D activity. Bernstein (1989) and Bernstein
and Nadiri (1989, 1991) estimated the effect of intra- and inter-
industry spillovers on firms' cost structures, finding evidence that
inter-industry effects have a strong downward effect on average
costs of production. These cost benefits would be greater in firms
with larger R & D spending.

It is fair to conclude from this evidence that substantial spillovers can be found in practice, both between firms and between industries, leading to productivity gains and even to changes in the structure of production. There is also evidence that spillovers have an important effect on innovative activity itself— or at least on patenting activity—as shown by Jaffe (1986). These effects vary according to R & D intensity in both firms and industries.

Sources and beneficiaries of spillovers

Although most of the available evidence on knowledge externalities is based on empirical studies of spillovers between firms and industries, it must be remembered that technological spillovers may also come from outside the industrial structure. Jaffe (1989) and Acs et al. (1992) found evidence that corporate patenting activity responds positively to research expenditures in universities. Moreover, Acs et al. (1992) also provide evidence that geographical proximity seems to play an important part in this, since there is strong co-location of university and corporate R & D at the state level, and this co-location of activity has a positive impact on the generation of knowledge. Another non-industrial source of knowledge spillovers is government expenditure in R & D. Nadiri and Mamuneas (1991, 1994) showed that the stock of government financed R & D makes a significant contribution to reducing the average industry costs, and to increased labour productivity—though the magnitude of this effect differs between industries.

The literature appears, therefore, to confirm that there are unobserved externalities associated with R & D activity carried out by different sources. Firms appear to be the main beneficiaries of these spillovers, obtaining productivity gains and cost reductions, and also increasing their own innovative output. An important question here is which type of firm tends to profit most from the different kinds of spillover? Although it has been shown that the bulk of corporate R & D expenditure is concentrated amongst the largest firms (Scherer and Ross 1990), studies such as Pavitt et al. (1987) and Acs and Audretsch (1987) have found that, in some markets, small firms seem to have the edge in innovative activity. This could mean that small firms benefit more from R & D spillovers than their large counterparts, since their own R & D investment is comparatively small. Using data for US firms, Acs et al. (1994) found evidence suggesting a differential capacity to absorb spillovers. Their results suggest that large firms tend to benefit more from R & D efforts carried out by private corporations, while research activities carried out by universities would be an essential resource for small firms.

2.4 CLUSTERS IN PRACTICE: REGIONAL NETWORKING AND USER–PRODUCER RELATIONSHIPS

The literature suggests that networks of related innovating firms, such as those found in successful clusters, make an important contribution to innovative effort and output (Freeman 1991). Proximity to rivals also seems to procure improvements in the firms' internal organization, boosting both incumbents' and new entrants' chances of growth. This happens because these regions provide both low transaction costs and high external economies (Cooke and Morgan 1994). Some of the earliest research in this area took the form of detailed case studies examining the creation and evolution of well-known and successful clusters in Europe and the USA. Studies of Silicon Valley (California), Route 128 (Massachusetts), the Emilia-Romagna region in Italy, and Baden-Württemberg in Germany are probably the most obvious examples.

Most studies on the success and failure of specific clusters (see, for instance, Saxenian 1994; Brusco 1982), and on national and regional systems of innovation (see Nelson 1993; Aydalot and Keeble 1988), demonstrate that the existence of localized networks of innovators and the establishment of close user–producer relationships seem to be distinguishing features of successful clusters. In some European regions, strong institutional support at the local level also appears to play an important part. However, the origins and dynamics of these agglomerations vary from one region to another, and are conditioned by a large number of factors, especially technological factors.

Debresson and Amesse (1991) found that localized networks appear to be more durable than formal, international strategic alliances. This is because regional networks are reinforced by social, cultural, and symbolic bonds that result in a kind of 'social solidarity' made possible by geographical proximity and frequent contact. Technological collaboration increases the partners' scope of activities, allows for risk sharing, and improves the firms' ability to deal with increasing technological complexity (Teece 1986*a*; Dodgson 1994). At the same time it needs to be remembered that joint ventures can incur substantial transactions costs.

Integration between customers and suppliers allows for spillovers and feedbacks that induce innovation and organizational improvement (Fagerberg 1995). Close and stable communication and interaction between users and producers of a technology decrease the costs of technology transfer and accelerate diffusion (Lundvall 1988). The presence of strong user–supplier relationships in the value chain allows for better performance by sustaining flexibility and adaptability in product and process development. Slaughter (1993) found that, in some cases, users appear to be a greater source of ideas to enhance technology development than the producers of that same technology.

American high-technology clusters: Silicon Valley and Route 128

Interest in the emergence and prosperity of the high-technology clusters located in Santa Clara, California (Silicon Valley), and in the area surrounding Boston–Cambridge, Massachusetts (Route 128), has generated a stream of literature. This has sought to establish the reasons for the success, decay, and revitalization of these and other, less important, high-tech industrial centres in the United States (see, for instance, Hall and Markusen 1985).

The decline of the traditional US 'manufacturing belt' region (see Krugman 1991*a*) in the north-east was accompanied by the rise of the high-tech 'sunbelt' (California) from the late 1960s onwards. According to Scott (A. J. 1994), this succession of events can be interpreted as a locational outcome of the crisis of Fordist mass production, and the consequent rapid growth of new kinds of flexible production systems. These innovative changes were radical enough to be indifferent (or even adverse) to the specific kinds of skills and benefits agglomerated in the old industrial regions. In both the Californian and Massachusetts high-technology complexes, these developments were the result of entrepreneurial efforts drawing on the existent network of universities and research laboratories in the area.

Dorfman's (1985) study of Route 128 points out that the explosive growth in the high-tech sector, fuelled by the advances in computers and electronics, encouraged new firm start-ups not only from university researchers but also from existing companies. It was the tendency for these spin-offs to remain near their source that fostered geographical concentration.

Among the factors that fostered the growth of the Boston–Cambridge high-technology complex, Dorfman emphasizes the existence of physical resources, the availability of critical human capital, the support of venture capital, and a technological infrastructure composed of research facilities and specialized suppliers. From the mid-1970s onwards, however, Route 128 entered a period of decline, due to its excessive dependence on government contracts, to its vulnerability to increased foreign (Japanese) competition, and to failures in diversifying into new technologies with future market potential.

The story of Silicon Valley has much in common with the story of Route 128, though there are some very important differences. Silicon Valley provided the scientific and industrial base for the development of the semiconductor industry. As in Boston, university research was a focal point for innovation and new firm entry (Saxenian 1994). As with Route 128, the Silicon Valley cluster faced crisis by the end of the 1970s. At that point, the performance of the two centres started to diverge (Saxenian 1994). While Silicon Valley regained its former vitality, and successfully moved into new semiconductor technologies, Route 128 showed few signs of reversing the decline. Saxenian (1990, 1994) believes that one of the main reasons for the difference in performance was that in Silicon Valley, companies were better at drawing on the rich infrastructure of social, professional, and commercial relationships. The establishment of informal networks of contact that had started in the 1960s and 1970s was replaced in the 1980s by the founding of formal and effective partnership and cooperation agreements.

Networks became powerful forms of institutional collaboration designed to cope with systemic innovation, though some were formal in structure and others informal. Firms organized to learn from customers, suppliers, and competitors about what to make next and how to make it. This approach clashes with the individual, isolated, and vertically integrated large firm approach that remained characteristic of the Boston–Cambridge cluster. As Saxenian (1994) observes, 'Corporations that invested in dedicated equipment and specialized worker skills find themselves locked into obsolete technologies and markets, while their hierarchical structures limit their ability to adapt quickly as conditions change. Their inward focus and vertical integration also limit the development of a sophisticated local infrastructure, leaving the entire region vulnerable when the large firms falter. . . . Route 128 firms continued to generate technological breakthroughs but were not part of an industrial system that would have enabled them to exploit these successes as a region' (p. 9).

The contrast between the cases of Silicon Valley and Route 128 suggests that innovation and its communication are key factors in the development of clusters. Cluster success, at least in the case of highly complex and ever changing technologies, seems to reside in the ability of firms to establish networks of relations that allow them to keep up with the latest developments.

The European case: different approaches to the development of a regional creative environment

The European experience has been different, and the differences in patterns of agglomeration can be related to differences in local environment. Although it is possible to find many different, hybrid types within the same country, there is a distinctly national pattern to the form of clusters—associated with different national innovation systems. The regional agglomerations in France, Italy, Germany, and the UK all have important differences.

The classical French *dirigiste* approach (Cooke and Morgan 1994) was modelled on the concept of *growth poles* (Perroux 1950). Based on strong government orientation and funding, it led to the construction of innovative areas (*technopoles*) such as Meylan in the Rhône-Alpes, and Sophia-Antipolis in the south. These areas were constructed as concentrations of universities, research centres, small and medium enterprises, and also some branches of

large multinationals. Although these regions have grown, some
studies have shown that a lack of innovative synergies and interaction has led to shortcomings in innovative performance
(Charbit et al. 1991; Colletis 1993). More recently, attempts have
been made to tone down the centralist approach, to make local
structures more flexible, and to foster the interaction between
large and small firms, with the aim of enhancing the technological
diversification of these poles (Loinger and Peyrache 1988).

Italy's infrastructure of innovation support emerges from the
concerted efforts of local private and municipal organizations.
Regions like Emilia-Romagna and Tuscany have grown rapidly
in a remarkably cohesive local social and political environment.
Two vital factors in this success have been the creation of producer and trade associations, and the close supplier–customer
relationships in mono-industrial towns or districts. Strong examples of this are in Carpi and Prato (clothing), Sassuolo (ceram-
ics), and Modena (mechanical engineering); in all of these the
small and medium enterprise dominates. Urban structure reinforces a kind of communal solidarity that encourages specialization and the exchange of information.

Commenting on the success of the 'Emilian Model', Brusco
(1982) points out that, in addition to supportive local networks
and institutions, a key factor is the presence of a 'secondary'
industrial sector. This sector, consisting of mainly small, competitive, and innovative enterprises, provides flexibility to the productive structure of the 'primary', internationally competitive,
industrial sector, which is composed of larger firms. This secondary sector provides labour or absorbs redundant labour over
the business cycle, and responds to subcontracted orders with a
guarantee of high-quality performance.

The German approach, identified with the Baden-Württemberg
region, is based on a well-defined hierarchy of institutions supporting innovation. These range from the large-scale government
and private institutions to multiple technology-transfer institutions, providing business services to small and medium
enterprises, and supporting supplier–customer relationships that
lend themselves to new innovations, through 'simultaneous engineering' (Cooke and Morgan 1994). As noted before, hybrid forms
of these models can be found in other places in Europe. The
Neuchâtel region in Switzerland, for instance, is an example of
how the flexibility of the scientific framework and the existence of

regional labour mobility chains help to secure the survival of small and medium firms in periods of recession (Maillat and Vasserot 1988).

Of the various European approaches, the British model for high-technology clusters is perhaps the closest to that in the United States. The location of innovative (and, more particularly, high-technology) industries results from a more spontaneous, unplanned choice. Keeble (1988) argues that the most important determinants of high-technology industry location in Britain are the spatial distribution of highly qualified labour and the residential preferences of senior management.

The characteristics of clusters are highly dependent on the social, political, and economic environment of the region. It seems clear, however, that three properties are common to all successful innovative clusters:

- formal and informal networking, allowing for effective transfer of technology and other organizational capabilities;
- close user–producer collaboration allowing for production flexibility and joint development;
- mobility and flexibility in the local labour market, allowing for low redundancy costs and easy adaptation to changes in products and processes.

This flexibility in the scientific and production structures of firms and workers lies at the heart of Piore and Sabel's (1984) concept of 'flexible specialization', and indeed has much in common with Marshall's (1927) concept of an 'industrial district'.

However, it is clear that these regional economies cannot all be assimilated into the same model, and their survival depends ever more on their ability to evolve, and to adapt to a widening global landscape of hierarchically integrated territories and functions (Amin and Robbins 1991).

2.5 THE GEOGRAPHY OF INNOVATION

Theoretical background

The foundations for the modern theories of innovation were established by Schumpeter (1928, 1934, 1939, 1943). Schumpeter argued that innovation continues to change economic structures through a process of *creative destruction* that is *the essential fact about capitalism* (1943: 83). Schumpeter's theory of innovation was closely related to his theory of entrepreneurship since the entrepreneur plays such a key role in the process of innovation.

Schumpeter recognized, however, that innovation has an incremental, cumulative characteristic that cannot solely be attributed to the will and persistence of entrepreneurs. It is also dependent on the technological and scientific knowledge that defines technological trajectories: 'When some innovation has been successfully carried into effect, the next wave is more likely to start in the same or a neighbouring field than anywhere else. Major innovations hardly ever emerge in their final form or cover in one throw the whole field that will ultimately be their own' (Schumpeter 1939: 167).

Schumpeter's works provide a foundation for the analysis of innovations deriving from cumulative advances in science, technology, and knowledge accumulation within specific sectors (Freeman 1990). The literature in this tradition has also shown that there are both technology-push and demand-pull forces at work in the innovative process (see Kamien and Schwartz 1982 for a review). The cumulativeness of the innovative process is one of its most important characteristics. Some of the most influential subsequent work in the Schumpeterian tradition, notably Rosenberg (1976) and Nelson and Winter (1982), has further stressed the importance of cumulativeness as a feature of industrial innovation, and has demonstrated this both theoretically and empirically.

Cumulativeness is also highly relevant in the context of clustering. As Breschi (1995) shows, the cumulativeness of innovative activity is also relevant in geographical space, and plays a key role in shaping the geographical pattern of innovative activity and performance. The scientific base supporting innovation, besides being industry-specific, is also place-specific. Likewise, different regions provide different forms of demand-pull on innovative activity, according to their dimension, growth, and social development, and to the presence of user firms in related industries, increasing the demand for inputs. As these effects can differ between geographical regions, so the innovation patterns will also differ and, furthermore, these differences should be cumulative or self-reinforcing.

Why is innovative activity localized?

During the last two decades, the globalization of markets has led industries to disintegrate vertically and seek out the lowest cost locations for production (Hymer 1979). Technology-intensive businesses tend to disperse their manufacturing units, leading to the fragmentation of enterprises into global webs (Reich 1991). The rationale for multinational dispersion rests on two principles (Flaherty 1986). First, multinational firms derive competitive advantage from intangible assets (e.g. technology) that can be transferred with ease within the company, but outside a company only with difficulty. Second, in using its own technology in foreign manufacturing, a company can earn a larger return on its technology than by just selling it.

On the other hand, non-routine activities associated with innovation, such as research and development units, tend to become more spatially concentrated (as we saw above). The geographical rigidity of R & D activities in multinationals is confirmed by Zander and Sölvell (1995). Patel (1995) moreover finds no evidence of a growing fragmentation of R & D activities. On the contrary, his study shows a tendency for firms to keep the production of technology for global markets localized, usually close to their home base. Why does location matter for innovative activity? Feldman (1994) shows that locations which contain knowledge inputs that are critical to the innovative process will tend to be locations with higher than average levels of innovation.

The nature of the innovative process

The innovative process has an internal dimension, consisting of those sources of knowledge that a firm finds it advantageous to internalize, and an external one, comprising those sources which the firm does not attempt to internalize, on grounds of high cost, high level of specialization, or because of other constraints. The latter are procured by a variety of formal and informal strategic arrangements with other organizations which have these knowledge bases.

The simplistic 'linear' view of innovation saw innovation as a straightforward one-directional process whereby the fruits of 'ivory tower' scientific research were translated through product development into marketed products. In this context, the origins of innovation are always in research. This 'linear' model is known to be flawed. It is clear, for example, that there are other knowledge-producing activities that make a major contribution to the innovation process, and that internal sources of new knowledge can be found in each stage. Moreover, the bi-directional flow of information between the stages is crucial. Hippel (1988) found that the knowledge and experience gained through activities such as product testing and development, producer and customer services, and market research create a greater understanding of the potential of a technology, and of the modifications and improvements it needs.

Kline and Rosenberg (1986) presented an alternative formulation of the 'linear model', which they called the chain-linked model. This recognizes the interdependencies and dynamic feedback between the stages of the process: in a model of this sort, innovation can be initiated at any stage, and in any part of the organization.

It seems clear that each of the stages of the innovation process receives inputs from external sources, whether formally or informally. As noted in the previous section, technological externalities or spillovers constitute an important source of innovative output. The origins of these knowledge inputs make up the technological infrastructure that supports innovation activity (Feldman 1994). Innovation activity will tend to be geographically concentrated close to this infrastructure, which is relatively immobile and place-specific (Tassey 1991). An area with specialized resources for innovative activity has a comparative advantage, and, since knowledge is cumulative, this advantage is self-reinforcing and leads to the geographical clustering of innovative activity (Arthur 1990).

We have seen that the literature suggests that university R & D has a positive effect on private research output (Jaffe 1989; Acs et al. 1992). Government-financed academic research enhances the stock of basic knowledge, therefore expanding technological opportunities and increasing innovative activity. Nelson (1993) found evidence that academic research is more important for technological progress in the early stages of development of an industry than in its maturity, where industrial and academic research tend to grow apart.

While information may be easily transmitted across great distances, translating information into usable knowledge is a more complex, cognitive process. It requires a shared language and a set of common frames of reference. In the initial stages, this language may not even exist, and there is a need to create common codes of communication. Innovation becomes an interactive process that involves questioning and interpretation, which is facilitated by face-to-face contact (Feldman 1994). The development of a common cognitive structure between people in all the three stages of the innovative process is essential to allow for learning and knowledge accumulation.

Uncertainty is another distinctive characteristic of the innovative process (Dosi 1988b). The close presence of other innovators sharing similar experiences makes regional networking important, and offers a mechanism that enables risk sharing and reduces uncertainty (Camagni 1991a). Allen (1983) describes how spillovers resulting from close contact and observation can reduce uncertainty. Another important local source of knowledge is the presence of suppliers and users of the products/processes introduced. Hippel (1988) showed that suppliers and end-users of a technology are an important source of outside knowledge and ideas. This interaction involves direct cooperation and the exchange of qualitative information, by which suppliers gather feedback for further innovation and users learn about new products/processes and construct plans for implementation (Webb and Cleary 1993).

This kind of interaction is again highly dependent on geographical proximity. Lundvall (1988) points out that, when a technology is complex and ever changing, proximity can be very important for the competitiveness of both users and producers. When user needs or technological paradigms change rapidly and radically, the need for proximity in geographical and cultural terms becomes even more important.

Specialized business services can also be considered as part of the *knowledge infrastructure*. These include sources of expertise on government regulations, standards, product testing, market research, and financial services. Case studies such as Dorfman

(1985) and Saxenian (1994) note the crucial role played by these kinds of businesses in the growth and success of Route 128 and Silicon Valley.

The nature of technology

Technological conditions differ across firms, industries, regions, and over time. But the sectoral and spatial patterns of innovation should be related, since there are common factors in their determination. It seems clear then that technological conditions, or *regimes* (Nelson and Winter 1982; Malerba and Orsenigo 1990, 1993), will affect the location of innovative activity (Breschi 1995). When technological opportunity affects the rate of innovation, then the spatial location of innovators will be affected by where such opportunity is available and effectively accessible to firms; that is, it depends on the location of the sources of knowledge spillovers, and also on the availability of relevant specialized labour.

In industries with a higher level of technological opportunity, there is more scope for innovators to derive competitive advantage through innovation. These industries therefore have stronger selective pressures (Nelson and Winter 1982), permitting successful innovators to acquire and maintain high levels of market power. In such cases, market structure will exhibit a strong tendency towards concentration.

Turning to the variation in technological opportunity over time, Brezis and Krugman (1993), Audretsch and Feldman (1995), and Klepper (1996) suggest that the propensity for innovative activity to cluster depends on the stage of the industry life cycle. Clustering is important at an early stage, when the level of innovative activity is high, and when the exchange of tacit knowledge is vital. The forces for clustering weaken as the industry life cycle enters maturity because most knowledge is codified, and cost conditions rather than local sources of expertise become the dominant factor in location.

Finally, if appropriability is high and diffusion is slow, competitive advantage and super-normal profits can be maintained, leading, again, to high sectoral concentration. The precise effect of increased sectoral concentration on the spatial distribution of innovation is unclear, but it seems reasonable to expect that when there is a smaller number of innovators, geographical concentration of innovative activity is more likely.

The geography of innovation and R & D spillovers: empirical evidence

As noted above, economic geographers have offered extensive descriptive evidence on the location of innovative activity (Malecki 1980; Howells 1984, 1990), but have not sought to quantify the strength of the economic forces that lead to clustering.

One of the first studies on the location of patented inventions was Thompson (1962). His work sought to identify the inventing population and to determine the relationship between the geographical concentration of patents and industry employment. He found that more than 90 per cent of the patents in the sample had their origin in central metropolitan areas, suggesting that invention was essentially an urban phenomenon. Thompson's results show high correlation between distribution of inventions and employment in related industries. His work anticipated some of the ideas that would appear later in the literature: 'The reasoning here is that new products and techniques are largely spawned by persons who work for, or are otherwise closely associated with, the industry most closely linked with the particular idea or device. To the extent that this is so, a substantial, persistent and even cumulative advantage would accrue to any region which gained a head start in a particular industry' (Thompson 1962: 260).

One of the most influential studies in this area was Jaffe's work (1989) on the results of university research. Jaffe found that corporate patenting activity within a particular state increases with the level of research expenditures undertaken by universities in that state. Acs et al. (1992), replicating Jaffe's study, found a strong correlation between university and corporate R & D at the state level, with both having a positive impact on the generation of knowledge.

Jaffe et al. (1993) used data on patent citations to determine the extent to which knowledge spillovers are geographically localized. They studied whether a patent filed by a company in one particular location tended to cite other patents filed by companies (or universities) located nearby. Their rationale for this is that patent citations can be treated as a paper trail left by spillovers. Obviously it is an incomplete paper trail, since not all spillovers can be tracked in this way. But nevertheless it is an imaginative approach to studying this difficult question. Their results find a strong localization of spillovers. Most spillovers occur within a metropolitan area, but some occur within the same state. Localization appears more significant for patents registered by universities and by medium and small firms than for the patents filed by top corporations.

Feldman (1994) found an important correlation between the location of innovative output and of manufacturing value-added. Her results indicate that regional innovative output increases in the presence of high private and academic research expenditure within the state. However, it is the presence of related industries that has the most significant effect, which seems to demonstrate the importance of regional networks of innovators, at least in highly innovative industries. Specialized business services in the region also have a significant role. In later work, Audretsch and Feldman (1996) also found evidence for the clustering of innovative output. Baptista and Swann (1996) found that firms located in strong clusters, where employment in their own (two-digit) industry is high, are significantly more likely to innovate than firms located in more sparsely populated clusters.

2.6 CONCLUDING REMARKS

This chapter has surveyed some of the main theoretical and empirical work on industrial clusters and the geographical concentration of innovative activity. We have seen that while this phenomenon is pervasive, the forces leading to agglomeration (especially in high-technology industries) differ between Europe and the USA. As we have seen, the spatial organization of production and innovation can be approached from several perspectives. Nevertheless, a recurrent theme in the survey has been the effects of agglomeration externalities in general, and of knowledge spillovers in particular.

Industrial clusters arise from the pervasiveness of agglomeration externalities, leading to a dynamic, self-reinforcing process that will only be stopped by congestion effects or by radical technological discontinuities. These clusters are constituted as transactions-intensive regional economies which are in turn interdependent across the globe, setting up the foundations for much contemporary international trade (A. J. Scott 1994).

The examination of agglomerations also leads to the conclusion that a localized pattern of development facilitates a collective learning process, increasing the speed of diffusion by reducing uncertainty. Innovation becomes, first and foremost, a collaborative social endeavour (Allen 1983) where the costs and burdens are shared by a wide range of regional participants: the workforce, suppliers, customers, universities and research institutes, government bodies, and, of course, competing companies. The networking of firms engaged in related research and sources of novel scientific knowledge in universities and public research laboratories play an important role in this process. Interaction with suppliers and clients also assumes an important role, as do specialized business services. The cumulative nature of innovative activity creates a clear, self-reinforcing advantage for firms who locate in areas that are abundant in these resources, leading innovation to exhibit pronounced geographical concentration.

3

Towards a Model of Clustering in High-Technology Industries

G. M. PETER SWANN

Drawing on the literature review, the aim of this chapter is to set out a simple model of clustering in high-technology industries that forms the basis of the empirical analysis in the later chapters. Much analysis of clusters has focused on the initial formative stages, or what could be called the *rise* of clusters. In these formative stages there is an important positive feedback mechanism which reinforces the development of clusters. But this positive feedback rarely continues indefinitely. Within most clusters, even the most successful, diminishing returns are liable to set in beyond a certain point. This means that the rate of growth of the cluster will start to decline. Eventually, indeed, the cluster will stop growing, and start to decline. Most analysis of cluster-ing tends to stop there: the cluster enters a phase of decline from which there is no apparent recovery. But this is not the inevitable outcome. In a few cases, clusters that reach maturity do not nec-essarily then decline into oblivion. Some of them experience a *renaissance* or revival in a new age with a new set of industries.

The first section of this chapter gives an overview of the life cycle of the industrial cluster, beyond the rise described in Chapter 2, through its fall and to its possible rebirth. Section 3.2 summarizes the advantages and disadvantages of clustering from the perspective of the firm trying to optimize its location. The next three sections (3.3 to 3.5) focus in more detail on each of these phases. Section 3.6 describes the general structure of the econometric models that are used for empirical analysis, while sections 3.7 and 3.8 (and Appendix 3A) give details. Section 3.9 concludes.

3.1 OVERVIEW, FROM RISE TO FALL
AND RENAISSANCE

The model of cluster life cycles developed in this chapter has three basic features:[1]

Agglomeration externalities and positive feedback. The empirical analysis in Chapters 4–7 demonstrates that firms in clusters grow faster than those in isolation, and that clusters attract a higher rate of entry at least during the early and growth phases of the life cycle for a particular industry. This happens because of agglomeration economies, which impact on entry and growth and hence lead to a form of positive feedback. These effects operate more strongly within a confined geographical area, in part because of the tacit nature of much technological knowledge (Pavitt 1987).

Congestion effects. Our empirical analysis also suggests that the rate of entry and possibly also the rate of growth start to tail off (and perhaps even decline) in very large clusters—essentially because the costs of locating in a cluster start to detract from the benefits.

Convergence of technologies. Two technologies, and the industries producing them, are assumed to be *distinct* if the strength of industry A in cluster X has no effect on the rate of growth and rate of entry into industry B at that cluster—and vice versa. The technologies are assumed to be converging when the strength of A in cluster X does have a positive effect on the rate of growth and entry into industry B at that cluster—or vice versa. Our empirical analysis of Chapters 4–7 suggests that cross-sectoral effects of this sort are important.

We assess the growth of clusters, meanwhile, by reference to two variables: first, the extent of entry, and second the growth of incumbent firms in a cluster. While to a first approximation it might seem likely that these follow a similar pattern over the cluster life cycle, in fact our empirical analysis suggests that they do not necessarily behave in exactly the same way.

---

[1] The ideas in this section are developed in greater detail in Swann (1998, forthcoming).

Rise, fall, and renaissance

The essence of the cluster life cycle is this. When the cluster starts to emerge, ahead of other regions or cities, it attracts further entry and firm growth is faster. This reinforces its position, and it continues to forge further ahead. At this stage the first feature of the model is the dominant one. But beyond a certain size, the costs of locating in the cluster start to rise. The cluster may still be the preferred location if the benefits are high enough to offset these congestion costs. But as the industry enters its maturity stage, the benefits of clustering start to tail off, and eventually the costs of clustering will outweigh the benefits. This is where the second feature of the model starts to dominate.

At this stage the cluster is approaching its peak, but has not entered the decline phase as such. It may be growing very slowly, but it is not getting smaller. That stage starts when the industries located in this cluster start to decline. This could be because activity is being relocated to other countries with lower costs. Or it could be that the industry itself is in decline. At this point, the cluster will start to decline too, and will be left with large mature firms in a mature industry. These are not the sorts of organizations that generate significant spillovers, and hence further entry to the cluster is unlikely. So even if the cost of locating at this mature cluster starts to fall, so also do the benefits, and so the price mechanism on its own does not reverse this decline.

As new industries emerge, firms in those industries may then be faced with location decisions of the following sort. Should they locate in an old cluster, where they have little commonality with incumbents, where the established infrastructure is dated, and where congestion costs are still relatively high, though admittedly declining? Or do they locate in a new cluster where the incumbents, though new and small, are generating the sorts of spillovers that attract entrants and are based in more relevant industries, and where the infrastructure is better? Not surprisingly, many choose the new cluster, and so the decline of the old cluster, based on traditional industries, continues with few firms in new industries to replace the old.

This process could in principle continue until the old cluster disintegrates. But in some cases we believe that the third feature of the model can come into play. Convergence between traditional industries and old industries means that the mature and declining cluster may in fact offer an attractive location for certain types of entrants in newer industries. Thus, for example, computer services companies find it attractive to locate near to mature companies in traditional industries, who are starting to exploit the potential of computer technologies in reviving their business. Or indeed, computer software companies find that the most powerful attractor in locational terms is no longer a strong hardware base in that cluster, but a strong publishing sector with a large stock of intellectual property rights. When old and new technologies converge in this way, then the mature cluster becomes once again an attractive location. And with luck (or planning) the new entrants attracted in this way themselves act as attractors for a new generation of entrants.

As noted before, this process of convergence is not the only process by which old clusters may be revived. In principle this could happen simply through the price mechanism. The oldest, derelict clusters are also the cheapest, and this on its own can attract a wave of new entry. In fact we do not find this very compelling as an explanation on its own. No doubt the price mechanism plays some role, but so too does technological convergence. Of course, the policy of *urban renewal* can be seen as an attempt to revive moribund clusters—not always with success, however (Jacobs 1961).

Sections 3.3 to 3.5 explore each stage of this cycle of rise, fall, and renaissance in more detail. First, it is useful to classify the advantages and disadvantages of clustering—from the perspective of the firm choosing where to locate.

3.2 THE ADVANTAGES AND DISADVANTAGES OF CLUSTERING[2]

It is natural to split the forces generating clusters into two groups: demand side and supply side. But it is also important to note that there can be disadvantages as well as benefits from clustering. Indeed, some firms actively choose to locate some activities outside the main industry cluster. The location strategies of Japanese car firms in the UK and especially the USA could be interpreted as an example of this (Rubinstein 1992).

[2] This section draws on Swann (1993c).

Table 3.1 classifies the various forces for and against clustering. Starting in the top left-hand corner (demand-side benefits), firms may cluster in a particular location to take advantage of strong local demand. But it is worth remembering that the source of this demand need not necessarily be firms in the same industry. A second, and slightly different demand-side motive for clustering is that under certain conditions, a firm stands to take market share from rivals if it locates in a cluster. This gain may admittedly be short-lived if further firms enter, or if the incumbents in a cluster react to this unwanted competition. Models in the tradition of Hotelling (1929) can generate a clustering outcome, essentially because under certain assumptions one firm stands to gain market share if it moves its location closer to another.

A third demand-side motive for clustering can be more long-lived. Firms may choose to locate in a cluster because they are more likely to be *found* by customers. A clear example of this applies in the context of antique shops. Many of the potential customers are discriminating, and wish to search before purchase to find the item that most closely fits their requirements. Searching is costly, especially if long distances have to be covered, and a shop located in a cluster will enjoy more chance visitors than an isolated shop. Antique shops (for example) often cluster together, in part because their consumers are discerning, and wish to search before purchase. A shop located in a cluster will enjoy more spillovers (chance visitors) than an isolated shop. Another is the informational externality about the strength of market demand that accrues to the new entrant who sees an established supplier trading successfully (and profitably?) at a particular location. A fourth motive arises because customers are a good source of ideas for innovation (Hippel 1980), and firms can exploit these information spillovers by locating near to key users, and maintaining frequent contact.

Turning now to supply-side benefits, these consist of technology spillovers from widespread tacit technology transfer (Jaffe et al. 1993), and also the benefits of access to a large pool of specialized labour, which can be found in a cluster, but may be harder to attract to an isolated location. We can add to that the infrastructure benefits of locating in a cluster. For example, access to major motorways is often cited as an attractor. Another form of informational externality accrues to the new entrant from seeing an estab-

Table 3.1 *Advantages and disadvantages of clustering from the perspective of the clustered firm*

	Demand side	Supply side
Advantages	Input-output multipliers	Technology spillovers
	Hotelling	Specialized labour
	Search costs	Infrastructure
	Info. externalities	Info. externalities
Disadvantages	Congestion and competition in output markets	Congestion and competition in input markets (real estate, labour)

lished firm *producing* successfully at a particular location. A natural example of this is the informational externality from one successful gold-digger to the new entrant. An analogous example applies in drilling for oil.

These are the advantages enjoyed by a firm that locates in a cluster. But there can be disadvantages for that firm too. And as with the benefits, these can accrue on the demand side as well as the supply side. The disadvantages of clustering are obvious enough on the demand side. Congestion and increased competition in output markets can detract from firm performance. In a Cournot model, for example, an increased number of competitors will reduce per-firm sales, prices, per-firm profits, and per-firm growth. It seems likely that these effects will start to dominate the demand-side benefits when congestion becomes heavy, and that in turn suggests that there may be diminishing (and ultimately negative) returns to locating in a cluster, as the degree of congestion increases. On the supply side, the disadvantages of clustering again relate to congestion and competition in input markets, whether it be the cost of real estate or the cost of labour (Forester 1980). Again, it is plausible to expect that these effects may come to dominate when the cluster becomes very congested.

The benefits may be most important at an early stage of the cluster's life cycle, while the disadvantages start to build up at a later stage. Accordingly, it seems likely that beyond some point in the cluster's history, the disadvantages will start to dominate the benefits, especially when congestion becomes heavy.

3.3 THE RISE OF CLUSTERS

A very simple model which does, however, have all the required properties is in two parts.[3] Let entry of firms into industry i at cluster c be defined as E_{ic} and let the rate of growth of firms in industry i at cluster c be defined as G_{ic}. Then we shall refer to two measures of the *strength* of a cluster c: one is the strength of cluster c in industry i (S_{ic}), and the other is the strength of cluster c in all industries (k) other than i (S_{kc}). In some of our empirical analysis (Chapters 4–6), we have used estimates of employment as a measure of the strength of a particular industry in a particular cluster.

$$\text{Entry}_{ic} = f\left(S_{ic}, S_{kc}\right) \tag{1}$$

$$\text{Growth}_{ic} = g\left(S_{ic}, S_{kc}\right) \tag{2}$$

A simple case is where $df/dS_{ic} > 0$ and $dg/dS_{ic} > 0$, but $df/dS_{kc} = dg/dS_{kc} = 0$. This means that entry to industry i is higher and firms in i grow faster in clusters that are already strong in i, but the cluster's strength in other industries k does nothing to attract entry or promote growth. In this case it is easy to see that when a cluster in industry i gets ahead of rival clusters, it will tend to forge further ahead. Moreover, in the absence of any cross-sectoral effects to attract entry or promote or growth, the model will tend to predict that clusters specialize in a single industry. At least, there is no advantage to the cluster in diversifying its industrial base. And while there is no disadvantage either in the model as it stands, it is not difficult to see that if congestion effects are a function of $S_{ic} + S_{kc}$, then there are clear merits in specialization, and clear costs in diversification. To put it simply, if like firms convey benefits on incumbents while unlike firms do not, then if space is limited, it is better to group together with like firms.

Of course this simple case ($df/dS_{ic} > 0$, $dg/dS_{ic} > 0$, $df/dS_{kc} = dg/dS_{kc} = 0$) is not the only possibility. As an empirical matter, the

---

[3] The model in sections 3.3–3.5 is developed in more detail in Swann (1998, forthcoming).

magnitudes (and even the signs) of these derivatives are not likely to be constant. Moreover, the signs and magnitudes are likely to depend on the level of aggregation at which one is operating. We deal with these two points in turn. One aspect of this is the sort of congestion effect noted above, so that there are diminishing returns to clustering. More subtly, we find in our research that the relationship between the strength of the cluster and entry may follow a bell-shaped curve (Chapter 4). Below a certain size (the critical mass) the cluster does not attract entry and the effect of increases in strength on entry (df/dS) are small. But when this critical mass is reached, entry starts to take off sharply $(df/dS$ gets large, and d^2f/dS^2 is maximized). Then as the cluster grows it reaches a point of peak entry, at which $df/dS = 0$. Note that at this point the cluster is still growing, as entry is high. But beyond this point, entry starts to drop off and it then approaches zero.

In short, the magnitudes and signs of these derivatives may be very dependent on the size of the cluster. They may also be dependent on the stage of the industry in its life cycle. Thus in the formative (introduction and growth) stage of the life cycle, geographical proximity may be critical to tacit technology transfer—which is so essential to industry development—and hence the positive effects are large. But by the maturity stage, the technological knowledge that requires to be transferred is largely codified, so that geographical proximity is no longer such an important issue, and the derivatives used in the model are much smaller.

The second important empirical matter is that the signs of these derivatives depend on the level of aggregation at which one is working. In Chapters 4–6, the consensus seems to be that when one is working at a fairly aggregated level (two-digit SIC industries, for example), there is a clear dichotomy: the effect of strength in 'own industry' (i) on growth and entry is positive, while the effect of strength in 'other industries' (k) is negative (rather than zero).

When the level of aggregation is much smaller, more subtle effects comes into play. In our study of the USA computing industry (Chapter 4) we shall look at the effect of cluster strength on entry and growth when the industry is broken down into eight sectors (this is below the four-digit level of aggregation). As with the aggregated studies, we find that the effect of other sectors on incumbent growth is negative (though often statistically insignificant), but (in contrast) we find that the effect of other sectors on entry can be positive and rather significant. And moreover, while the effect of own sector strength on growth is positive (as with aggregated studies), the effect on entry can be negative. This can easily be rationalized by asking, 'who would enter a densely populated cluster?'

Why are the results so dependent on the level of aggregation? Consider entry by a firm X. Suppose that companies in related, but not identical, fields to X attract X's entry. On the other hand, suppose that companies that are identical to X may deter X's entry—a little reflection on the Cournot model of oligopolistic competition is enough to convince us that this second assumption is fair. At a *high* level of aggregation, related firms come into the *same* category as identical firms, and so the net effect of own sector strength on entry may be positive. Conversely, at a *low* level of aggregation, these related firms which attract entry come into a different sector, while the identical firms count as the same sector and deter entry.

3.4 THE MATURITY AND DECLINE OF CLUSTERS

The last section showed that positive feedback in the clustering process has its limits. Indeed, beyond a certain point congestion limits the attractiveness of an existing cluster for new entry— particularly if the industry located at that cluster is entering a maturity phase in which geographical proximity is not so important for technology transfer and industrial development.

The maturity of clusters arises (in the language of the bell-shaped entry curve of the last section) because the cluster has reached a size at which further entry is no longer attracted—and perhaps the growth externality to incumbent firms no longer operates. But this of itself does not explain decline. Entry may stop, and the factors that promote growth may disappear, but that simply implies stabilization at a particular size. It does not imply decline. To explain that, we have to invoke two additional effects. First, that the industry located at a mature cluster is in the decline stage of its industry life cycle; and second, that the cluster fails to attract sufficient new entrants into new industries to compensate for the exit and decline of mature incumbents. Not, however, that there is anything particularly implausible about these two assumptions—as we shall argue.

First consider the maturity of industries in mature clusters. We saw above that, in some circumstances, clusters would tend to specialize in one industry, and at least during the growth phase of the cluster this specialization is advantageous. Specialization becomes less desirable, however, later in the cluster life cycle. For if the cluster depends on one industry (or all the industries in the cluster mature at the same time) then maturity and decline—when they arrive—hit the cluster very hard. It is perhaps invidious to single out cities that have suffered especially because of an over-reliance on one industry, but examples (at some stages of their respective histories) include Detroit (cars), Glasgow (shipbuilding), and Manchester (cotton). All clusters face the maturity of some of their industries, and yet some of them ride through this because new industries are still attracted to replace the declining ones—we come to this in the next section.

Now we turn to the second characteristic required for the decline of clusters: that the cluster fails to attract sufficient new entrants into new industries to compensate for the exit and decline of mature incumbents. The question is why? This is exceptionally difficult to answer. To approach an answer let me draw an analogy to the Leontief input-output table. This table indicates how growth in sector X generates demand for the output of sector Y. As such it could be described as a *demand-side* sector-to-sector spillover chart. Imperfect as they may be, input-output tables of this sort exist, and are rather widely trusted. If we had the equivalent *supply-side* sector-to-sector spillover chart, then we would know which industries *attract* which other—where I use the word attract to describe attractive forces that derive from the sorts of agglomeration economies defined above. Then we could answer the question.

We see below in Chapters 4 and 6 that the econometric models of the US computer and biotechnology industries map out a set of sector-to-sector supply-side attractive forces. These define how strength in sector X (say) attracts entry into sector Y (say). In biotechnology we find few cross-sectoral effects, but in computing these cross-sectoral effects are rather significant (see Chapter 8). There is no doubt that it would be difficult to calibrate such a matrix on an economy-wide basis. But this matrix would be so helpful in explaining why some clusters have industries which—even if mature—are still capable of attracting successors, while other clusters are dominated by the sorts of industries and firms who are incapable of that.

Some have conjectured that there is a hierarchy of industries on a spectrum between *introvert* at one end and *extrovert* at the other. Some would place the chemical industry at the extrovert end of the spectrum. Indeed, to quote the chapter by Clow and Clow (1958: 230) in Singer et al.'s monumental *History of Technology*: 'The chemical industry is the most polygamous of all industries.' In our current frame of reference, this means that the supply-side sector-to-sector spillover chart should show that the chemical industry is unequalled as a suitor—it forms alliances with many other industries, or generates spillovers to many other industries. A cluster strong in this particular industry should be capable of surviving the decline of that industry—essentially because it is good at attracting successor industries to the same location.

Some would place distribution towards the other end of the spectrum—though it has to be said that there is limited evidence for this. The argument is that if (in effect) we knew this invisible supply-side input-output table, it would indicate that while distribution sectors were undoubtedly successful at absorbing spillovers from manufacturing industry, they are less successful at generating spillovers to the successive generation of entrants.

We can sum up this section as follows. Clusters enter maturity, and can start to decline when the cluster gets large enough to suffer from congestion, when the indigenous industries in that cluster start to decline, and particularly when the indigenous industries and firms are ones that do not attract the next generation of entrants into new industries. The lucky clusters are those that sustain a mix of industries and firms which continue to attract entry—as we see below.

3.5 THE REVIVAL (RENAISSANCE) OF CLUSTERS

We have seen why some clusters enter a phase of unremitting decline. The next issue for our attention is why some clusters—far from entering oblivion—actually recover in a most spectacular way. Let us start with the example of London. London seems to be an evergreen cluster. Is this because London is a cluster that through luck or design happens to have mature industries which attract the new industries? Or is it simply, as many have put it (including Porter 1990), that London is a nice place to live? Not of course that the latter explanation, London's beneficent industrial archaeology, is independent of its economic history. A city that invests a large share of its (large) economic rents in cultural infrastructure can expect to survive as a 'cluster'. But we submit that London's success as a cluster also derives from its history of attracting a diverse mix of industries, and its pre-eminent success at exploiting convergence between technologies.

Now let us turn to cities or clusters that recover. Boston is cited as a city that declined as an agricultural centre and port, but revived as a high-technology centre, building in some part at least on its retained cultural capital—including its world-renowned universities (Dorfman 1985). Norwich in the UK is a city whose wool industry declined at the start of the industrial revolution, as that industry relocated northwards to Yorkshire, but has re-vived recently as a centre for biotechnology in the UK. The theory of business cycles offers some obvious parallels here. The macro-economy can recover because of the price mechanism: if investment is cheap enough then firms will invest, and the investment-led growth will ensue.

Few macro-economists believe that the price mechanism alone is the key to macro-economic recovery: Keynes certainly did not. He referred instead to *animal spirits*. And we can draw a parallel here: just as the macro-economic recovery is related to qualitative business expectations, so also is the cluster recovery a function of qualitative factors. The key issue, as we saw in the last section, is for mature (even moribund) clusters to attract new entry into new industries at that cluster. If the price mechanism will not make this happen, then it must happen through the attractors, or supply-side spillovers.

It seems clear that some entry phases into mature but *renascent* clusters are generated by attractive mature industries. An impor-tant concept here is *convergence* between technologies. If two tech-nologies (A and B) are distinct, then however strong a cluster may be in industry A that strength does nothing to attract entry into

B—and vice versa. On the other hand, if two technologies (A and B) converge, that means either that a cluster strong in industry A generates spillovers that attract entry into B, or *vice versa*, or possibly both. (We return to this question of the direction of effects shortly.) If industry A generates spillovers of some value to new entrants in industry B, then the cluster, while an early centre for industry/technology A, will subsequently become a centre for B. This, as much as movements in relative prices, is the key to cluster revival. It also makes very clear just how important to the future development of clusters is what we shall call here *industrial archaeology*.

In Chapter 4, we examine a simulation study of the growth of industrial clusters based on an econometric analysis of entry and growth patterns in computer industry clusters. This finds that single technology clusters, while they might grow faster in the formative stages, did not have the lasting power of diversified clusters. The key concept here is an exceptionally evolutionary one: 'Diversity promotes longevity.' This seems to be sound human genetics and sound industrial economics!

The process of convergence

But if this thesis is to convince, we must say more about the process of convergence. Why and how does convergence happen? Are its effects symmetric (A attracts B and B attracts A) or not? Let us start with the question of symmetry, because it is easy to answer. There can be no general supposition that convergence has symmetric effects on the two industries A and B. Thus, in our computer industry study (Chapter 4) we find that software and hardware converge in the sense that clusters with strength in hardware and components were more successful at attracting entry into software, but the reverse is not true. Indeed, software does not appear to be an attractor in that study. And when we turn to convergence between a mature technology and a new one, symmetry would be most unlikely. The strength of the mature industry at a cluster may start to attract some sorts of entrants into the new industry. But it is unlikely that the strength of the new industry will attract entry into the old—though it may serve to promote growth in the old.

Now let us turn finally to the harder question—indeed the hardest question in this entire chapter. Why and how do technologies and hence industries converge? First let us consider an example. One of the most widely quoted examples is the convergence of telecommunications and information technology (Guy and Arnold 1986). At the simplest level a growing proportion of telephone traffic is in fact in the form of digital messages. At the next level we find that some computing and electronics companies start to specialize in the branches of technology required to make this interaction happen (modems, communications cards, digital exchanges, etc.). At the next level we start to find that the giants in one industry start to diversify into the other: thus AT&T started to make computers. Systems houses start to offer online databases. Alternatively joint ventures that cut across the two technologies start to blossom (Hagedoorn and Schakenraad 1992).

Indeed, what we have observed with information technology (IT) recently is that some of these joint ventures (notably with multimedia) have cut into a variety of traditional industries. For example, the key to success in multimedia may be nine parts intellectual property rights and one part technology. Thus a key component of multimedia strategy is to have the right publisher(s)—with IP rights over a wide range of 'software' (images, music, text, poetry, and so on). If geography matters in the multimedia industry, then it seems likely that the leading clusters of this industry will be those with a strong base in the 'publishing' industries (broadly defined). It is more plausible to expect the great galleries, recording studios, television-producing communities, and so on to attract computer industry entrants than vice versa.

IT is converging on most industries, in the sense that many industries have created entry opportunities to supply IT applications for that industry. Perhaps in the quote above, 'the chemical industry is the most polygamous of all industries', we should really replace chemical by IT.

But why does it happen? Is it a technological imperative? Or is it purely a socio-economic construction? This is one of the big (and perhaps unanswerable) questions in the philosophy of science. For while technologies—and the convergence between them—are indubitably developed as a product of a socio-

economic system, technological developments cannot be scientifically arbitrary. The answers to these questions have to be that
convergence is not a technological imperative, but neither is it
purely socio-economic and technologically arbitrary. Convergence between IT and other industries is not a technological imperative, and it will not happen as a matter of course. But if it can
be done, many companies will try to make it happen in the belief
that such an alliance would prolong the life cycle of their products, and hence their growth and profitability. Convergence does
not drop on them like 'manna from heaven'. But they cannot
create such convergence out of nothing.

The profitability of convergence depends in part, of course, on
the nature of demand for new products that emerge from the
convergence of old and new technologies. Almost by definition,
the products arising from this convergence will embody characteristics for which there has been no revealed demand in the past.
It is always exceptionally difficult to forecast demand for products with new characteristics. Many such products may fail, but
some succeed. But the record shows that convergence between
traditional technologies and new ones can sometimes yield substantial dividends.

3.6 TOWARDS AN ECONOMETRIC MODEL OF GROWTH AND ENTRY INTO HIGH-TECHNOLOGY CLUSTERS

Chapters 4 to 7 summarize our empirical studies of clustering
processes. In Chapters 4 to 6 we have used the same econometric
approach to analyse these questions. In Chapter 7, because the
biotechnology industry in the UK has a much shorter history to
date, it was not possible to use these detailed econometric models,
and instead some simpler models have been used. Nevertheless,
the same basic ideas underlie all of this empirical work. The
historical episodes we have studied are periods of cluster growth,
with only the beginnings of maturity in some parts of the USA
computer industry. Accordingly the econometric models developed here relate mainly to the first (growth) stage of the cluster
life cycle. But the models are also capable of detecting the onset of
congestion effects and therefore the beginnings of maturity—at
least in a few USA computer industry clusters. We have not been

able, however, to carry out any econometric study of decline and revival.

In Chapters 4 to 6 we summarize our estimates of two econometric models. The first examines whether the growth of firms is influenced by the strength of the cluster in which they are located. If a firm in sector i (say) is located in a cluster that is strong in firms *from that same sector* (i), does it grow faster or slower as a result—or does it make no difference? Again, if a firm in sector i (say) is located in a cluster that is strong in firms *from other sectors* (k), does it grow faster or slower as a result—or does it make no difference?

The second examines to what extent a strong cluster acts as an attractor to new entrants. If a cluster is strong in sector i (say), does that lead to higher or lower average entry into sector i at that cluster? Or does it make no difference? Again, if a cluster is strong in sector i, what effect does that have on entry into other sectors (k)? Or again, does it make no difference?

Figure 3.1 provides quite a concise summary of these models. Three groups of factors summarize the composition of a cluster: industry strength, fixed effects, and the science base. The clustering effects are felt through the entry of new firms and the growth of incumbents. As the diagram shows, any positive effects of industry strength (measured for example by relevant industry employment) on entry or growth lead to a positive feedback loop, or virtuous circle. The fixed effects are all the factors that make a cluster attractive, and hence promote entry and/or growth, but are not themselves changed by that entry or growth. These could include the climate—a factor often cited as part of California's success as an industrial cluster. Fixed effects could, in the short run, also include certain infrastructure factors (such as transport networks, cultural capital, and so on). In the models that follow, we do use the traditional econometric approach of fixed effects to model these factors.

The science base is an important attractor and potentially a growth promoter—especially in biotechnology (see Chapter 6). Here we have filled in the feedback loop as a dotted line, indicating that while there can be positive feedback from new entry and firm growth to the growth and strength of the science base, the link is more indirect and may take longer than the feedback to industry strength.

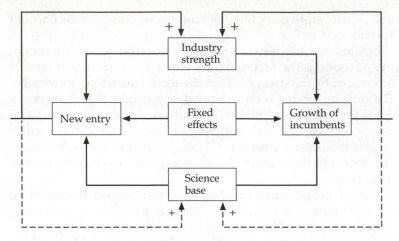

Fig 3.1 *Positive feedback in the growth of clusters*

3.7 THE MODEL OF ENTRY

To what extent are new entrants to an industry drawn towards
existing clusters? And what sorts of firm in the cluster may act as
the strongest attractor? This question could be treated at an individual firm level in which case we would need to model the
discrete choice of location selection *for each entrant*. For various
reasons, however, it is much easier to model this at an aggregate
level, that is the number of entrants to a particular subsector at a
particular cluster, in a particular time period. For reasons that will
become clearer when we study the data problems encountered
in the empirical studies (see especially Chapter 4), we use three
approaches to modelling entry to clusters.

A latent variables model of entry using principal components

This method is useful when we have a reasonably accurate time
series of entry by cluster, sector, and time period, but do not have
such accurate data on the strength of each cluster by sector and
time period. This is indeed the case in our studies in this book.
This method can then be summarized formally as follows. We
take time series of entry for each cluster and sector, and turn this

into a matrix of dimensions T^*C by S—where T is the number of time periods, C is the number of clusters, and S is the number of sectors. Call this matrix E. The latent variable approach postulates that $E = FA$, where F is a matrix of dimensions T^*C by S representing the latent (or unmeasurable) variables that attract entry, and A is an S^*S matrix summarizing the effect of each latent variable on entry into each sector. Although the interest of this may appear to be limited if F is unknown, it is still interesting to know whether each latent variable works independently to attract entry to a different sector, or by contrast whether some latent variables attract entry into several sectors simultaneously.

It can be shown (see appendix to this chapter) that A can be estimated as follows:

$$A' = XM \tag{3}$$

where X is the matrix of eigenvectors of the matrix $E'E$, and where M is a diagonal matrix whose elements are the square roots of the eigenvalues of $E'E$, placed in the same order as the eigenvectors are in X.

In practice—see Chapters 4–6—two eigenvalues tend to account for most of the variation in $E'E$, and accordingly two latent variables do most of the work in attracting entry. The interpretation of the technique is as follows. Those sectors for which a latent variable has a strong effect (as indicated by a large value of the relevant element in A) are sectors into which the latent variables (whatever they are) attract a lot of entry; those sectors for which coefficients are small are sectors into which these latent variables attract little entry. The attraction of this technique is that it works even if cluster strength data is problematic on a time series basis. The snag, of course, is that we are just left with latent variables, and no interpretation of them.

Average entry models

Again, where time series data are limited, it is useful to estimate a quasi-cross-section model summarizing how average entry to a cluster relates to a measure of cluster strength. To do this, for any cluster/sector combination, we simply compute average entry across all years for each sector and cluster. Then for any sector, we can plot a graph of average entry for that cluster/sector against (say) total employment in the cluster at end-period. Or, as appropriate, these plots can be summarized by a simple regression, where there are C observations per regression (C = number of clusters). Indeed, in the biotechnology study of the USA (Chapter 6), we have found it useful to compare the effects of total industry strength (employment in all sectors of biotechnology) with the effects of employment in the science base. In principle, one could run a regression of average entry against employment in each of the different sectors, but in practice this is unlikely to be very well determined given collinearity and limited degrees of freedom.

A full model of entry

In this model, total entry into a particular sector (i) at a particular cluster (c) in a particular year (t) is assumed to be a function of industry strength (usually employment) in each sector at that cluster at the start of that year. Loosely speaking, the model is as follows:

$$n_{cit} = \alpha_{ci} + \beta_i n_{.it} + \sum_{j=1}^{8} \gamma_{ij} \ln E_{cjt-1} + \sum_{\theta=2}^{4} \delta_{i\theta} \left(\ln E_{c.t-1} \right)^{\theta} \qquad (4)$$

where:

$$n_{.it} = \sum_{i=1}^{C} n_{cit} \qquad E_{c.t-1} = \sum_{i=1}^{8} E_{cit-1} \qquad (5)$$

n_{cit} is entry into sector i at cluster c in year t. $n_{.it}$ is a macro variable representing total entry into sector i in year t. The E_{cjt-1} variables represent employment in sector j at cluster c in year $t-1$ (i.e. at the start of period t). The α_{ci} parameters represent fixed effects: if these are strong and positive they represent factors which attract entry to sector i at cluster c, irrespective of industry strength and macro variables. The final polynomial terms in ln (Total Employment) in equation (4) are included to allow us to capture critical mass and congestion effects in clusters—as will become clearer in Chapter 4.

As the appendix shows, it is in practice efficient to use a slightly different form of this model, but with the same basic structure. This more sophisticated model will be used in Chapter 4, but not in other chapters. This full model allows us to separate out the effect of different types of industry strength at a cluster on entry, and in that sense is more interesting than the average entry model, which cannot do that. Moreover, it allows us to identify the character of cross-sectoral attraction: i.e. the capacity of strength in one sector to attract entry to another. The latent variable approach may imply that such cross-sectoral effects exist, but it cannot identify exactly what they are.

In Chapter 4, we use this full model to identify what we call congestion and Cournot effects. These are defined as follows. Let $\gamma_{i,\min}$ be the smallest attractor coefficient in the estimated entry model for sector i. There are two possibilities: that $\gamma_{i,\min}$ is in fact γ_{ii}, the effect of strength in sector i on entry into i; or that $\gamma_{i,\min}$ is γ_{ij}, where j is some other sector. In the first case, we also compute $\gamma_{i,\min}^*$ which is the smallest coefficient excluding γ_{ii}. Then if γ_{ii} is the smallest coefficient, we say that the Cournot effect is $\gamma_{ii} - \gamma_{i,\min}^*$ and the congestion effect is $\gamma_{i,\min}^*$. But if γ_{ii} is not the smallest coefficient, we say that the Cournot effect is 0 and the congestion effect is $\gamma_{i,\min}^*$. The rationale of this is that is the least attractive attractor of entry into i is sector i itself, then it appears that Cournot-type effects are reducing entry into sector i. But if the least attractive attractor is another sector, then that is simply a measure of the way in which cluster congestion is reducing entry.

3.8 THE MODEL OF GROWTH

Two approaches to modelling growth of firms have been used. The most successful, used in Chapters 4–7, works at the firm level, and identifies whether firms located in strong clusters (with strong industry employment and/or strong science base employment) grow faster than isolated firms. But we also use an aggregate growth model comparable to the full entry model in the previous section.

Growth model at the individual firm level

The firm-level growth model is simply:

$$\ln e_{nT} = a_0 + b_1 \cdot (T - t_n) + b_2 \cdot \ln E_{icT} + b_3 \cdot \ln E_{kcT} + b_4 \cdot \ln S_{cT} \quad (6)$$

where:

firm n is active in sector i, and located in cluster c;

e_{nT} is employment in firm n in year T;

the index k summarizes all the other sectors beside i, in which n is not active;

t_n is the date of foundation of firm n;

accordingly, $T - t_n$ represents the age of the firm;

E_{icT} is employment in sector i at cluster c in year T;

E_{kcT} is employment in other sectors k at cluster c in year T;

S_{cT} is science base employment at cluster c in year T.

Thus the model estimates the trend rate of growth b_1, but also makes allowances for the fact that growth may be influenced by the presence of like firms (b_2) or unlike firms (b_3), or the science base (b_4). In principle, $b_2 \ln E$ can be replaced by a sum of effects, one for each sector at cluster c, but given the likely collinearities, this does not usually work very well.

Growth model at the aggregate level

This growth model examines how growth of employment in each sector depends on cumulative exposure to employment in different sectors at that cluster. It has essentially the same structure as the full model of entry. Once again, polynomial terms are included to capture the effects of congestion. No adding-up restriction can (or need) be applied here, so the model is a good deal simpler as a result:

$$\Delta \ln E_{cit} = \mu_{ci} + \sum_{j=1}^{8} \psi_{ij} \ln E_{cjt-1} + \psi_i \sum_{j=1}^{8} \ln E_{cjt-1} + \sum_{\theta=2}^{4} \pi_{i\theta} \left(\ln E_{c.t-1} \right)^{\theta} + v_{cit}$$

(7)

The variables are equivalent to those defined above in section 3.7.

The interpretation of the parameters for the growth model is similar to that of the entry model, though slightly different in detail. The parameters here are elasticities, which is convenient for interpretation, while those in the entry model were not. The μ_{ci} terms are cluster fixed effects on growth, and summarize the extent to which a particular cluster (c) tends to experience above (or below) average growth rates in sector i. The ψ_{ij} parameters describe how an increase in employment in sector j at a cluster will increase (or reduce) the growth of sector i at that cluster. Finally, the $\pi_{i\theta}$ parameters in the growth model summarize the extent to which congestion sets in and constrains further growth.

As indicated above, this model is little used in what follows, essentially because it yields rather poorly determined results. But it is very useful for the simulation model developed at the end of Chapter 4, and is included for that reason.

3.9 CONCLUSION

The econometric models set out here do not pretend to capture more than a few of the findings summarized in the literature review of Chapter 2. Moreover, they can only address the effects summarized in the growth and maturity sections of this chapter (sections 3.3 and 3.4). Nevertheless, they allow us to compare the clustering dynamics observed in two of the most dynamic high-technology industries. And these comparisons generate some very interesting, and novel, findings of considerable policy significance.

APPENDIX 3A: ENTRY OF FIRMS TO CLUSTERS

1. Latent variable analysis of entry

Let E be a T^*C by S matrix of entry, where T is the number of time periods, C is the number of clusters and S is the number of industry sectors. The latent variable model postulates that $E = FA$, where F is a T^*C by S matrix of latent variables (giving the value of each of the S latent variables in each time period and cluster). Then:

$$E'E = A'F'F'A \tag{8}$$

and it is customary in such models to assume that the latent variables are orthonormal, so that $F'F = I$. Hence $E'E = A'A$. We compute the eigenvectors of $E'E$ and call these $X = [X_1 \ldots X_S]$. Let the associated eigenvalues of $E'E$ be given by $L_1 \ldots L_S$, and summarize these in a diagonal matrix L made up of the elements $L_1 \ldots L_S$. Since X is orthonormal, $X' = X^{-1}$. Hence:

$$E'E = XX'E'EXX' = XLX' \tag{9}$$

And the diagonal matrix L can be decomposed into $L = MM'$, where M is also diagonal, and the elements on its diagonal are the square roots of the eigenvalues. Hence:

$$E'E = XMM'X'$$

It is then easy to compute:

$$A' = XM \tag{10}$$

This enables us to estimate the effect of the latent variables F on entry into each sector.

2. Full model of entry

This model treats the entry of firms into sector k at location c in year t as a function of the total extent of entry in sector k (across all locations) in period t, and a function of the current size of the cluster (at the end of year $t - 1$) at location c. The basic model of entry is:

$$n_{cit} = \alpha_{ci} + \beta_i n_{.it} + \sum_{j=1}^{8} \gamma_{ij} \ln E_{cjt-1} + \sum_{\theta=2}^{4} \delta_{i\theta} \left(\ln E_{c.t-1} \right)^{\theta} \tag{11}$$

where:

$$n_{.it} = \sum_{i=1}^{C} n_{cit} \quad E_{c.t-1} = \sum_{i=1}^{8} E_{cit-1} \tag{12}$$

The problem with this model is that ideally it should satisfy the adding-up condition, so that the sum of predicted entry across all clusters c is equal to actual total entry in all clusters. In fact it is not possible to design parameter restrictions to ensure that this adding-up condition is satisfied.

For the present chapter, therefore, we work with the latent macro variable M_{it} which defines macro conditions as they would affect entry into sector i in period t. The base model is then:

$$n_{cit} = \alpha_{ci} + \beta_i M_{it} + \sum_{j=1}^{8} \gamma_{ij} \ln E_{cjt-1} + \sum_{\theta=2}^{4} \delta_{i\theta} \left(\ln E_{c.t-1} \right)^{\theta} \tag{13}$$

As M_{it} is a latent variable, we shall substitute for it in our working model by using the adding-up condition. Summing (13) over 1 to C, gives:

$$\sum_{c=1}^{C} n_{cit} = \sum_{c=1}^{C} \alpha_{ci} + \beta_i C M_{it} + \sum_{c=1}^{C} \sum_{j=1}^{8} \gamma_{ij} \ln E_{cjt-1} + \sum_{c=1}^{C} \sum_{\theta=2}^{4} \delta_{i\theta} \left(\ln E_{c.t-1} \right)^{\theta} \tag{14}$$

We define:

$$\overline{n}_{it} = \frac{1}{C}\sum_{c=1}^{C} n_{cit} \quad \overline{a}_{i} = \frac{1}{C}\sum_{c=1}^{C} \alpha_{ci} \tag{15}$$

$$\overline{\ln E}_{.jt-1} = \frac{1}{C}\sum_{c=1}^{C} \ln E_{cjt-1} \quad \overline{\left(\ln E_{..t-1}\right)^{\theta}} = \frac{1}{C}\sum_{c=1}^{C} \left(\ln E_{c.t-1}\right)^{\theta} \tag{16}$$

Using these abbreviated expressions, equation (14) can then be rearranged to give:

$$\beta_{i}M_{it} = \overline{n}_{it} - \overline{\alpha}_{i} - \sum_{j=1}^{8}\gamma_{ij}\overline{\ln E}_{.jt-1} - \sum_{\theta=2}^{4}\delta_{i\theta}\overline{\left(\ln E_{..t-1}\right)^{\theta}} \tag{17}$$

We can substitute for $\beta_{i}M_{it}$ in equation (13) using equation (17). With a little rearrangement, this yields:

$$n_{cit}^{*} = \alpha_{ci}^{*} + \sum_{j=1}^{8}\gamma_{ij}\ln E_{cjt-1}^{*} + \sum_{\theta=2}^{4}\delta_{i\theta}\left(\ln E_{c.t-1}\right)^{\theta*} \tag{18}$$

where:

$$n_{cit}^{*} = n_{cit} - \overline{n}_{it} \quad \alpha_{ci}^{*} = \alpha_{ci} - \overline{\alpha}_{.i} \tag{19}$$

$$\ln E_{cjt-1}^{*} = \ln E_{cjt-1} - \overline{\ln E}_{.jt} \quad \left(\ln E_{c.t-1}\right)^{\theta*} = \left(\ln E_{c.t-1}\right)^{\theta} - \overline{\left(\ln E_{..t-1}\right)^{\theta}} \tag{20}$$

Equation (18) can be used for estimation purposes using OLS, and it is readily apparent that it satisfies the adding-up condition. It is clear from (15), (16), (19), and (20) that:

$$\sum_{c=1}^{C} n_{cit}^{*} = \sum_{c=1}^{C} \alpha_{ci}^{*} = \sum_{c=1}^{C} \ln E_{cjt-1}^{*} = \sum_{c=1}^{C}\left(\ln E_{c.t-1}\right)^{\theta*} = 0 \tag{21}$$

In our analysis we sometimes work with a slightly different normalization of (18):

$$n_{cit}^{*} = \alpha_{cit}^{*} + \sum_{\substack{j=1 \\ j \ne j_{min}}}^{C}\gamma_{ij}^{*}\ln E_{cjt-1}^{*} + \phi_{i}\sum_{j=1}^{8}\ln E_{cjt-1}^{*} + \sum_{\theta=2}^{4}\delta_{i\theta}\left(\ln E_{c.t-1}\right)^{\theta*} \tag{22}$$

where j_{min} is defined as follows:

$$\gamma ij_{min} = \min_{j\in[1,8]}\left\{\gamma ij\right\} \tag{23}$$

where the γij parameters refer to the estimated parameters for equation (18). In short, j_{min} is the sector with the smallest (usually, the most negative) attractor effect. The merit of this alternative normalization (22) is that all the γ_{ij}^{*} parameters in (22) are positive and the ϕ_{i} parameter can be

G. M. Peter Swann

interpreted as a congestion effect. This is the (probably negative) effect on
entry of an increase in the least useful sort of employment.

Finally, it is worth adding that (18) can obviously be rewritten
as follows, which is at first sight a little like (11) using the restriction
$\beta_i = 1/C$:

$$n_{cit} = \alpha_{ci}^* + \frac{1}{C} n_{.it} + \sum_{j=1}^{8} \gamma_{ij} \ln E_{cjt-1}^* + \sum_{\theta=2}^{4} \delta_{i\theta} \left(\ln E_{c.t-1} \right)^{\theta*} \tag{24}$$

Note however that the right-hand side variables in (24) are of course in
'deviation from average' form, rather than the 'levels' form used in (11).

4

Clusters in the US
Computing Industry

G. M. PETER SWANN

This chapter applies the models set out in the previous chapter to analyse the clustering process in the US computing industry. Section 4.1 describes the data used for this study. Section 4.2 examines the models of entry: the simple latent variable model, the average entry model, and the full entry model. Section 4.3 examines the models of growth: a firm-level model of growth and an aggregate model. Section 4.4 uses these models in a simulation exercise to explore what sorts of clusters will prosper in the long term. Section 4.5 offers an interpretation of the main research results.

4.1 DATA

This study explores clustering patterns with reference to the growth of the US computer industry over the period 1960–88. For this study, the computer industry is broken into eight sectors, as follows: (1) communications; (2) components; (3) computer hardware; (4) computer distributors; (5) computer peripherals; (6) computer services; (7) software; (8) systems.

Three US states account for more than half of the computer companies in 1988. Moreover, the same three states (California, Massachusetts, and New York) tend to dominate all sectors of the computer industry. More generally there is a close correlation between state shares of the different computer industry sectors. This suggests that clustering patterns are especially closely related for software, peripherals, and computer hardware, and

Table 4.1 *Top four states ranked by numbers of firms per state*

	California	Massachusetts	New York	Texas
All sectors	1	2	3	4
Communications	1	4	3	9
Components	1	3	2	6
Computer hardware	1	2	4	3
Computer distributors	1	4	2	3
Computer peripherals	1	2	3	19=
Computer services	1	3	2	5
Software	1	2	4	7
Systems	1	3	11=	8

Source: Based on data in Juliussen and Juliussen (1989).

Table 4.2 *Correlation matrix of state shares in different sectors (%)*

		1	2	3	4	5	6	7	8
Communications	1	100							
Components	2	91	100						
Computers	3	85	96	100					
Distributors	4	81	94	95	100				
Peripherals	5	84	94	97	92	100			
Services	6	75	82	76	83	72	100		
Software	7	84	93	97	93	98	76	100	
Systems	8	84	88	90	88	89	69	90	100

Source: Based on data in Juliussen and Juliussen (1989).

indeed the patterns for all sectors except computer services are quite close. The reason why services may show a different clustering pattern is that the factors that attract service companies to a particular location are much broader than supply-side spillovers from the computer industry. Indeed, it seems likely that location close to key users is equally (if not more) important. That is consistent with the work of Hippel (1979, 1980, 1988) and others (Webb and Cleary 1993) which has shown just how important the user can be in the innovation process.

Data for the entry and growth models

The source used was the *Brady Computer Industry Almanac* for 1989 (Juliussen and Juliussen 1989). This lists about 750 of the top computer companies in the United States—the criterion for inclusion being that revenue is above \$2 million (1987/8 financial year), or employment above ten people.[1] The almanac classifies companies into at least sixty-five sectors—and indeed, if the line of business descriptors were used carefully, an even finer disaggregation could be achieved. For our present purposes, however, we have used the eight-sector classification given above (section 2). The source lists date of foundation, sectors in which the firm operates, location (headquarters), employment, and revenue. However, as the revenue data is somewhat patchy (for unquoted companies, in particular), the growth model described below looks at the lifetime growth of employment in the firm (not the growth of revenue).

The growth and entry models described below do not require complete time series of employment for individual companies, but they do require estimates of the level of employment in each sector (by state) for 1960–88. We do not have accurate state data on this at the required level of sectoral disaggregation, and hence it has had to be built up from company data. It should be stressed at the start that the data available for this econometric model had a number of limitations. Moreover, a number of reasonably strong assumptions were required to estimate these models. First, the data on 'entry' are in fact data on surviving entry. Transitory entrants who do not survive to the end of the period analysed (1988) are not counted. For the purposes of the present chapter, however, it is arguable that this is not too serious because after all it is the contribution to growth made by surviving entrants that matters rather than the more transitory contribution of entrants who do not survive.

Second, we do not have employment histories for our sample of firms—only a few isolated points. While it was possible to assemble a reasonably accurate time series of the number of surviving firms in each sector at any date, this is a poor measure of the

---

[1] Some of the companies in the almanac, however, seem to be smaller than this. Also, the lower limit for inclusion as a computer distributor is \$20 million revenue (1987/8 financial year).

strength of a cluster because it takes no account of size: IBM is treated the same way as a one-man computer services company. For that reason we have computed a rough estimate of employment in each cluster by estimating the size of each relevant firm in each year, assuming that the firm grows steadily at its long-run exponential growth rate—which can differ significantly from one firm to another. This is obviously quite a strong assumption, and makes no allowance for cycles in growth, resulting from business cycles, for example. But again, given that these estimates are aggregated across firms, then for the exploratory purposes of the present chapter, the data can still give a rough indication of cluster strength.

Third, a substantial number of firms are active in more than one sector of the computer industry, and it is usually difficult to say exactly how to split the workforce between different sectors. Moreover, some giant firms, Boeing, for example, are important participants in parts of the computer industry, but clearly only a proportion of their employment should be counted for our present purposes. To handle these questions, a number of simplifying—and quite strong—assumptions had to be made. Nevertheless, a number of cross-checks using much simpler models confirm the essential character of the models used for simulation in this chapter.

Fourth, there is a problem concerning the geographical breakdown of a firm's activities. In the smaller firms, it may be fair to assume that the bulk of spillovers emanate from the company headquarters, but this is unrealistic for the largest firms. Yet it is difficult to obtain systematic data on the geographical breakdown of activity in more than a few companies. In this chapter, the assumption is that all spillovers flow through the company headquarters, except in the case of identified subsidiaries—which account for quite a few firms in the database. Obviously this is very crude. Accordingly, as described in the previous chapter, we also use a latent variable analysis of entry, and a model of average entry per state (over all years). These tell us something about entry patterns: if we are prepared to make the stronger assumptions required for the full model, then that can tell us something more.

A few companies had to be omitted from the sample used for analysis because key data were unavailable. Moreover, for esti-

Table 4.3 *Classification of firms in sample*

	1 sector	2 sector	3 sector	4 sector	Sum
Date of foundation					
1960 and onwards					
All sectors	500	144	24	0	668
Communications	25	8	2	0	35
Components	14	8	1	0	23
Computer hardware	57	18	3	0	78
Distributors	32	1	1	0	34
Computer peripherals	128	32	5	0	165
Services	37	21	2	0	60
Software	183	41	6	0	230
Systems	24	15	4	0	43
Date of foundation					
before 1960					
All sectors	63	48	15	8	134
Communications	14	6	0	1	21
Components	8	12	3	0	23
Computer hardware	6	9	3	0	18
Distributors	4	1	0	0	5
Computer peripherals	12	7	4	2	25
Services	9	5	1	1	16
Software	2	3	1	2	8
Systems	8	5	3	2	18

Source: Based on data in Juliussen and Juliussen (1989)—see section 4.

mating the growth and entry models, we chose to use companies that were active only in one sector (we return to the performance of multi-sector firms below), and only those that were founded in 1960 or later.[2] Table 4.3 shows how the firms are distributed between these various classifications—or, to be precise, how the different firm divisions are distributed (since each division of a multi-sector firm is treated as a separate entry here). To make the

---

[2] A large number of the pre-1960 firms started in other (related) technologies, and entered the computer industry at a later stage. The date 1960 is somewhat arbitrary, but it represents the earliest volume production of integrated circuits, which, it can be argued, did as much as anything to foster the very rapid growth of this industry thereafter.

following analysis tractable, the unit of location was the state. In certain respects this is unsatisfactory because the distances involved are far too great to constitute a cluster. However, the state data can in some cases be taken to represent a group of distinct clusters.

4.2 ENTRY MODELS

1. A latent variables model

As described in Chapter 3, this approach gives us a rough idea of the nature of entry attractors when time series data on the strength of clusters are unreliable. It identifies the principal components of the time series of entry data, and as demonstrated in Chapter 3, allows us to identify the effect of each latent variable on entry into each sector. The results are summarized in Table 4.4. Two eigenvalues account for the vast majority of the variation in entry patterns. If the entry model is defined as $E = FA$, where F are the latent variables, and A is a matrix of coefficients, then the coefficients for these two most important latent variables are given in the table. The other latent variables have little effect on entry, and indeed their only effect is to promote entry in one particular sector. As such these other latent variables could be described as idiosyncratic variables attracting entry into particular sectors. The two presented here are much more interesting,

Table 4.4 *Latent variables for entry*

Eigenvalue	0.14	0.59
Weighted eigenvector		
Communications	−0.01	0.03
Chips	−0.01	0.06
Hardware	−0.08	0.10
Distributors	−0.01	0.06
Peripherals	−0.28	0.43
Services	0.08	0.02
Software	0.21	0.62
Systems	−0.01	0.03

because the first one has a joint effect on entry in several sectors, and the second one acts to attract entry towards some sectors and drive it away from others.

How should these two latent variables be interpreted? One is a general attractor, which attracts entry to software, peripherals, and to a lesser extent into hardware. From these latent variable models we cannot know exactly what it is, but the full entry model summarized below suggests that it relates to core strength in hardware, chips, and systems. In contrast, an increase in the second latent variable increases entry into software and reduces entry into peripherals. (A decrease in the latent variable would have the reverse effect.) Again, the results of the full entry model below suggests that this may be an increase in core strength in systems and computer hardware at the expense of 'chips'—holding total core computer manufacturing constant.

The important thing about these latent variable results, however, is that they demonstrate that there are some attractors which work on more than one sector. If the attractors relate to industry strength, then there must be some cross-sectoral effects. And as we shall argue below, this is a key part of the story of clustering in computing. If the attractors of entry in different sectors were distinct, then each latent variable would be made up of zeros except for a non-zero value for one element. That is, each latent variable would specialize in attracting entry to one and only one sector.

2. The average entry model

Here, we compute average entry to each sector and cluster over the period 1960–88. In this case, that gives us a 39 (cluster) by 8 (sector) matrix. Then, for each sector, we regress average entry for each of the 39 different clusters against a constant and ln total employment in the cluster at end-period. This gives the results shown in Table 4.5 (we report only the slope coefficients here). In each regression there are 37 degrees of freedom. These indicate reasonably strong correlation between entry and employment in some sectors, but not in others. The three sectors where this entry attraction is strongest are software, peripherals, and to a lesser extent computer hardware. But again, all we know is that some

84   *G. M. Peter Swann*

Table 4.5 *Average entry model*

Sector	Coefficient on	
	ln (tot. employment)	s.e.
Communications	0.0105	0.0034
Chips	0.0080	0.0046
Hardware	0.0212	0.0103
Distributors	0.0089	0.0029
Peripherals	0.0534	0.0249
Services	0.0160	0.0040
Software	0.0634	0.0241
Systems	0.0120	0.0043

aspect of industry strength attracts entry in these cases. We do not know which, and that is where the full model will help.

3. The full entry model

We have already indicated that there are some significant difficulties with the data required for this full model. Nevertheless, we present estimates of it here because it supplements the two preceding models in such a useful way. The full model is set out in Chapter 3. Table 4.6 summarizes some of the results, using OLS on the full data set described above. It shows the attractor coefficients—that is the power of employment in one sector to attract entry to another. These attractor coefficients are presented as gross attractors: that is employment in any sector is postulated to have a non-negative attractive effect and a negative repellent effect (through the combined congestion and Cournot effects described in Chapter 3). To work out the net attractor effect, simply add the gross attractor to the (negative) figure in the SUM row. Thus for example, sector 2 (chips) has a strong positive gross attractor effect on sector 7 (software) as shown by the coefficient 0.206 (row 2, column 7). But this has to be attenuated by −0.055 because an increase in sector 2 employment increases congestion in this case. The lower half of the table shows the coefficients on the polynomial terms in total computer industry employment.

Table 4.6 *Entry model gross attractor and congestion effects*

	Equation for sector							
	1	2	3	4	5	6	7	8
1	0	0.002	0.011	0.029	0.012	0.024	0.024	0.023
	(–)	(0.009)	(0.013)	(0.009)	(0.027)	(0.013)	(0.034)	(0.009)
2	0.018	0	0.076	0.054	0.167	0.022	0.206	0.036
	(0.011)	(–)	(0.018)	(0.012)	(0.036)	(0.017)	(0.048)	(0.012)
3	0.018	0.008	0	0.030	0.069	0.009	0.130	0.033
	(0.008)	(0.009)	(–)	(0.009)	(0.027)	(0.012)	(0.033)	(0.010)
4	0.009	0.001	0.002	0	0.003	0.021	0	0.024
	(0.009)	(0.010)	(0.014)	(–)	(0.026)	(0.012)	(–)	(0.011)
5	0.016	0.005	0.005	0.019	0	0.021	0.024	0.021
	(0.009)	(0.010)	(0.014)	(0.008)	(–)	(0.010)	(0.033)	(0.012)
6	0.014	0.000	0.021	0.025	0.032	0	0.055	0.024
	(0.009)	(0.010)	(0.013)	(0.008)	(0.021)	(–)	(0.031)	(0.012)
7	0.014	0.006	0.018	0.021	0.045	0.031	0.013	0.030
	(0.008)	(0.008)	(0.014)	(0.008)	(0.029)	(0.013)	(0.031)	(0.010)
8	0.014	0.003	0.028	0.046	0.100	0.018	0.137	0
	(0.008)	(0.009)	(0.014)	(0.010)	(0.034)	(0.016)	(0.039)	(–)
SUM	–0.013	–0.005	–0.011	–0.024	–0.035	–0.020	–0.055	–0.023
	(0.006)	(0.008)	(0.009)	(0.006)	(0.019)	(0.008)	(0.023)	(0.008)
SUM^2 (*10)	–0.057	–0.025	–0.134	–0.077	–0.385	–0.085	–0.349	–0.039
	(0.036)	(0.031)	(0.057)	(0.036)	(0.110)	(0.052)	(0.140)	(0.041)
SUM^3 (*10)	0.011	0.004	0.023	0.014	0.064	0.016	0.054	0.006
	(0.006)	(0.005)	(0.010)	(0.006)	(0.019)	(0.009)	(0.024)	(0.007)
SUM^4 (*100)	–0.006	–0.002	–0.012	–0.007	–0.030	–0.009	–0.023	–0.003
	(0.003)	(0.002)	(0.004)	(0.003)	(0.009)	(0.004)	(0.011)	(0.003)
R^2	0.15	0.27	0.36	0.14	0.47	0.14	0.36	0.18
ESE	0.17	0.14	0.27	0.17	0.52	0.24	0.65	0.19

Note: Figures in parentheses are standard errors.

These are hard to interpret as they stand, but we present these graphically, which yields some interesting conclusions.

Graphical summary of the full entry model

The model can be summarized in a series of graphs which bring out the essential character of the results. Figure 4.1 shows the principal net (i.e. net of congestion and Cournot effects) attractors in a simple graphical fashion. An arrow running from one box to

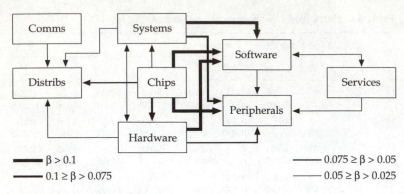

Fig. 4.1 *Attractors in the US computer industry*

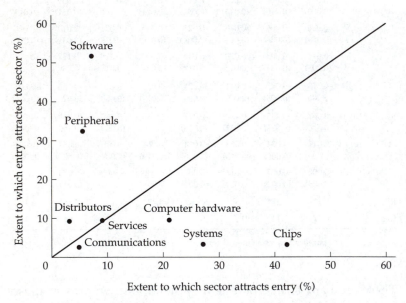

Fig. 4.2 *Attractors and attracted*

another indicates that the first sector attracts entry into the second, and the width of the line indicates the strength of the effect as the index shows. This shows that the main forces attracting entry are from the hard sectors (systems, chips, and hardware) on other sectors such as software and peripherals. There is also an effect from chips to entry into hardware. The other effects are on the whole small. The coefficient beta describes the gross entry attractor coefficient, as shown in Table 4.6.

Figure 4.2 summarizes this in a different way: it shows the attracted sectors and the attractive sectors—by summing up the the gross coefficients in each column to obtain the 'attracted' score, and the gross coefficients in each row to get the 'attractive' coefficient. This shows even more clearly perhaps that entry into software and peripherals is attracted by cluster strength, but software and peripherals do much less to attract. Conversely, hardware, systems, and chips are attractive, but little entry is attracted into these (except perhaps hardware). The other three (communications, distribution, and services) are neither attracted nor attractive: they neither attract entry, nor is much entry attracted into these by cluster strength.

Figure 4.3 offers one other perspective on the coefficients. It groups together the hard sectors (hardware, chips, systems, and communications) and the others (software, services, distribution,

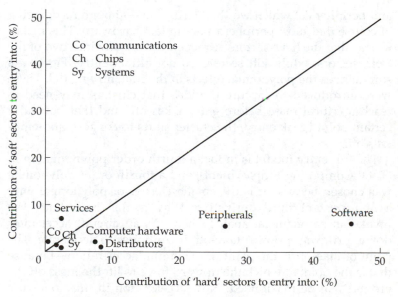

Fig. 4.3 *The contribution of 'hard' and 'soft' sectors to entry*

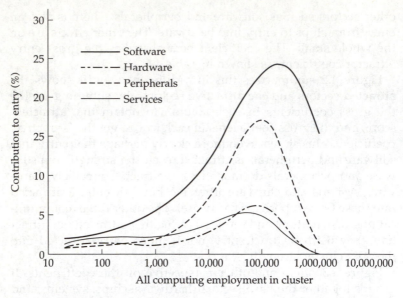

Fig. 4.4 *Cluster strength and entry*

and peripherals) which we shall term 'soft'—though recognizing of course that most peripherals are in fact hardware. This makes it clear that the hard sectors attract entry—mostly into two of the 'soft' sectors, while soft sectors do not attract entry. Figure 4.4 summarizes the polynomial effects in the full entry model. These were introduced to capture the idea that clusters may need to reach a critical mass before entry takes off, and that beyond a certain point (peak entry) the cluster starts to congest, and entry tails off.

The full entry model is in fact a fourth order polynomial in ln (Total Computing Employment), and a fourth order polynomial was chosen because it is the smallest order of polynomial with a non-constant third derivative. Why is this important? We invoke an aeronautical analogy here. As an aircraft accelerates down a runway prior to take-off, it continues to accelerate. The point of take-off is the point of maximum acceleration—because that is the point at which the upward force to lift the mass off the ground will be maximized. Now acceleration in this context is the second derivative of place with respect to time. Accordingly, to maximize acceleration requires setting the third derivative equal to zero.

Shifting back to the entry context, we can say that acceleration in entry is the second derivative of the entry function with respect to total cluster computing employment. To maximize the acceleration of entry (and so achieve entry take-off to the cluster) requires that we find the point at which the third derivative is zero. But if we use a polynomial of third degree or less, the third derivative is either constant or zero. In that case there is no unique point of take-off. If we use a fourth order polynomial, the third derivative is a linear function of total cluster computing employment—and so there is a unique point of take-off.

Figure 4.4 shows that, for software, peripherals, hardware, and services, the entry curves follow a highly intuitive shape. (The curves for the other four sectors are not shown since entry is so modest in these sectors.) In all cases, there is a slow take-off followed by an acceleration, a peak entry around 100,000 employment, and then entry tails away to zero. Figure 4.5 looks at this in

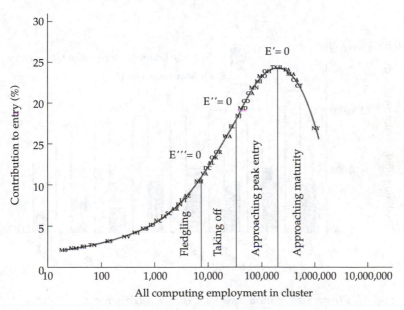

Fig. 4.5 *Entry 'life cycle' in software*

more detail for one sector, software. It plots the same entry curve as before, but also marks the points at which acceleration is maximized ($E''' = 0$), the point of inflexion ($E'' = 0$) and the point of peak entry ($E' = 0$). Finally, the graph also plots each state's total computing employment in 1988.

There are several points of interest here. First that take-off takes place when the cluster reaches a little under 10,000 total computing employment. There are quite a few states in the USA that were past or well past take-off in 1988. Second, that peak entry is above 100,000. This point of peak entry is not the end of the cluster—moreover, entry still continues beyond that point, but it starts to tail off. The diagram indicates that several states (New York, California, Connecticut, and Massachusetts) were past the point of peak entry while others were approaching the peak in 1988. The graph identifies several clusters that are coming—what have been called by some commentators (e.g. Herbig and Golden 1993*a*, 1993*b*) 'innovative hot spots'.

Figure 4.6 summarizes the estimated critical mass (or take-off points) and points of peak entry for different sectors. Critical mass is usually between 2,000 and 10,000, while peak entry is generally

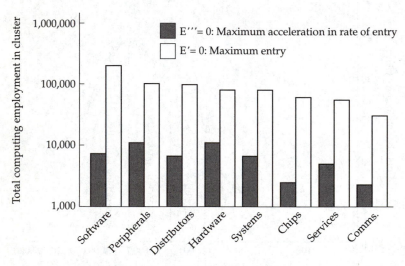

Fig. 4.6 *Cluster size: 'critical mass' and size for maximum entry*

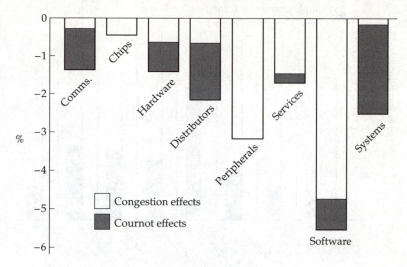

Fig. 4.7 *Congestion and 'Cournot' effects on entry*

only reached at around 100,000. Figure 4.7 summarizes the Cournot and congestion effects described earlier. Because, in all but one of the entry equations, own sector employment is the least attractive sector, all sectors but one are deemed to have Cournot effects. These summarize the extent to which own sector employment deters entry, over and above any effect it may have on cluster congestion. It is clear that, in a number of cases, the Cournot effect makes up a large part of the overall deterrent to entry, though this is not true in chips, software, services, or peripherals.

Figures 4.8 and 4.9 are a useful postscript to this discussion of the entry model. They show (Figure 4.8) that while post-1960 entrants may account for a large proportion of the firms in each sector, they still do not account for so large a proportion of employment—except in distributors, perhaps. And Figure 4.9 shows that except in chips and distributors, the post-1960 entrants are still small relative to the pre-1960 incumbents. Despite these last observations, entry has been desperately important in this industry, as a vehicle (the main vehicle) of technological change.

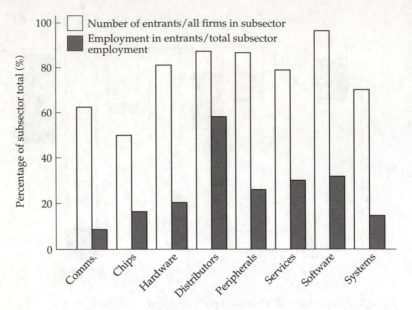

Fig. 4.8 *Relative number and size of entrants*

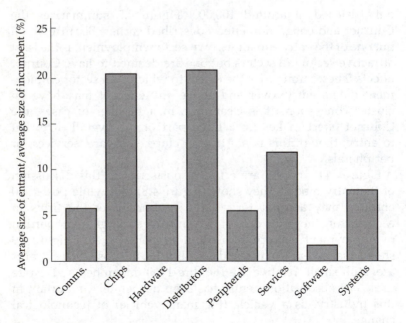

Fig. 4.9 *Relative size of entrants and incumbents*

1. Growth model at the individual firm level

The firm-level growth model described in Chapter 3 gives the results in Table 4.7. The results are striking, even if not all coefficients are statistically significant. They show that a firm located in a cluster with strong own sector employment tends, usually significantly, to grow faster than the isolated firm. Some of the effects here are very strong. Conversely, a firm located in a cluster that is strong in 'other sector' employment will tend to grow slower than average, sometimes significantly so. The effects here are not, typically, so strong, but in all cases negative coefficients are

Table 4.7 *Firm-level growth models*

Sector	Age	Own employment	Other employment
All sectors	0.109	0.218	−0.155
	(0.009)	(0.037)	(0.037)
Communications	0.105	0.162	−0.211
	(0.043)	(0.168)	(0.113)
Chips	0.162	0.305	−0.222
	(0.034)	(0.195)	(0.220)
Hardware	0.118	0.422	−0.291
	(0.027)	(0.127)	(0.157)
Distributors	0.050	0.470	−0.202
	(0.049)	(0.128)	(0.099)
Peripherals	0.066	0.107	−0.043
	(0.019)	(0.096)	(0.100)
Services	0.104	0.025	−0.149
	(0.031)	(0.219)	(0.125)
Software	0.105	0.073	−0.056
	(0.014)	(0.061)	(0.052)
Systems	0.087	0.202	−0.271
	(0.044)	(0.286)	(0.470)

Note: Figures in parentheses are standard errors.

G. M. Peter Swann

found. We offer some interpretations of these findings in the concluding section.

2. Aggregate level growth models

Table 4.8 summarizes the results of the aggregate growth model. This is only reported here for completeness, because as indicated above the results here are not well determined. However, this model was needed for the simulation exercise in the next section,

Table 4.8 *Growth model gross promotion and congestion effects*

	Equation for sector							
	1	2	3	4	5	6	7	8
1	0.034	0.014	0.007	0.004	0	0.025	0.004	0.019
	(0.009)	(0.005)	(0.013)	(0.019)	(–)	(0.011)	(0.017)	(0.009)
2	0.009	0.033	0.022	0	0.029	0.026	0.018	0.021
	(0.012)	(0.008)	(0.019)	(–)	(0.019)	(0.016)	(0.022)	(0.012)
3	0.029	0	0	0.012	0.005	0	0.065	0.033
	(0.010)	(–)	(–)	(0.019)	(0.014)	(–)	(0.019)	(0.010)
4	0.011	0.008	0.027	0.036	0.011	0.016	0.014	0.033
	(0.011)	(0.006)	(0.014)	(0.021)	(0.015)	(0.012)	(0.018)	(0.011)
5	0.038	0.020	0.045	0.036	0.013	0.008	0.034	0.027
	(0.012)	(0.006)	(0.015)	(0.020)	(0.015)	(0.012)	(0.022)	(0.012)
6	0.025	0.001	0.047	0.024	0.015	0.011	0.020	0.030
	(0.013)	(0.005)	(0.014)	(0.020)	(0.015)	(0.012)	(0.020)	(0.012)
7	0.021	0.006	0.027	0.011	0.017	0.035	0	0.032
	(0.010)	(0.006)	(0.014)	(0.017)	(0.013)	(0.012)	(–)	(0.010)
8	0	0.001	0.004	0.056	0.043	0.011	0.011	0
	(–)	(0.006)	(0.015)	(0.018)	(0.014)	(0.012)	(0.019)	(–)
SUM	−0.020	−0.007	−0.023	−0.019	−0.012	−0.017	−0.030	−0.028
	(0.008)	(0.004)	(0.009)	(0.016)	(0.010)	(0.008)	(0.012)	(0.008)
SUM^2 (*10)	0.080	0.016	0.104	−0.034	0.033	0.125	0.129	0.027
	(0.037)	(0.021)	(0.053)	(0.054)	(0.055)	(0.045)	(0.072)	(0.037)
SUM^3 (*10)	−0.012	−0.002	−0.015	0.014	−0.000	−0.020	−0.012	−0.003
	(0.007)	(0.004)	(0.010)	(0.010)	(0.010)	(0.008)	(0.013)	(0.007)
SUM^4 (*100)	0.005	0.000	0.006	−0.007	−0.002	0.009	0.006	0.001
	(0.003)	(0.002)	(0.005)	(0.005)	(0.005)	(0.004)	(0.006)	(0.003)
R^2	0.28	0.41	0.17	0.20	0.15	0.24	0.09	0.29
ESE	0.19	0.11	0.26	0.27	0.27	0.23	0.36	0.18

Note: Figures in parentheses are standard errors.

and that is why we report it here. Our main observation is that the clustering effects here are generally much weaker than in the entry model.

4.4 SIMULATION OF CONVERGENCE
AND THE GROWTH OF CLUSTERS

This section applies the aggregate entry and growth models from the previous sections to analyse the possible effects of convergence between technologies on the growth and longevity of industrial clusters. The discussion that follows draws heavily on an earlier paper by this author (Swann 1996). The aim of these simulations is to look at how technology evolution influences the relative success of different sorts of cluster. In particular, we focus on technology evolution that follows from the convergence of distinct technologies. The concept of convergence has already been discussed in Chapter 3. The index of convergence between two sectors (i and j) used here is the extent to which a cluster that is strong in industry i attracts entry into j. And we focus on the effects of convergence on the relative success of specialized clusters (where activity is concentrated in one industry sector) and more general purpose clusters (where activity is dispersed across a number of industry sectors).

To explore this question we proceed as follows. The aggregate growth and entry models are used in a series of simulation experiments. The entry attractor and growth promoter matrices can be taken to summarize the interaction between different subsectors—rather like the input-output matrix. If there has been no convergence between the technologies then it is reasonable to expect that the off-diagonal elements of these matrices will be small or zero. If on the other hand there has been convergence between two or more technologies, then it is reasonable to expect that some at least of the off-diagonal elements in the matrix will be strong and positive. The rationale for this is that when there are such connections, the performance of one subsector at a cluster will be dependent on the strength of other convergent subsectors at that cluster.

It is reasonable to conjecture that specialized (i.e. single technology) clusters might do best when the technologies are distinct, but when the technologies start to converge, the specialized cluster will be at a disadvantage compared to the more general purpose cluster. The results that follow find some support for this in the context of the US computer industry, though the results also suggest that the ideal degree of diversity in the cluster is to have strengths in three to five sectors, but not all.

1. Simulations

The simulation model is based on the estimates in sections 4.2 and 4.3 for the normalized entry model and the growth model. The only difference is that the fourth order employment effects in some of the growth equations had to be constrained to zero, since as they stand they would employ explosive growth in the largest clusters—an implausible, if not physically impossible, implication. The estimated matrices presented above do have some strong and positive off-diagonal elements, which suggests a degree of convergence. To explore the implications of this convergence process, we perform simulation experiments using a set of possible *entry attractor* and *growth promotion* matrices based on these actual matrices. In particular, if the estimated matrices are defined (respectively) as β and γ, then the simulations encompass hypothetical attractor and promotion matrices defined as follows (for different values of σ):

$$\text{If} \quad i = j: \quad \gamma_{ii}^* = \gamma_{ii}, \; \beta_{ii}^* = \beta_{ii}$$

$$\text{If} \quad i \neq j: \quad \gamma_{ij}^* = \sigma * \gamma_{ij}, \; \beta_{ij}^* = \sigma * \beta_{ij} \quad \left[0 \leq \sigma \leq 1\right]$$

The rationale for this is that, when $\sigma = 0$, we have no convergence, but when $\sigma = 1$, we have the level of convergence suggested by our econometric estimates.

The other dimensions of variation in the simulations relate to the initial conditions. Given the autoregressive character of the model, the simulation model needs some sort of 'kick' to get it started on a growth path. This could be in the form of a pioneering firm (or group of firms) setting up in a new location—and thereby making the foundations of a subsequent cluster. In the simulations we experimented with different sorts of 'kick-start'. In particular we explored a grid of the 256 possible permutations: $\{E_i = 0 \text{ or } 100 \text{ employees in sector } i, \, i \, \varepsilon \, [1,8]\}$.

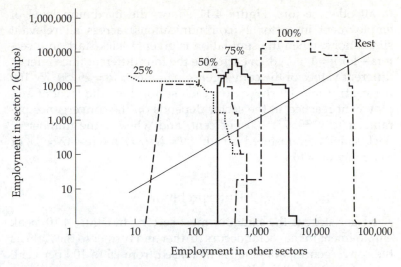

Fig. 4.10 *Employment in sector 2*

Starting with a vector of initial conditions for employment in a cluster, the simulation model computes entry and growth in each period, and then accumulates that entry and growth into the employment estimates for the next period. The simulations are run forward for 50 periods, and final employment in each sector is recorded. In short we have simulations for the 256 types of kick-start and 4 values of the convergence parameter σ. These are far too bulky to reproduce in full, but Figures 4.10 and 4.11 describe two typical sets of results for two particular sectors, and Table 4.9 summarizes the main points of importance in the set of simulations for all sectors. Note that no simulations are summarized for sector 8 (systems) because the model fails to predict any endogenous growth or entry in this sector.

Figure 4.10 shows the maximum[3] level of employment in sector 2 (chips) obtained in the simulations for a given total employment

---

[3] As such, these lines represent the upper hull of the data. Though not drawn here, if the other simulations were plotted on the graph, the points would all lie below the lines shown. Strictly speaking, this is an *undominated* hull and not a *convex* hull, since convex combinations are not taken when computing these lines.

in all other sectors. Figure 4.11 shows the maximum level of employment in sector 1 (communications) across all relevant simulations, when the simulation is given a 'kick-start' in n sectors—for $n = 1, \ldots, 8$. In each case the four different lines refer to different values of the convergence parameter ($\sigma = 25, 50, 75, 100$ per cent). Table 4.9 shows, for each sector, how the level of employment reached in the sector depends on the convergence parameter ($\sigma = 50, 75, 100$ per cent) and whether the number of 'kick-starts' administered is right ($N = N\text{MAX}$), too few ($N = 1$), or too many ($N = 8$).

2. Interpretation

The basic story is the same for most sectors. In Figure 4.10, peak employment in the sector occurs further and further to the right as the convergence parameter is increased from 25 to 100 per cent. Moreover, the peak itself increases as the convergence parameter is increased. Finally, the curves for different convergence parameters intersect. With low employment in other sectors, the peak employment in sector 2 is reached with a low convergence parameter (25 per cent) while with a high level of employment in other sectors, the peak employment in sector 2 is reached when convergence is high (100 per cent).

How are these observations to be interpreted? First, if convergence is low, peak employment in a sector is reached when employment in other sectors is low, but if convergence is high, then peak employment is reached when employment in other sectors is higher. This is really just the observation that when convergence between technologies is low, the best performing clusters are the single-technology clusters. Clusters which have moderate employment in several subsectors will tend to get congested, and this detracts from employment growth in any one subsector. Conversely, when convergence is high, the best way to grow employment in a particular subsector is to exploit the many spillovers between sectors,[4] and this requires high employment in other sectors. Even here, congestion eventually sets in. In Figure 4.10, when convergence is high (100 per cent), it is clear that employ-

[4] There is an interesting parallel with the study by Mensch (1979) which recognizes that a trigger is needed to fire a new wave, or cluster, of innovations; the convergence of technologies offers just such a trigger.

ment in other sectors must exceed 1,000 to reach peak employment in sector 2 (Chips), but when employment in other sectors goes far above 10,000 then the employment level reached in sector 2 starts to dip—again a result of congestion.

Second, the fact that peak employment increases as the convergence parameter increases follows simply from the observation that as the technologies converge, so too does the degree of positive feedback in the simulation model. The increase in the peak is not spectacular, but important nevertheless. Third, the fact that with low convergence peak employment is found where other-sector employment is low, while with high convergence the peak is found where other sector employment is high, suggests the following. With low convergence, single-technology clusters have an advantage over multi-technology clusters, because the latter do not generate much in the way of useful spillovers, but do generate congestion effects. Conversely, with high convergence, it is necessary to be in a multi-technology cluster to take best advantage of the rich spillovers—though not an omni-technology cluster, because there congestion sets in too fast.

Figure 4.11 gives perhaps an even simpler illustration of the simulations. It shows the relationship between peak employment in sector 1 (Communications) and the number of sectors in which a kick-start is administered. Three main observations can be made. First, for any particular level of convergence, the peak level of employment is reached when a 'kick-start' is administered in an intermediate number of subsectors. Second, the optimum number of sectors in which to apply a kick-start increases as the level of convergence increases. And third, the peak employment level reached increases as the rate of convergence increases.

The third observation has already been made in the context of Figure 4.10. The first and second observations are also broadly compatible. When convergence is 100 per cent, peak employment is reached with a kick-start in four sectors: as before, the diversified, multi-technology cluster does best when technologies converge. But when convergence is low (25 per cent), the best initial conditions are to apply a kick-start in one sector only—the 'home' sector indeed. With little convergence there is little cross-sector positive feedback, and congestion effects set in sooner in multi-technology clusters.

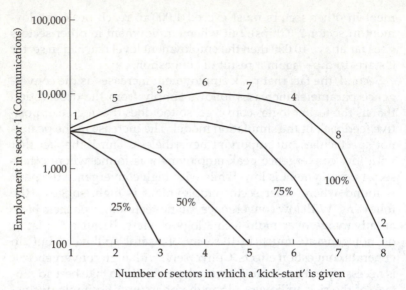

Fig. 4.11 *Employment in sector 1*

Table 4.9 summarizes these results across all sectors. For sectors 1–5, the right number of sectors in which to apply a 'kick-start' is four or five—while in sector 7 (software) and sector 6 (services) the number is smaller. For each sector, the employment levels achieved with 100 per cent convergence and when the optimum number of kick-starts is given are normalized at 100. The table then shows how the employment level reached declines as the convergence parameter is reduced (to 75 and 50 per cent), and if 'kick-starts' are administered in only one sector ($N = 1$) or in all sectors ($N = 8$). What this shows is that the employment levels reached in sectors 4 and 5 are very sensitive to the value of the convergence parameter, and in sectors 1, 2, 3, and 7 there is a fair degree of sensitivity. It is also clear that in sectors 1, 4, and 7 a kick-start in all sectors is seriously counter-productive, with ultimate employment much reduced because congestion effects start to limit the growth of the sector quite early on. Sectors 4, 5, and 7, on the other hand, will not flourish in isolation: the employment levels reached when only one 'kick-start' is given, in their own sector, is much less than the maximum attainable.

Table 4.9

	Relative Employment with					'Kick Start' in Sector							
	Convergence (%)	Nmax	N = Nmax	N = 1	N = 8	1	2	3	4	5	6	7	8
1	100	4	100.0	32.1	1.2	1		1		1	1		1
	75	3	43.0	29.8	0.9	1		1		1	1		
	50	1	28.6	28.6	0.9	1							
2	100	5	100.0	39.1	27.3		1		1	1			
	75	3	27.6	8.0	0.4		1			1			
	50	3	14.1	5.3	0.0		1			1			
3	100	4	100.0	21.7	32.1			1	1				
	75	4	26.4	11.4	14.7			1	1				
	50	2	11.8	11.5	11.5			1					
4	100	4	100.0	6.5	0.2						1	1	1
	75	3	6.7	0.1	0.1							1	1
	50	2	0.3	0.1	0.1								1
5	100	5	100.0	4.6	30.6					1	1	1	1
	75	4	7.3	0.2	0.2						1	1	1
	50	2	0.8	0.2	0.2								1
6	100	2	100.0	77.4	33.8					1			
	75	2	68.6	52.3	33.9					1			
	50	1	52.0	52.0	33.9					1			
7	100	3	100.0	11.6	8.9					1			
	75	2	75.6	5.1	1.9			1					
	50	2	13.6	2.2	1.9			1					
Frequency						3	3	5	3	10	5	4	7

The right-hand side of the table also shows the optimum set of 'kick-starts' for each sector and convergence rate. If a 1 is shown, then a kick-start is required in that sector; if not, then it is not. In all cases, the optimum kick-start for sector i (say) requires a kick-start in that sector i. These are shown in bold. The last row of the table (frequency) shows the number of times that a kick-start is required in sector i to achieve an optimum outcome in another sector j. (The fact that a kick-start is required in i to achieve the optimum result in i is not counted.) Sector 5 (peripherals) emerges as the sector most in demand: for the six other sectors shown (1–4 and 6–7), and the three convergence parameter values considered, a kick-start is desirable in this sector in 10 out of 18 cases. The systems sector (8) is also in demand. This means that the most successful performance in other sectors will be observed in clusters where the peripherals sector is at least reasonably strong. On the other hand, communications (sector 1), chips (sector 2), and distributors (sector 4) are less in demand. Clusters weak in these three sectors are less likely to see other sectors suffer as a result.

3. Conclusions from the simulations

The main implication of these simulations, therefore, is that the performance of a particular subsector of the computing industry at a particular cluster depends on both the diversity of the cluster and the degree of convergence between the different computer technologies. When technologies have not converged, so that positive spillovers between different subsectors are limited, then the single-technology cluster outperforms the multi-technology cluster. This happens because in the latter (multi-technology), congestion starts to restrain growth in one subsector earlier than in the former (single-technology). When the technologies converge, on the other hand, the multi-technology cluster outperforms the single-technology cluster because the former exploits the inter-sectoral spillovers that the latter cannot have. The optimum degree of diversity is to have strengths in somewhere between three and five sectors. If a cluster starts with strengths in all subsectors of the industry, then congestion sets in too soon to allow full development of any one of these subsectors.

The results suggest that single-technology clusters grow most rapidly when there is little or no convergence. But when technologies start to converge and when congestion emerges in early-established clusters, then the most successful clusters at a later stage may be multi-technology, and the single-technology cluster declines in relative importance.

4.5 CONCLUSIONS FROM THE ECONOMETRIC ESTIMATES

We can draw four main conclusions from this econometric study. First, there are three sectors that seem to play an important role at attracting entrants to a particular location: components, computers, and systems. Most of the entry they attract is to the software and peripheral sectors, but little to the core manufacturing sectors. The other sectors do not appear to attract much entry. The entry attractor effects tend to work across sectors rather than within sectors. Indeed, most sectors have a Cournot effect—whereby strength in a sector deters further entry into that sector. Second, firms tend to grow faster when located in a cluster that is strong in own sector employment. But if the firm is co-located with other industries, then growth appears to be reduced. Third, the clusters that seem to grow to be the largest in the long run are not single-technology clusters, nor do they have strengths in all areas of computing. They tend to have strengths in an intermediate number of sectors (about three to four). Fourth, if the size of the core manufacturing sector is constrained, the growth of the peripheral, service, and software sectors will be reduced, because entry will be limited. Conversely, the growth of core manufacturing sectors is little affected when other sectors decline, because the latter would in any case do little to attract entry to the core. In summary, we can conclude that the absence of a strong manufacturing core appears to reduce entry to other sectors, and in that sense these other sectors cannot flourish if the core does not.

1. Discussion of these results

It is instructive to reflect on how these results relate to some recent strands in the literature on organizational structure and innovation. First, this difference between the growth and entry models is consistent with the thesis that entrants and incumbents have different capacities to absorb the spillovers from incumbent firms in core manufacturing sectors, and that radical innovations in core manufacturing tend to provoke *entry* in the core and other sectors, rather than promoting rapid growth amongst incumbents. A striking example of this is the way in which the introduction of the microprocessor (a radical innovation in core manufacturing) provoked entry of many new PC manufacturers, and in due course new software companies. It did less to help the growth of large incumbents.

These propositions stem from the different organizational structures of large and small firms, and the implications of this for their ability to absorb knowledge. Absorptive capacity, in the sense used by Cohen and Levinthal (1989, 1990), summarizes the ability of firms to assimilate knowledge from the external environment and to transfer knowledge across and between the subdivisions of the firm. Nelson and Winter (1982) point out that absorptive capacity depends less on individuals than on organizational structure, and that large complex organizations depend on tried and tested innovative routines. This makes large organizations poor at improvising responses to novel situations (or what Tushman and Anderson 1986 would call *competence destroying* technological change). Large firms cope better with technological change that is compatible with their technological vision or paradigm—Dosi (1982), Metcalfe and Boden (1993), Swann (1992*a*). With a perceptive vision, firms can develop routines, and hence reduce the range of technological challenges that are *competence destroying*. Hannan and Freeman (1977), moreover, stress that the internal political balance of the large organization can be severely disrupted by the sorts of organizational restructuring required to respond effectively to new challenges, and in the light of this managers may choose to defer reorganization. This goes some way towards explaining why large incumbents are not especially good at absorbing spillovers from different subsectors, while new entrants are much better at it.

Second, it is worth noting that the special role of core manufacturing sectors here suggests that they are, in Bresnahan and Trajtenberg's (1992) terminology, *engines of growth*. As we saw, the core manufacturing parts of the computer industry could grow the rest, but not vice versa. Third, and last, entrants in this analysis play an important role in soaking up spillovers that might otherwise be lost, even if those entrants do not grow to be especially large. It is consistent with Simon's (1985) observation that it is learning from diverse knowledge bases which is most likely to yield innovation.

5

Clustering Dynamics in the UK Computer Industries: A Comparison with the USA

RUI BAPTISTA AND G. M. PETER SWANN

This short chapter compares the dynamics of the process by which clusters have emerged in the UK and US computer industries. It summarizes growth and entry models for the computer industries in the two countries. A full technical account of these models is given in Baptista and Swann (1996). In both countries, clusters of industrial strength in particular sectors attract new entrants to the industry, and incumbent firms located in a cluster that is strong in their own subsector of the industry tend to grow faster than average. While there are some second order differences between the models estimated for the USA and the UK, it appears that the dynamics of clustering are similar. In particular, there is no evidence that clustering effects are weaker in the UK than in the USA. This last conclusion is surprising, perhaps, but it suggests that the more modest clustering effects in the UK are a function of the smaller scale of the market, rather than a weaker clustering dynamic *per se*.

The chapter is organized as follows. Section 5.1 summarizes the industry structure in computing in the UK, while section 5.2 summarizes the data used for the UK study. Sections 5.3 and 5.4 respectively summarize the growth and entry models used in this comparison, which are slightly different from those used in the previous chapter. Section 5.5 compares the UK and US results obtained in this study, and section 5.6 concludes.

5.1 INDUSTRY STRUCTURE IN COMPUTING

The computer industry, and especially the personal computer, provide a most striking case of organic growth. Much of this growth was the result of the creation of external capabilities within networks of specialized firms whose major nexus of coordination is the market, rather than in large organizations enjoying internal economies of scale and scope (Langlois 1992). In the case of the PC, the size, diversity, and rapid development of the market meant that no single organization could develop the necessary technological capabilities internally with the required speed. A decentralized network of firms and users allowed for a diversity of approaches and led to a rapid learning process whereby new procedures spilled over to competitors. But the geographical concentration of firms and employment observed from the origins of the industry to the present day suggests that such positive feedback effects are geographically bounded.

Clustering in the UK

Arguably the main determinant of high-tech industry location in Britain is the spatial distribution of highly qualified labour, and its residential space preferences (Keeble 1988). It is not surprising, therefore, to find the largest concentration of firms in the south-east region. Associated with this functional and spatial division of labour is the concentration, in particular areas, of substantial scientific research capacity. Universities and public and private research establishments provide opportunities for new business ventures through spin-offs from basic research.

Kelly (1987) has cited a series of factors explaining the location of high-tech industries and, more specifically, computer hardware and software. These include: the existence of university–industry links, the availability of labour skills and venture capital, and government policy. The region's inherited industrial structure also has a very important influence on location. A large majority of new high-tech firms were founded as spin-offs from university research or from other firms, and studies such as Beaumont's (1982) show that more than 90 per cent of the initial locations are found within 40 miles of the founder's previous employer. The prior accumulation of firms in a region provides it with a self-reinforcing advantage in attracting new entrants.

Two regional areas—Cambridgeshire–Hertfordshire and Berkshire—have, in this way, become major technology-oriented complexes. The Cambridge region has seen the growth of mainly small and medium research-oriented firms, resulting from university research spin-offs, and which tend not to engage in hardware manufacturing. Berkshire contains a wider range of small, medium, and large firms, with a larger scale of activity and benefiting from scientific research carried out by large public and private research institutes. From 1980 onwards, however, regional incentive policies have played a larger role in the location of high-technology industries. An example of this is the development of a high-tech concentration in central Scotland—Silicon Glen—where government policy has attracted a range of mainly foreign-owned companies. However, although R & D activity has grown recently in this location, the main activities have been in production and operative labour (Kelly and Keeble 1989).

5.2 DATA FOR THE COMPARATIVE ECONOMETRIC STUDY

1. Data characteristics

The database used for the US study has already been described in Chapter 4. The database set up for the UK related to a census of firms in 1991. As described in the previous chapter, both databases represent snapshots at a single date, although it is possible to construct a quasi-time series from information on dates of foundation of companies. In principle, a sequence of such snapshots could have been put together, but this would have been an extremely time-consuming exercise, and would have led to a less complete dataset or, at least, to an unbalanced panel. Consequently, our efforts have been directed at exploring what could be learned about the clustering process from these single snapshots of the industry for the two countries.

Obviously, as described in the last chapter (section 4.1), this approach creates several difficulties, notably: first, the data on entry are in fact 'surviving entry' since exits before the census year are lost; second, we do not have employment histories, and hence our estimates of sector employment are in fact size-weighted numbers of firms; third, we have to estimate how each firm's activities are spread across different sectors, in the absence of detailed data on this; and fourth, equally, we have to estimate how each firm's employment is distributed across regions. Nevertheless, as described in Chapters 3 and 4, some of the simpler models that can be used use the data in a simpler way, and hence do not need to make such strong assumptions.

The data in the UK census include information on employment and location of each firm, with its corresponding date of foundation. In assembling the dataset, only firms above a certain size were included. For the UK, the criterion for inclusion was that the firm should have a level of employment above ten people. In the US dataset, however, the cut-off size was much higher; firms with a revenue below \$US2 million were excluded. This produced a US sample which is actually a much smaller subset of the total number of companies than the one for the UK. As a description of the industry, the two datasets are therefore very different in scope. Nevertheless, in comparing the clustering dynamics we can adjust for this.

Technically, these restrictions are a source of sample selection bias (see Heckman 1979), and we are aware that this should affect the results for the models presented. As Geroski (1991*a*, 1995) points out, entry rates are far higher than market penetration, survival rates are low, and successful entrants may take some time to achieve a size comparable to the average incumbent. Moreover, selectivity between new entrants is greater in markets where innovation and rapid technical change are important. Audretsch (1995) finds that, in industries where innovation is a critical factor, successful entrants are usually more innovative, but survival rates are lower. This should certainly be the case for the computer industry.

Nevertheless, it seems reasonable to assume that the kind of bias introduced counteracts the effects tested, since any positive spillover effects on entry and growth that might have arisen from these unsuccessful firms are ignored by the models. Therefore, since our aim is to test whether regionally bounded spillovers within and across sectors have significant effects on growth and entry, omitting these firms should reduce the amount of positive spillovers that are actually picked up by the analysis. Besides, it seems probable that successful firms would be the ones which showed a higher level of absorptive capacity for external spillovers, while unsuccessful or moribund firms would have little or none. Hence, since the aim of the study is to evaluate how spillovers affect entry and growth, there is a case for excluding ephemeral entrants from the sample, and our main interest should be concentrated on the growth and entry behaviour of the successful surviving firms.

2. Data classification

Firms were classified and aggregated into the same eight major sectors of the industry as in Chapter 4: communications, components, hardware, distribution, peripherals, services, software, and systems. In both datasets, a proportion of firms are active in more than one of these sectors. The average number of employees per firm in the sample is more than 23 times as large for the US (9137.4) as for the UK (395.7). The narrower criterion used in assembling the US dataset partly accounts for this difference, although as we shall see, US firms do appear to grow faster, for reasons apparently unconnected with clustering.

The regional units used were the state for the USA and the standard region as defined by the Central Statistical Office (CSO) for the UK. The US sample includes firms located in a total of thirty-nine states, while UK firms are distributed among the ten CSO regions of Great Britain (excluding Northern Ireland). Both units have their limitations, since some clusters might spread across more than one state or region and, alternatively, there may be more than one cluster in large states or regions (notably in California). However, studies such as Glaeser et al. (1992) and Jaffe et al. (1993) have shown that external effects of the kind that are explored here seem to grow stronger as the regional unit becomes smaller. Any bias introduced here should be to underestimate the strength of clustering effects. Nevertheless, the use of states and regions as a spatial unit has some administrative sense, since in the USA individual states have their own tax regimes, utility pricing, and industrial policies, while in the UK government policies and incentives towards new industries are to a limited extent defined at a regional level.

The strong agglomeration of firms within the south-east region of Great Britain leads us to subdivide this region into five different subregions: a central area, corresponding to Greater London; a north-west (NW) area, approximately corresponding to Oxfordshire, Gloucestershire, Hertfordshire, Middlesex, and Berkshire; a north-east (NE) area corresponding to Essex; a south-west (SW) area, including Hampshire and Surrey; and a south-east (SE) area, roughly matching Kent and East and West Sussex. Although it would have probably been useful to do a similar breakdown for some US states such as California, New York, Massachusetts, or Texas, this was not done. However, we considered this a more important issue in the UK, since about two-thirds of the firms in the UK sample are concentrated in the combined south-east region. Not even California has such a monopoly in the USA.

3. Data description

As we saw in the last chapter, the three US major states (California, Massachusetts, and New York) account for more than half the total number of firms. In the UK, the three top subregions (Greater London, the NW and SW areas of the south-east) represent 62 per cent of the firms. In terms of employment, however, concentration is more pronounced in the UK, where Greater London accounts for about 70 per cent of employment, but 35 per cent of the firms. In short, the number of employees per firm in this region is roughly double that in the rest of the country.

The distribution of firms across sectors in the USA and the UK is rather different, though in some measure this reflects the different sample sizes. In the UK the services and distribution sectors account for almost 60 per cent of the number of firms and about 50 per cent of total employment. The corresponding figure is smaller in the US, because many small service and distribution companies have been excluded from that sample. In the US, the peripherals and software sectors account for more than 55 per cent of firms, but only about 16 per cent of total employment. Although the manufacturing sectors (components and hardware) account for similar proportions of firms in both countries (15 per cent in the

UK, 17 per cent in the USA), employment in these sectors is just 10.5 per cent of total employment in the industry for the UK, while it reaches 35.5 per cent for the USA.

This suggests divergence in the development and sectoral specialization within the computer industry in the two countries. The US industry contains a relatively large manufacturing base, which (as we saw in the last chapter) seems to encourage the entry of a large number of small firms in software and peripherals. In the UK, employment in core manufacturing is relatively low, while the main area of activity is in services and distribution.

5.3 GROWTH MODELS

The absence of a time series of data on firm size is not a serious problem, since our main interest is in the trend rate of growth over the firm's lifetime. The growth model used is basically that in Chapter 3 (section 3.8), though with a number of additional variables. A different model is estimated for each sector, and then a pooled model for all sectors. In this model, the logarithm of total employment in the sample year is regressed on the (log of) employment in the firm's own sector, employment in all other sectors, and on the age of the firm. The estimated coefficient on the age variable yields the average growth rate of firm since its foundation.

The individual sector models were estimated including only those firms active in that one sector alone. The pooled models include both single sector and multi-sector firms. Employment in each multi-sector firm was assumed (in the absence of any better information) to be equally divided into the constituent sectors. For these firms, therefore, the regional employment variables are defined as follows: own sector employment is calculated as the average regional employment in the sectors where the firm is active; while other sector employment is calculated as the average regional employment in those sectors where the firm is not active. Full results of these models and the additional variables used are set out in Baptista and Swann (1996). In this chapter we simply concentrate on the cluster-related growth effects, and the trend growth rates.

5.4 ENTRY MODELS

Again, the modelling of entry follows the approach set out in Chapter 3, and employed in Chapter 4. We have estimated latent variable models of entry and what we have called in previous chapters the full model of entry. A cross-section regression of mean entry (averaged over all years) into each sector in each region against sample year employment, such as in Chapter 4, is not a feasible option for the UK dataset. That is because there are only fourteen regions (or subregions) in the UK dataset.

Entry in our samples of the US and UK computer industry is measured using the date of foundation of successful firms to count the number of entrants per year. As noted before, this means that the time series is strictly of 'surviving entry' rather than total entry. Multi-sector firms were counted as one entrant in each of the sectors where the firm was active in the sample year. That may be an unsatisfactory assumption when the firm has diversified from one original sector into others, but, in the absence of detailed information on such diversification in each firm, this seems a reasonable working assumption.

1. Exploratory latent variable analysis

This approach avoids some of the strong assumptions that have to be made to estimate the full models of entry. As described in Chapter 3, the method postulates that there is a set of latent variables which 'explain' entry into the eight sectors in each region. These latent variables are unobservable and difficult to interpret, but can indicate if there are common factors attracting entry into several sectors simultaneously. If so, that implies that there are some common aspects of cluster strength which attract entry into more than one sector, but may deter entry into others. If not, then the factors attracting entry into different sectors are unrelated and peculiar to each sector. While we do not reproduce the detailed results here, in both countries one latent variable accounts for a large portion of entry variation. This first latent variable attracts entry into all sectors together. That means that there is one common factor that attracts all types of entry.

As we saw in the previous chapter on the US case, there is a second latent variable that attracts a significant amount of entry into software and peripherals but deters entry into other sectors. That was then seen to be a fundamental distinction in the full entry model: there were common factors about clusters that attracted entry to software and peripherals in particular. In the UK case, however, none of the other latent variables is especially important, though taken together they are large enough to mean that the determinants of entry are not uniform across all sectors of the computer industry in the UK. But the inference is that in the UK there is no single strong common factor that attracts entry to one group of sectors and deters entry into others.

It is of course impossible to determine the nature of these latent variables. But this simple comparison indicates that the strong distinction between clustering behaviour in hardware and software/peripherals observed in the US case is unlikely to be repeated in the UK case.

2. Full entry econometric models

As with Chapter 4, the regional employment time series for each sector had to be assembled from firm data. This raises a number of non-trivial problems that were dealt with in the following manner.

1. All spillovers are assumed to flow from companies' headquarters, except for known subsidiaries, and multi-sector firms' employment is presumed to be equally divided between the sectors in which the firm is active.
2. Each firm's history of past employment since the date of foundation was constructed by interpolation, assuming an exponential growth path, calibrated individually for each firm since the starting-up date (with employment equal to one) up to the level of employment in the sample year. This would produce very imperfect data for individual company growth, since it smooths out all the cycles, but when aggregated across all firms in each cluster, we believe that the overall measure of cluster size is not too bad.

For the USA, firms founded from 1960 are included in the entry model. For the UK, the entry sample extends from 1961 to 1990. We have, thus, a 29-year panel for the USA (1960–88) and a 30-year panel for the UK. The *full* entry model used is similar to that in Chapters 3 and 4, though with some additional explanatory variables. The models explain entry of successful firms into sector i at location c in year t as a function of the size of the cluster, as measured by (log of) employment in each of the eight sectors.

In addition, the econometric methods used were different. Chapter 4 uses ordinary least squares to estimate the entry model. This is not entirely appropriate since entry is an integer-valued variable $(0, 1, 2, 3, \ldots)$ rather than continuous. The results described below use instead Poisson and negative binomial methods of estimation, which recognize this property of the dependent variable. However, this use of limited dependent variable techniques is not costless: it is much less flexible at identifying different sector by cluster fixed effects on entry, and, as we saw in Chapter 4, these fixed effects are important.

Again, Baptista and Swann (1996) set out the technical details. Here we simply focus on the differences and similarities between the US and UK models.

5.5 ECONOMETRIC RESULTS

1. Growth

The pattern of results in the growth models is reasonably similar for the USA and the UK. Table 5.1 shows the coefficients for the model using pooled data for all firms in the datasets. The coefficients for age show that the average rate of growth for US firms was about twice the rate for the UK firms over the periods. In both countries, specialization seems to have a positive effect on individual firm growth, since employment in the sector(s) where firms are active has a positive significant effect on size, while employment in other sectors has a negative significant effect.

Coefficients are larger, in absolute value, for the USA. However, since the dimension of the US states in terms of employment is larger, the same percentage increase in regional employment represents a larger absolute increase for the USA than for the UK, so this does not necessarily mean that effects are less important for the UK case. Indeed, for the specific case of own and other

Table 5.1 *Growth promoters: pooled data for all sectors*

	Growth in USA		Growth in UK	
	GLS (White standard errors)	Robust regression	GLS (White standard errors)	Robust regression
Observations	674	674	1339	1339
R-Squared	0.5501	—	0.1226	—
F-Statistic	—	114.57	—	21.69
Variables				
Age	0.0611	0.0641	0.0319	0.0271
	(0.004)	(0.0033)	(0.0035)	(0.0024)
Log own Sector	0.2378	0.2244	0.1417	0.114
	(0.0378)	(0.0452)	(0.044)	(0.0383)
Log own Sector	–0.1917	–0.1872	–0.1125	–0.1197
	(0.0386)	(0.3481)	(0.0444)	(0.0376)
Constant	2.5536	2.6393	4.5423	4.7839
	(1.2208)	(1.2177)	(0.542)	(0.4889)

sector employment, coefficients for the USA are about two-thirds larger, in absolute terms, than for the UK, while the average regional size (in terms of total employment) is about four times as high. One could conclude, therefore that, on average, the effect of cluster strength on growth in the UK computer industry is comparable to that in the USA.

Results for individual sector models are presented in Table 5.2. We simply note that, in cases such as communications and hardware in the UK, and components for the USA, the size of the samples is probably too small to allow for reliable estimates. The estimated coefficients show that average growth rates are always larger for US firms, confirming the result from the pooled model. The individual models show, again, a positive effect of own sector employment in the region, and a negative effect of employment in other sectors on growth, although these are not significant for all sectors, particularly in the UK.

Table 5.2 *Growth promoters: individual sector models*

	US or UK	Growth in							
		Communications	Components	Hardware	Distribution	Peripherals	Services	Software	Systems
Number of observations	US	40	22	64	36	140	46	185	32
	UK	15	129	9	242	42	286	67	57
R-squared	US	0.6617	0.5625	0.3611	0.1641	0.4655	0.5372	0.5628	0.4918
	UK	0.4	0.0754	0.9522	0.0387	0.2328	0.101	0.148	0.0895
Variables									
Age	US	0.0499	0.0667	0.09	0.0448	0.0716	0.0626	0.0619	0.033
		(0.0092)	(0.0207)	(0.0221)	(0.0363)	(0.0087)	(0.0141)	(0.0141)	(0.0161)
	UK	0.0207	0.0179	-0.2319	0.016	0.0279	0.0282	0.0418	0.0184
		(0.0147)	(0.0062)	(0.0308)	(0.0084)	(0.0126)	(0.0052)	(0.0262)	(0.0189)
Log own Sector	US	0.2654	0.3533	0.3146	0.2696	0.1694	-0.0033	0.1832	0.3483
		(0.1318)	(0.1663)	(0.0819)	(0.1302)	(0.0726)	(0.2303)	(0.07)	(0.2019)
	UK	0.9859	0.4338	0.0677	0.1907	0.3539	-0.0387	0.4248	0.0633
		(0.3204)	(0.2597)	(0.1713)	(0.2167)	(0.3661)	(0.1939)	(0.3132)	(0.2815)
Log own Sector	US	-0.4803	-0.1578	-2.8967	-0.1161	-0.1726	0.1426	-0.0666	-0.4176
		(0.2089)	(0.0829)	(0.0856)	(0.1082)	(0.125)	(0.1971)	(0.053)	(0.3074)
	UK	-1.7044	-0.2417	-0.062	-0.1797	-0.2356	0.1603	-0.5512	-0.2409
		(0.5811)	(0.1637)	(0.2787)	(0.1532)	(0.2411)	(0.2313)	(0.3171)	(0.2787)
Constant	US	9.6614	3.683	5.3934	4.2514	5.6589	4.45	2.8413	6.1513
		(2.4204)	(2.1439)	(1.6187)	(1.7084)	(1.7197)	(2.2089)	(0.6287)	(3.181)
	UK	8.2794	2.5413	12.629	3.5091	3.6405	2.9864	3.198	2.4529
		(2.8376)	(1.0338)	(0.6194)	(0.732)	(1.4839)	(0.4148)	(1.008)	(0.8896)

2. Entry

The full entry model was estimated using a panel of 29 years by 39 regions for the US (1,131 observations) and 30 years by 14 regions for the UK (420 observations). As we observed earlier, since entry is a count variable, a Poisson model was fitted to the data. This kind of linear exponential model offers an improved methodology for repeated count models, as shown by Hausman et al. (1984), and Blundell et al. (1995*a*) for the cases of patents and innovation counts. Poisson models have been applied to the entry phenomenon by Chappell et al. (1990) and Mayer and Chappell (1994) with useful results. For technical reasons, we have estimated a generalization of the Poisson model—the Negative Binomial model, allowing for a quadratic relationship between variance and mean, as suggested by Blundell et al. (1995*a*), following Gouriroux et al. (1984).

Since we have Poisson-type linear exponential models, interpretation of the coefficients is different from the growth models above, or the ordinary least squares model of the last chapter. The Poisson parameter λ is defined as the average number of entrants per sector, per region, in each period. A rough estimate of the elasticity between this number of entrants (i) and the *log of employment* (x_i) is given by $\beta' x_i$. Consequently, if the (log of) employment in sector i in region c increases by 1 percentage point, then the average number of entrants in that region should increase by an amount equal to the product of the coefficient β_{ic} and (log of) employment in sector i in region c. Thus the percentage change in entry following a percentage change in cluster employment depends not only on the estimated coefficient, but also on the number of employees in the entry-promoting sector within that region. This makes the comparison of estimated parameters for the USA and UK a little less complex.

Estimates of the entry model parameters for each sector in the USA and the UK are presented in Table 5.3. Constants and a range of other parameters are omitted—again full details are in Baptista and Swann (1996). Note that because of the different form of the model, and because a variety of other explanatory variables are included, the results for the USA are not easily comparable with those presented in the last chapter. There is a similar pattern for the USA and UK. Employment in core sectors (hardware and

Table 5.3 *Entry attractors into computing*

	US or UK	Entry into							
		Communications	Components	Hardware	Distribution	Peripherals	Services	Software	Systems
Observations	US	1131	1131	1131	1131	1131	1131	1131	1131
	UK	420	420	420	420	420	420	420	420
Attracted by									
Communications	US	0.0673	-0.2071	-0.0159	-0.0399	0.0037	0.0314	0.0355	0.0329
		(0.0729)	(0.1615)	(0.0579)	(0.0709)	(0.0348)	(0.0422)	(0.0277)	(0.0557)
	UK	-0.021	0.0623	-0.1882	-0.0919	-0.1775	-0.0402	-0.0847	-0.0242
		(0.0974)	(0.0574)	(0.1205)	(0.3541)	(0.1973)	(0.0376)	(0.0572)	(0.0636)
Components	US	0.1356	0.1447	0.1075	0.0322	0.01043	0.0648	0.0564	-0.0139
		(0.0872)	(0.133)	(0.0579)	(0.071)	(0.039)	(0.0598)	(0.0312)	(0.0672)
	UK	0.1037	0.2308	0.5731	0.1599	0.384	0.1276	0.0556	0.1413
		(0.2265)	(0.1264)	(0.2681)	(0.0918)	(0.2273)	(0.0919)	(0.1582)	(0.1848)
Hardware	US	0.2735	0.3161	0.0988	0.1847	0.111	0.0907	0.1732	0.1113
		(0.1020)	(0.1913)	(0.0507)	(0.0866)	(0.0475)	(0.0499)	(0.0394)	(0.0609)
	UK	0.2654	0.2067	0.1651	0.209	0.3243	0.0047	0.0165	0.1064
		(0.1382)	(0.0915)	(0.2052)	(0.0526)	(0.121)	(0.0574)	(0.088)	(0.0982)
Distribution	US	-0.1932	-0.2843	-0.0499	-0.1355	-0.1985	-0.0694	-0.1656	-0.2169
		(0.1348)	(0.2598)	(0.0863)	(0.1006)	(0.0604)	(0.0907)	(0.0458)	(0.1166)
	UK	0.1281	-0.1107	0.4187	-0.043	-0.0578	-0.1229	0.0581	-0.1733
		(0.2332)	(0.1228)	(0.2642)	(0.0893)	(0.213)	(0.0896)	(0.1496)	(0.1682)

Table 5.3 *Continued*

	US or UK	Communications	Components	Hardware	Distribution	Peripherals	Services	Software	Systems
		Entry into							
Peripherals	US	-0.0571	-0.0465	0.0082	-0.1423	-0.0201	-0.0458	-0.0494	0.1334
		(0.1099)	(0.1951)	(0.0715)	(0.1098)	(0.0536)	(0.0733)	(0.0418)	(0.0941)
	UK	0.0563	0.0161	0.0463	0.1622	0.2125	0.09	0.3285	0.2301
		(0.1297)	(0.0681)	(0.1428)	(0.0504)	(0.117)	(0.0515)	(0.0885)	(0.0951)
Services	US	0.1155	-0.336	0.0191	0.0886	-0.0154	-0.0679	0.1257	-0.0013
		(0.1108)	(0.2237)	(0.0894)	(0.1092)	(0.0582)	(0.0849)	(0.0387)	(0.1031)
	UK	0.1219	-0.0751	-0.1735	0.105	0.2278	0.1365	0.1971	0.2686
		(0.1857)	(0.0929)	(0.2139)	(0.0672)	(0.1617)	(0.0687)	(0.1138)	(0.1248)
Software	US	-0.0189	0.1959	-0.045	0.0838	0.1455	0.2684	-0.0277	0.181
		(0.1426)	(0.2688)	(-0.1078)	(-0.1506)	(0.0791)	(0.0973)	(0.0547)	(0.126)
	UK	-0.2125	-0.0881	0.2968	-0.0475	-0.2613	0.1412	0.0566	0.0059
		(0.2133)	(0.1212)	(0.258)	(0.0836)	(0.1937)	(0.0878)	(0.1455)	(0.1612)
Systems	US	0.1784	0.0407	0.0773	0.1339	0.06	0.024	0.0431	0.1055
		(0.0881)	(0.1824)	(0.0648)	(0.0776)	(0.0404)	(-0.0668)	(0.0282)	(0.0796)
	UK	-0.0405	-0.1969	0.2341	-0.3464	-0.0155	-0.2641	-0.3015	-0.4354
		(0.0904)	(0.0978)	(0.2293)	(0.2736)	(0.1842)	(0.2759)	(0.2267)	(0.1481)

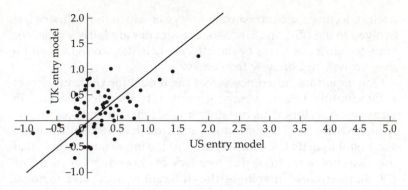

Fig. 5.1 *Scatter plot of Poisson model elasticities*

components) has a positive effect on entry into most other sectors. In the UK, employment in peripherals and services also has a positive effect on entry into some other sectors.

Figure 5.1 presents a comparison of the estimated Poisson model elasticities. It shows a scatter plot of US elasticities against UK elasticities. While these parameters are not all that closely correlated, there is no systematic tendency of the US estimates to exceed the UK estimates, although the larger ones are slightly bigger for the USA. One should bear in mind, however, that a 1 per cent change in regional employment in the USA will usually amount to a much larger number of employees than a 1 per cent change in a UK region. So the effect of the marginal employee on entry is as high on average in the UK as in the USA. In general terms, a striking result of these *full* entry models is that, unlike the case of incumbent growth, where regional specialization seems to be the main promoter, some regional cross-sectoral effects are important in attracting new entrants into a cluster. And this observation applies both to the USA and to the UK.

5.6 CONCLUSIONS

One remarkable conclusion that can be drawn from the results is that clustering dynamics do not appear to be stronger in the USA than in the UK. This is the case despite significant differences between the composition of the samples for the two countries, itself reflecting the contrast in the ways in which the industry has evolved in the USA and UK. Model estimates are fairly similar for both countries, in terms of the effects of cluster strength both on firm growth and on new firm entry.

One important difference is that the model for US firms shows a significantly larger average growth rate than for the UK, in virtually all sectors. This certainly implies that, in terms of underlying growth, the US computing industry has been much more successful than its UK counterpart. But the important point is that this does not seem to be due to a lack of clustering effects in the UK. Furthermore, in spite of the different sectoral and regional structures (e.g. distinct critical masses) of the US and UK computer industries, the broad dynamics of clustering as observed here are very much the same. We find, for both countries, that firms grow faster when they are co-located with other firms in the same sectors, but that if anything co-location with firms in other sectors reduces the rate of growth.

The entry models also yield similar results for the USA and the UK. Again, the magnitude of effects, although more difficult to compare, indicates that the capacity of clusters to attract entry is not weaker in the UK than in the USA. Unlike the case of incumbent growth, cross-sectoral effects appear to have an important impact on entry in both countries. In the USA, as we saw in the last chapter, spillovers coming from core manufacturing (hardware and components) attract new entrants, especially to software and peripherals. In the UK, hardware and components again attract entry into some other sectors, but peripherals (and, to a lesser extent, services) attract entry to remaining sectors.

As before, this contrast between the growth and entry models is consistent with the observation that entrants and incumbents have different capacities to absorb spillovers originating in different sectors. Incumbents find it easier to absorb spillovers emanating from the same sector, and grow faster as a result, but they find it harder to absorb spillovers from other sectors. The latter create an entry opportunity for new firms.

The computer industry, developing from mainframes to minicomputers, and from these to microcomputers, is certainly a case where radical innovation in both products and processes, associated with the existence of important network externalities, has changed the face of market structure. Incumbents may face restructuring problems that will hinder their absorptive capacity (Cohen and Levinthal 1989) in the face of radical innovation. This lack of absorptive capacity allows for successful entry of new firms to exploit the opportunities that arise along the boundaries between sectors. Successful entrants are likely to specialize in different subsectors of the industry, for example in different networks in the value chain, as suggested by Rosenbloom and Christensen (1994). On the other hand, localized spillovers in a sector, arising from innovations that draw upon existing skills or capabilities, and which are within the firms' value chain, will enhance the growth of incumbents that are already active in that sector.

To sum up, the story of clustering discussed at length in the previous chapter, in the context of the US computer industry, applies also to the industry in the UK. In the next two chapters, we examine how well this approach can explain clustering in a different high-technology industry. Chapter 6 looks at biotechnology in the USA, and Chapter 7 focuses on biotechnology in the UK. Chapter 8 will draw together and compare the studies of computing and biotechnology, to see what are the key differences between them.

6

Clustering in Biotechnology in the USA

MARTHA PREVEZER

INTRODUCTION

Chapters 4 and 5 looked at the phenomenon of clustering in the computing industry. The next two chapters look at another high-technology industry, biotechnology, that has also exhibited a marked propensity to cluster, particularly in the USA. To understand the phenomenon of clustering more generally, we need to establish why, in any particular industry, a cluster grows in one place rather than another.

This chapter has two parts. The first looks at what we have discovered about the clustering process in biotechnology in the USA through data and the construction of a series of models described in more detail in Chapter 3; at the entry of new firms into clusters in the USA, and at the growth of incumbent firms within clusters. This approach gives us an insight into how the clustering process worked in the USA during the 1980s. In part 2, from section 6.6 onwards, we use this view of process to understand in more detail some of the history of the industry in terms of why clusters formed in California in particular; what are the needs of different types of company, and how the industry has become diffused, spreading into separate clusters in several states. We look at the contribution of policy inducements to this clustering.

The clusters we are looking at here are of groups of firms within one industry based in one geographical area. This is different from the groups of firms in several industries based in one area, looked at by Porter (1990). The biotechnologies that we are focusing on here are based around the series of new scientific discoveries from the mid-1970s in the field of genetic engineering: in particular the technologies of recombinant DNA and hybridoma technology. We are not therefore referring to the use of traditional biotechnologies in the food and brewing industries which have been in use for centuries. Our focus is on the industry that was created out of scientific breakthroughs in the mid- and late 1970s. The biotechnology industry as we define it here includes not only those firms dedicated to biotechnology, DBFs as they are sometimes called, but also large multinational incumbent firms across a variety of industrial sectors—pharmaceuticals, agro-chemicals, food processing, and energy. These are the firms that use biotechnologies in-house. They are the firms that commercialize the new technologies in partnership with the DBFs. Thus the industry ranges from firms of one employee to those with many thousands. The DBFs were created since the mid-1970s, whereas the multinationals were born in an era when biotechnology as defined here did not exist.

Section 6.1 describes the biotechnology industry and how it differed in its genesis from the computing industry. We ask what are the advantages of clustering in biotechnology that create the momentum to congregate. These are the sharing of specialized labour, specialized inputs, and specialized knowledge, as well as a range of initial conditions that give particular locations or states an advantage over others in creating a new industry. In section 6.2 we give an overview of clustering in biotechnology in the USA: where the majority of companies are located and what has been the distribution of entry of new firms during the 1980s. Section 6.3 describes the data that we have used in looking at clustering in biotechnology in the USA—the unit of location, company data, and science base data, and the various problems or drawbacks that are associated with each type of data.

Section 6.4 sets out how we have used models to establish what common factors encourage clustering in several sectors simultaneously. There are two main types of model of cluster growth, one looking at what attracts entry of new firms to a cluster, and the other at what benefits incumbents in a cluster. Section 6.5 describes our results. The role of the science base emerges as the critical attractor to new firms, whereas 'own' sector strength is important for the growth of incumbents within a cluster. Strength in sectors other than the 'own' sector is not important for incumbents in biotechnology. It is important for new entrants into a group of sectors. New firms in health care and equipment sectors do tend to be commonly attracted into clusters together, suggesting some interaction between these sectors.

Part 2 takes a complementary, historical approach to understanding clustering in biotechnology. Section 6.6 finds the origins of the industry in the science base and in the knowledge race between west and east coast that established the west coast as the prime location for the new industry. However, it argues that the science was not the only factor that allowed the west coast to achieve this outcome. Other factors that may be considered as part of the infrastructure, or as part of the west coast's history, helped to determine California as the most fertile ground for a cluster of companies in a new industry to thrive.

Section 6.7 looks at the characteristics of entrant and incumbent companies and at their differing demands upon the local environment. We ask what the role of the science base is, and how it contributes to the industry. We find that new companies moved from being outcrops of the science base to become the typically industrially founded companies which predominated by the mid-1980s. As the industry matured it acquired legitimacy, and natural entrepreneurs, who had felt constrained within incumbent firms, left to set up their own businesses. We ask why cross-sectoral interactions within a cluster were less important in this industry than in computing. To answer this we look at the important issue of relationships between entrants and incumbents, which tend to be within a sector. Incumbents have not been replaced by entrants in this industry. Rather, their cooperation through strategic alliances has been central to the formation of the industry. In the main these have not been constrained by geography. They are not therefore specific to clusters but have occurred worldwide. However, looking at networks of alliances centred in particular states, firms local to those states are central within the network.

Section 6.8 inspects the structure of the industry and examines how this has shaped the clustering. The similarity of technologies and the lack of complementarities, together with the fact of divisions between the sets of users of that common technology, helps to explain why there has been more clustering in some industrial sectors than others. We conclude that the impetus to cluster in biotechnology is linked to the opportunities for innovation lying *upstream* in research. The opportunities for *entrants* to absorb spillovers lie in those sectors where opportunities for innovation are upstream in research. Opportunities for *incumbents* to absorb spillovers are found in sectors where more downstream activities such as marketing or processing are more important sources of innovation.

Section 6.9 looks at the role of policy in the USA to induce clustering activity in biotechnology, to shift activity away from the original centres in California and Massachusetts and to diffuse it more widely into many other states. Policy has been centred around the Regional Biotechnology Centres. We look at the mix of reliance on existing local specialisms and the construction of new infrastructure, and consider how far the successful rise of new clusters in North Carolina, Maryland, Washington, and Texas may have been helped by those Regional Centres.

PART 1

6.1 THE GENESIS OF THE BIOTECHNOLOGY INDUSTRY

In comparing the biotechnology industry with computing, we are also interested in which factors they had in common, causing both industries to cluster in California; and specifically, how far the biotechnology industry was influenced by the earlier clustering of computing in Silicon Valley. The factors creating the initial computing clusters in Silicon Valley were set out in Chapter 4. They included the spur that the Second World War and the Korean War gave to the electronics industry, the build-up by Frederick Terman of Stanford's electrical engineering department, and the decision of various key companies to settle in the area. In some measure the biotechnology industry benefited from the inheritance of clustering in computing in north California. There were experienced venture capitalists there who had helped to found and grow high-technology start-ups. The area was one of high job mobility and fluid communications networks, leading to the rapid spread of ideas. Furthermore, the experience of Stanford with its Research Institute and Industrial Park served as a useful model of how links between universities and companies could be fostered.

One key difference, however, between the growth of the computing cluster and that in biotechnology has been the much greater relative importance of the science base in biotechnology. In computing, the key links and information flows were between engineers in different companies; in biotechnology the important relationships have been between the science base and companies. Scientific breakthroughs provided the key external stimulus to the founding of the biotechnology industry. The two key discoveries, following Watson and Crick's discovery of the double helix structure of DNA in 1953, were the development of the recombinant DNA technique in 1973 by Cohen and Boyer at Stanford and the University of California at San Francisco (UCSF) and Kohler and Milstein's discovery of monoclonal antibodies in Cambridge (UK) in 1975. The earliest companies were based on the series of techniques that developed from these breakthroughs. The early companies were located near the most prominent centres of research, and the academic scientists who were responsible for the advances in the science were also leading figures in the founding of companies such as Genentech, Biogen, or Hybritech, which were based on the west and east coasts near their founders' universities. Above all, the area around San Francisco, with its collection of eminent research centres working together on these techniques, became the focus for the early industry. This closeness of the industry to the science base has continued, as relevant scientific advances have made the universities an important source of innovation for the industry.

Another difference from the computing industry has been a more prominent role played by the stock market in raising money for new start-ups in this industry. Genentech's very successful flotation in 1980 established a pattern whereby very young companies could make initial public offerings when 'windows of opportunity' opened. They were able to raise substantial sums publicly, and also to gain publicity and legitimacy whilst offering venture capitalists an exit route through the public market. This influence of the stock market was more prominent for the early biotechnology start-ups than it was in computing.

There were also significant differences between biotechnology and computing in the way the large established companies interacted with the new start-ups. These different interactions had an impact on the location decisions of both incumbents and start-ups. In computing the location of the large established companies served as a key attraction to new companies due to the interaction between them which required close geographical contact. In biotechnology, although large incumbents in pharmaceuticals and chemicals were involved in the start-up of new companies, this was largely in the form of alliances which were formed over geographical distances and did not require the incumbents to relocate at the centres of clusters, nor did it involve the start-ups locating near the incumbents. This has led to greater diffusion in biotechnology than computing, with clusters of small companies developing near research centres, at quite considerable distances from their large company partners in alliances. We look at this further in section 6.7.

The type of markets that the two industries have created have also been quite distinct. The computing industry has developed into sectors with different technologies, where markets for applications of the end-products are spread across other industries and the domestic and financial economy. The biotechnology industry has formed into sectors using similar technologies, but with applications confined to specific industrial sectors such as pharmaceuticals, chemicals, food, or agriculture. There are exceptions to this, with new diagnostics and instrumentation having applications in several industrial and research sectors. But broadly the new biotechnology companies have developed with clear dependencies on the existing industrial structure as consumers of their end-products. We explore this argument and its implications further in section 6.8.

We shall use the models that were developed in Chapter 3 and applied to computing in Chapter 4—tailored now to biotechnology. These are the series of entry models to estimate the main sources of attraction to new companies to enter into the biotechnology industry, together with a growth model that suggests why incumbent firms in clusters tend to grow faster than those outside clusters. The entry models distinguish between attraction of new firms to the science base and attraction to other industrial companies. The growth model looks at the benefits to incumbents of being located within a cluster. It examines whether companies benefit from being near other companies within their own sector or near companies in other sectors. It also looks at whether the science base is important in encouraging the growth of incumbent companies within clusters.

The types of attractions we expect to find are various. They exist on the demand side of the market through the presence of sophisticated buyers attracting new companies, and on the supply side through firms being attracted to new sources of technology in the science base or in other companies. The tacitness of the new knowledge created in the science base and companies require that companies locate nearby in order to be able to absorb the knowledge. These underlying theories for clustering have been explored in Chapters 2 and 3. Here we need only highlight the main factors that have emerged as critical to the underlying motivation to cluster in biotechnology. The key factors are the presence of specialized labour, specialized inputs, and knowledge spillovers, which Krugman (1991*a*) and Marshall (1920) before him highlighted as significant forces creating clusters. In the context of biotechnology, specialized labour means the scientific expertise in the collection of disciplines relevant to the industry, including for example microbiology, biochemical engineering, and genetics. It also includes other types of specialized labour such as those people with experience of raising venture capital, with management skills, and with sales and marketing expertise.

These human resources are present in the science base, in other companies, and in related business and venture capital companies with experience in starting new companies and handling the range of issues such as property rights, regulation, and distribution necessary in commercializing the science. The scientific and commercial networks of people within the science community and between the science and business environments also contribute to the specialization of labour which serves as an attractor to new companies to a particular location.

Specialized non-labour inputs in biotechnology may be interpreted as the new equipment, research tools, and related technologies to which companies need access in order to develop their products. Locating near these specialized sources of equipment and close to the leading-edge development of new instruments provides advantages to firms in this field. For instance equipment and instruments have ranged from reagents as chemical precursors, new biosensors, separation and purification equipment and testing devices, to a range of bioprocessing equipment necessary for scaling up scientific discoveries for manufacture.

Knowledge spillovers in this context are enjoyed by firms located close to the sources of such new knowledge as cannot be absorbed at a distance: so-called 'tacit knowledge'. There is evidence that this has been the nature of the new scientific discoveries in their early stages in the science base; it has required face-to-face collaboration between scientists in the science base and in companies and between scientists and entrepreneurs to make the science usable and adaptable to commercial purposes. We examine these arguments further in section 6.7.

As mentioned above, and laid out in Chapter 3, there are also reasons on the demand side of the market for companies to cluster. In biotechnology, therapeutics and diagnostics firms have been strongly motivated to locate and cluster close to the sophisticated end-users in hospitals. Such contact will have enabled new firms to test and develop drugs and diagnostic kits in consort with their end-users. There are also benefits for instrument and equipment makers in locating near their end-markets in companies and research centres; research establishments in particular have served both as customers of new instruments and as useful sources of ideas and innovations in the instrument sector.

The main costs of clustering in biotechnology which will deter companies from further congregating in an established cluster are the costs of competition in input and product markets, and the general congestion costs which drive up input prices and reduce profitability. In the case of biotechnology there have been many races between firms to produce a particular product, which will have decreased the likelihood of any one firm winning the race and securing monopoly profits. These races have often occurred between firms in the same cluster, competing for access to similar inputs. Congestion effects are thought to have been more important however in the case of the computing industry than in the younger biotechnology industry. However as some of the biotechnology clusters have overlapped with or are near to older computing clusters, saturation from earlier technologies may have affected the location decisions of new biotechnology firms.

6.2 A PRELIMINARY VIEW OF CLUSTERING

The easiest way to demonstrate that industrial clustering in biotechnology has occurred is to show the map of biotechnology companies in the United States in 1993, based on Ernst & Young's data (Figure 6.1). There are two distinct clusters in California—in the San Francisco Bay area and further south near San Diego and Los Angeles. There are also clusters on the east coast in the Boston area and in the New York Tri-State region and also significant groups of companies in Maryland, North Carolina, and Washington, DC. Table 6.1 and Figure 6.2, which we use in the series of entry and growth models, are based on our own databases for 1991 described in more detail below. In 1991 just under a quarter of firms were located in California.

The data include only those firms that have 'survived', i.e. entered the sample or were present already and have existed until 1991, the sample date. It does not include those firms that entered

Table 6.1 *Distribution of companies by state*

State	Number of companies	Proportion of companies (%)
California	197	23.2
Massachusetts	68	8.0
New Jersey	58	6.8
Maryland	57	6.7
Texas	41	4.8
New York	39	4.6
North Carolina	39	4.6
Pennsylvania	37	4.4
Total above	536	63.1
Out of	849	100.0

Source: Dibner 1991.

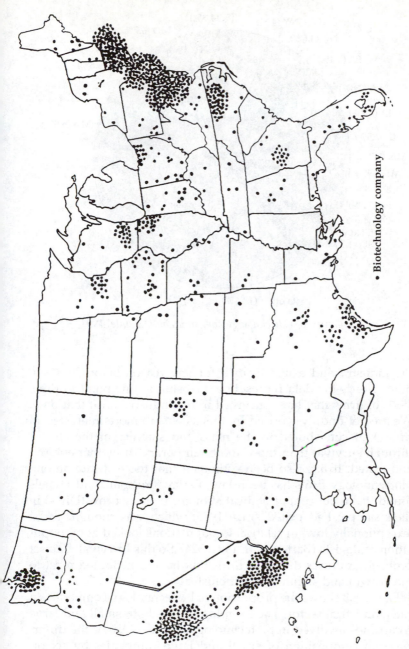

Fig. 6.1 *Location of biotechnology companies in the USA in 1993*
Source: Ernst & Young (1993).

• Biotechnology company

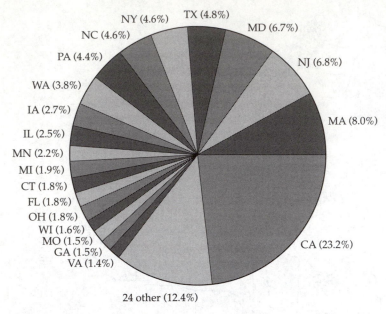

Fig. 6.2 *Distribution of biotechnology companies by US state, 1991*

the industry and exited from it for any reason before 1991. In other words the data represent a snapshot at one point in time, 1991, of firms that have survived in the industry until that date. We are not unduly worried by this as we are more interested in firms that contributed to the mass and stability of the cluster through survival than those more temporary firms that entered and exited. It has also been estimated that the exit rate among biotechnology firms has been low. Barley, Freeman, and Hybels found that 6 per cent of dedicated biotechnology firms (DBFs) in their sample had exited since 1975, which was thought to be 'exceptionally low' in relation to populations looked at by population ecologists (Barley et al. 1992: 324). So this 'survival' dataset probably captures the main firms that have contributed most to the growth and stability of our clusters.

Figure 6.3 shows the proportion of biotechnology companies in each industrial sector. The sample includes both small and large companies involved in biotechnology. Table 6.2 gives the differences in composition of small and large companies by sector.

(a) **Firms**

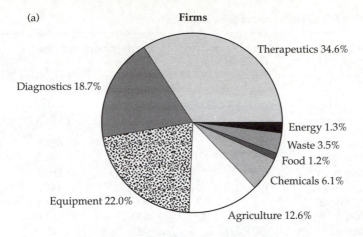

(b) **Employment**

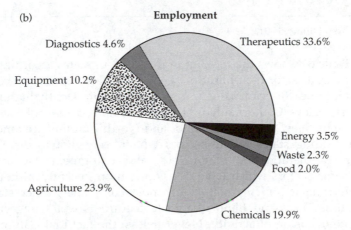

Fig. 6.3 *(a) Proportion of firms in US biotechnology by sector. (b) Employment in US biotechnology by sector*

There is a mix of small and large companies in the therapeutics, agricultural, and equipment sectors including large pharmaceutical, agrochemical, and equipment companies alongside small dedicated biotechnology firms (DBFs). Companies specializing in diagnostics and dealing with waste products and processes are mainly small, whereas there are relatively few small food or energy companies.

Table 6.2 *Classification of firms in sample*

	Number of firms small and large	Employment in firms	
		of which Small firm	Small and large
All companies	849	742	1,856.6
Therapeutics	293	265	624.5
Diagnostics	158	151	84.5
Equipment	186	156	189.5
Agriculture	107	87	444.3
Chemicals	52	41	369.4
Food	10	7	37.0
Waste	30	28	42.1
Energy	11	7	65.3

Source: Dibner 1991.

Table 6.3 shows the ranking of the top four states according to industrial sector of application, i.e. which states have most companies in each sector. The same states rank consistently highly in most sectors. California is first in almost all sectors, and Massachusetts, New Jersey, Maryland, and North Carolina are among the leading states in the sectors which were first to develop, namely therapeutics, diagnostics, and equipment. However, in some sectors which have developed more recently, although California is still the state with most companies, other states such as Texas and Illinois begin to feature as well, suggesting some diffusion of activity. Nevertheless, the fact that California and Massachusetts have significant numbers of companies in a number of sectors suggests that these are clusters which are not specialized in one sector but have a mix of companies from different sectors.

Entry of new firms and geographical concentration

Table 6.4 shows the entry of new firms into our sample over the period 1979–90. We give four-state concentration ratios for each year and rank the states for entry in each year. There were just

Table 6.3 *Ranking of top four states; numbers of firms per state (including large companies)*

	Ranking			
	1	2	3	4
All sectors	CA	MA	NJ	MD
Therapeutics	CA	MA	NJ	PA
Diagnostics	CA	NJ	MD	MA
Equipment	CA	MD	MA	NC
Agriculture	CA	IA	NC = NJ	TX
Chemicals	CA	NJ	NY = IL	MD, PA, TX, WI
Food	PA	—	—	—
Waste	CA	TX	—	—
Energy	—	—	—	—

Notes: CA = California; MA = Massachusetts; NJ = New Jersey; MD = Maryland; TX = Texas; PA = Pennsylvania; NC = North Carolina; IA = Iowa; IL = Illinois; WI = Wisconsin.
A dash denotes only one company per state.

over 600 entrants into our database which survived until the sample date. Entry occurred in the 1980s in waves, with peaks of entry in 1981, 1984, and 1986–7. There was more entry into therapeutics than into other sectors, but also a sizeable number of new companies went into the diagnostics and equipment sectors. The waves of entry coincided with the financing 'windows of opportunity' mentioned earlier, when particular enthusiasm for biotechnology stocks was evident. Entry was predominantly into those states which ranked high in Table 6.3, with California, Massachusetts, Maryland, New Jersey, North Carolina, and Texas capturing over 50 per cent of new entrants. In the first years of the 1980s, the geographical concentration of entry fell, but rose again to its previous levels in the second half of the decade. So entry patterns showed no signs of becoming less concentrated in the late 1980s, despite the diversification of entry of some companies into states such as Texas and Pennsylvania.

Table 6.4 *Number of new firms in our sample and the four-state concentration ratio of entry by new biotechnology firms across the USA*

	Number of new firms in sample (four-state concentration ratio)	Ranking of top four states by entry of new firms (% of new firms entering into that state)			
		1	2	3	4
1979	19 (64%)	NC (21%)	CA (16%)	MD (16%)	MA (11%)
1980	33 (51%)	CA (33%)	NC (6%)	TX = NJ = MA (6%)	
1981	81 (55%)	CA (31%)	MA (12%)	NJ (7%)	MD = WA (5%)
1982	40 (48%)	CA (24%)	MD (10%)	NJ = NY (7%)	
1983	57 (46%)	CA (18%)	MD (14%)	NJ (9%)	NY = NC = MO (5%)
1984	69 (46%)	CA (24%)	WA (9%)	TX (7%)	MD = NJ (6%)
1985	54 (44%)	MD (17%)	CA = MA (15%)		MN = NC (6%)
1986	64 (50%)	CA (25%)	MA (13%)	NC (8%)	PA = TX (5%)
1987	88 (47%)	CA (24%)	MA (9%)	MD (8%)	TX = NC (7%)
1988	56 (55%)	CA (30%)	MD (9%)	NC (9%)	NJ = NY = PA (7%)
1989	35 (60%)	CA (26%)	TX (17%)	MA (11%)	NC = WA = PA (6%)
1990	13 (69%)	CA (38%)	MA (15%)	CO = NY = MD = NJ = PA = WA (8%)	

Note: CA = California; MA = Massachusetts; NJ = New Jersey; MD = Maryland; TX = Texas; PA = Pennsylvania; NC = North Carolina; IA = Iowa; IL = Illinois; WI = Wisconsin; WA = Washington; NY = New York; MO = Montana; CO = Connecticut; MN = Minnesota.

6.3 DATA AND CLASSIFICATION OF THE INDUSTRY FOR THE MODELS

Unit of location

As with the computing models, the unit of location to define a cluster was taken to be the individual state in the United States. There are a few problems with this. As one saw in Figure 6.1, there was more than one distinct cluster in the state of California and on the east coast, clusters have spilled over state boundaries into more than one state. Some clusters develop *across* states, thanks to the unifying presence of a common neighbourhood factor. In this way, the location of the National Institutes of Health encouraged entry jointly into Maryland, North Carolina, and Washington, DC. There is, none the less, some justification for using the state as the unit of the cluster. Each state has had its own policies towards new and high-technology industries and has employed its own tax regime and utility pricing policy.

Company data

The models use a company database. The data are taken from Mark Dibner's *Biotechnology Guide USA, 1991*. There are 849 companies in our database, including small DBFs and large multinational companies involved in biotechnology. Data include date of foundation, location of the company, numbers employed, and the main field of application of each company. The field of application defines the sector in which the firm mainly operates. This classification distinguishes companies therefore according to the industrial sector in which they are making their applications, and not according to the technologies they use in doing so. In fact companies across most industrial sectors of application have employed very similar technologies (recombinant DNA, hybridoma technology, fermentation, and cell and tissue cultures), especially in the first generation of the industry. This contrasts with the structure of the computing industry, as we discuss in Chapter 8. So our classification into sectors in biotechnology, according to application, distinguishes between therapeutics, diagnostics, equipment and research tools, chemicals, agriculture, food, environmental and waste applications, and energy sectors. These eight sectors have been amalgamated out of the thirty-three sectors that Dibner gives. Companies may be active in more than one sector, but Dibner assigns a main field of application to each one and we adopt this to assign each company to one sector only. There may be some error for companies active across sectors, but we feel that our definition of eight sectors is sufficiently broad to ensure that almost all companies fall within one sector only.

We treat both small DBFs and large companies in our database identically. They are distinguishable by the earlier date of foundation of the large companies and because each large company employs many more people. The issue of how much of a large company is involved in biotechnology is not felt to be a serious problem in this industry, unlike computing. This is because in biotechnology all the capabilities of the large company have been relevant in the commercializing of the biotechnology product. Thus the proportion of the R & D department given over to the new techniques is not the only relevant factor; in the many alliances in biotechnology between DBFs and large companies, the main relevant complementary assets of the large company have been their clinical expertise, regulation, distribution, sales, and marketing departments. We have therefore used the numbers employed within the whole of the large company as a proxy for the extent of expertise and ability in these areas, without which the biotechnology products of the DBF would not have been commercialized.

The science base

We have also constructed a database on research expertise in biotechnology in the USA. We needed to be able to locate the areas of research strength within the science base relevant to this industry. These data are taken from the *Research Centers Directory, 1991*. We have picked out the life science research centres and ignored other sciences. The research centres include universities and all other research establishments with strength in the life sciences. Within the life sciences we have divided the centres into those connected to agricultural, food, and veterinary sciences, to biological and environmental sciences, and to the medical and human health sciences. From the description of the research centres' activities, we have picked only those with an interest relevant to biotechnology. We have defined this to include all types of microbiology, genetic engineering, biochemical engineering, cancer genetics, plant breeding and genetics, fermentation research, and biological instrumentation research using molecular or cellular approaches. We have excluded clinical and epidemiological research. We feel that this classification corresponds with the areas of research that have been closest and most relevant to the biotechnology industry. Again as with the company database, this is a 'survival' dataset and does not include research centres that exited from the sample before 1991. However, the exit rate for research centres is likely to be lower than that for companies and this problem is therefore ignored. Data on research centres include their address, date of foundation, and number of staff. From this we have aggregated different categories of staff, giving a crude estimate of numbers employed in each research centre.

6.4 ENTRY AND GROWTH MODELS

Entry models

Lacking a time series of data on employment by sector, by state, by year, we have employed two simple models to identify the main forces of attraction to new firms to enter into clusters and the main forces that benefited incumbents through being in a cluster. These are the latent variable analysis and average entry models, as described in Chapter 3. The first model uses an analysis of entry with a single estimate of employment per sector per state. We take the time series of surviving entry into each sector and perform a latent variable analysis upon it. The second model computes average entry into each sector and cluster per year (averaged over all years) and explores how this correlates with industry employment in each cluster in the sample year, 1991, and for biotechnology with employment in the science base in each cluster in 1991. We also consider the results of the full entry model, which was also described in Chapter 3, and applied to computing in Chapter 4.

Latent variable analysis

As described in Chapter 3, this approach to analysing the data on surviving entrants postulates that there is a set of eight latent variables which 'explain' entry into the eight sectors of the industry. These latent variables are unobservable (and difficult to interpret) but what this analysis can show is whether there are common factors which attract entry into several sectors simultaneously. If so, then that is suggestive of some common aspect of cluster strength which attracts entry into more than one subsector. If not, then the factors which attract entry into each subsector are idiosyncratic, and unrelated to those that attract entry into another. We computed a sector-by-sector covariance matrix, and then took principal components of this matrix. Each eigenvalue obtained summarized what proportion of entry into all sectors of biotechnology is accounted for by the corresponding latent variable and each eigenvector showed the effect of each latent variable upon entry into each sector.

In biotechnology there were two large eigenvalues, the first accounting for 69 per cent of the variation in entry, and the second eigenvalue accounting for a further 13 per cent of the variation. The eigenvector for the principal eigenvalue indicated that the first latent variable attracted entry mainly into therapeutics, with some entry into the diagnostics and equipment sectors. The second latent variable, as in computing, differentiated between sectors: entry is attracted into diagnostics and equipment but away from therapeutics. The other eigenvalues did not explain much of the variation in entry, and the latent variables represent factors specific to one sector. What this shows is that factors attracting entry into sectors are not uncorrelated, that there are some underlying common factors that attract entry into several sectors within biotechnology. We do not know, however, what exactly these latent variables are.

Average entry model

The next step was to estimate average entry, per sector, per cluster, per year, and to see how these correlated for each sector with sample-year employment in the industry, and sample-year employment in the science base in each cluster. We computed mean

Table 6.5 *Regression of mean entry in each sector and each state on industry employment and science base employment*

Biotechnology	Therapeutic	Diagnostics	Equipment	Agriculture	Chemical	Food	Waste	Energy
In science base employment	0.0710 (0.0382)	0.0408 (0.0178)	0.0439 (0.0168)	0.0180 (0.0074)	0.0110 (0.0057)	-0.0011 (0.0022)	0.0066 (0.0037)	0.0031 (0.0013)
In industry employment	0.0866 (0.0385)	0.0486 (0.0184)	-0.4428 (0.1888)	0.0215 (0.0080)	0.0172 (0.0065)	0.0005 (0.0008)	0.0117 (0.0039)	-0.0018 (0.0011)

entry across all years into each sector and state and regressed this variable on employment in that industry and employment in the science base. Results are summarized in Table 6.6. These regressions suggest that entry at a cluster into therapeutics, diagnostics, equipment sectors in particular in biotechnology is significantly related to the science base as well as employment within the biotechnology industry. Table 6.5 tells us that there are common factors in entry, and that entry does appear to be related to strength of employment in the science base in each cluster and to strength of industry employment at a cluster. It does not tell us anything about the specific sector-to-sector effects.

Full entry model

As explained in Chapter 3, there are some difficulties with the full entry model. The model is set out in that chapter. The results were found to be consistent with our two simpler models and are presented here in Table 6.6. The table shows the attractor coefficients—how much employment in one sector and in the science base affects entry in each other sector. It should be noted that the coefficients summarize the effect of a 1 per cent increase in relevant employment on mean entry and that a 1 per cent increase of science base employment represents far fewer people than a 1 per cent increase in industrial employment.

The results in Table 6.7 are summarized by the two flow diagrams, Figures 6.4 and 6.5, which show the direction of attraction (attractor → attracted) and the strength of attraction (indicated by

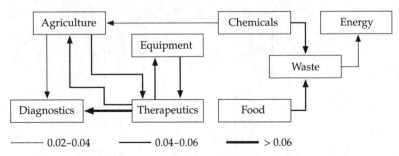

Fig. 6.4 *Principal new entry attractors in US biotechnology: sectors*

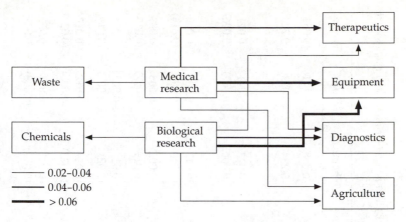

Fig. 6.5 *Principal new entry attractors in US biotechnology: science base*

the width and darkness of the line). We give attractor effects above an arbitrary cut-off point of 0.02. There are three degrees of strength of attraction: weak (coefficients between 0.02 and 0.04), medium (coefficients between 0.04 and 0.06), and strong (coefficients above 0.06). We can distinguish between two main types of attractor effect: attraction between industrial sectors and attraction of industrial sectors to the science base. These are given separately in Figures 6.4 and 6.5 respectively.

The results show that the science base—in particular medical and biological research—has acted as a more powerful attractor to new firms than have most industrial sectors. The only sector with a similar pull to the science base has been the therapeutics sector attracting new firms into the diagnostics, equipment, and agriculture sectors. As shown in Figure 6.4, most entry and interaction between industrial sectors is confined to those four sectors— therapeutics, diagnostics, equipment, and agriculture—with much less entry and interaction occurring in the other four sectors. We discuss some possible explanations for this in section 6.5. It is also noteworthy that the diagonal elements in the matrix of results of Table 6.6 are almost all negative, suggesting that own sector strength of employment does not attract entry. This is in marked contrast to the results below of the next model—the growth model.

Table 6.6 Entry attractors in biotechnology (mean change in the number of entrants for given percentage increase in employment in each sector)

Entry into	Therapeutics	Diagnostics	Equipment	Agriculture	Chemicals	Food	Waste
R^2	0.103	0.102	0.101	0.129	0.058	0.111	0.084
Std. error	0.696	0.52	0.56	0.395	0.234	0.083	0.223
Attracted by:							
Total entry into sector (all states)	0.022 (0.004)	0.021 (0.005)	0.02 (0.004)	0.022 (0.004)	0.023 (0.006)	0.021 (0.007)	0.021 (0.006)
Therapeutics	-0.01 (0.048)	0.091 (0.036)	0.043 (0.039)	0.048 (0.02)	0.017 (0.016)	0.005 (0.006)	0.000 (0.015)
Diagnostics	0.006 (0.057)	-0.089 (0.042)	-0.026 (0.046)	0.006 (0.024)	-0.002 (0.019)	0.003 (0.007)	-0.003 (0.018)
Equipment	0.037 (0.061)	-0.022 (0.045)	-0.064 (0.049)	0.019 (0.026)	0.01 (0.02)	-0.005 (0.007)	0.021 (0.019)
Agriculture	0.054 (0.068)	0.026 (0.05)	-0.007 (0.055)	-0.084 (0.029)	0.017 (0.023)	-0.012 (0.008)	-0.017 (0.022)
Chemicals	-0.019 (0.065)	-0.075 (0.048)	-0.022 (0.052)	0.025 (0.028)	-0.048 (0.022)	0.011 (0.008)	0.056 (0.021)

Table 6.6 *Continued*

Entry into	Therapeutics	Diagnostics	Equipment	Agriculture	Chemicals	Food	Waste
Food	-0.052 (0.084)	-0.057 (0.062)	0.014 (0.068)	-0.045 (0.036)	0.017 (0.028)	-0.061 (0.01)	0.042 (0.027)
Waste	-0.157 (0.089)	-0.06 (0.066)	-0.098 (0.072)	-0.013 (0.038)	-0.026 (0.03)	-0.009 (0.011)	-0.141 (0.029)
Energy	-0.14 (0.124)	-0.136 (0.092)	-0.317 (0.099)	-0.066 (0.052)	-0.019 (0.042)	-0.012 (0.015)	0.019 (0.04)
Science base							
Agriculture	-0.023 (0.157)	0.025 (0.117)	-0.006 (0.127)	-0.003 (0.067)	-0.019 (0.053)	0.003 (0.019)	-0.032 (0.05)
Biology	0.021 (0.09)	0.052 (0.067)	0.057 (0.073)	0.034 (0.038)	0.02 (0.03)	0.004 (0.011)	0.002 (0.029)
Medical	0.029 (0.104)	0.03 (0.077)	0.119 (0.084)	0.029 (0.044)	-0.011 (0.035)	0.017 (0.012)	0.029 (0.033)

Table 6.7 *Growth promoters in biotechnology (company employment as a function of age of company, own sector employment, and other sector employment)*

Growth in:	All biotech.	Therapeutics	Diagnostics	Equipment	Agriculture	Chemicals	Food	Waste
R^2	0.483	0.477	0.275	0.435	0.473	0.673	0.850	0.698
Std. error	1.707	1.794	1.678	1.539	2.031	1.657	1.534	1.273
Promoted by:								
Age of company	0.058 (0.003)	0.058 (0.005)	0.064 (0.009)	0.052 (0.007)	0.053 (0.006)	0.073 (0.008)	0.055 (0.012)	0.065 (0.021)
Own sector employment	0.203 (0.028)	0.252 (0.069)	0.200 (0.081)	0.316 (0.082)	0.107 (0.078)	0.114 (0.101)	0.262 (0.218)	0.324 (0.198)
Other sector employment	−0.006 (0.027)	−0.038 (0.076)	−0.033 (0.057)	−0.076 (0.054)	0.057 (0.082)	0.095 (0.068)	−0.173 (0.093)	−0.06 (0.088)
Science base employment	−0.023 (0.053)	−0.081 (0.102)	0.006 (0.127)	−0.131 (0.118)	0.066 (0.133)	0.043 (0.146)	0.335 (0.263)	−0.097 (0.15)

Company growth model

The growth model is a company-level model and is set out fully in Chapter 3. It examines how growth of employment in each company depends on the age of the company, own sector employment at that cluster, employment in other sectors than the sector to which the company belongs at that cluster, and also in the biotechnology case on employment in the science base at that cluster. The models for computing and biotechnology are basically the same, the only difference being the inclusion of science base employment in the biotechnology model.

Table 6.7 summarizes the growth-promoter parameters for biotechnology. (There are not enough companies in the energy sector of biotechnology to compute these growth promoters.) It is employment within the company's own sector and cluster which promotes growth of the company, whereas strength of employment in other sectors at that cluster in general detracts from company growth. The strength of the science base at a cluster does not assist company growth; more often coefficients are negative, suggesting that it discourages company growth. Note that the coefficients of 'age' simply represent the trend growth rate of a company in the relevant sector.

6.5 INTERPRETATION

The science base has been a significant attractor of new companies to particular locations in biotechnology, as seen in Table 6.6 and Figure 6.5. In section 6.7, we shall explore the nature of these significant links between the science base and new start-up companies. This attraction by the science base was in part due to many early founders of companies coming themselves from research establishments and also due to the continuing need for links to scientific expertise in the variety of specialist disciplines that companies required but could not possess in-house. Research centres also formed a market and source of ideas and input into the development of research equipment, and interaction between the science base and the equipment sector has been strong. We shall look at these equipment and instrument companies in section 6.8, and distinguish between those that have clustered near research centres and therapeutic companies and those (larger, established companies) that have been based elsewhere.

These links between the science base and companies have been supplemented by forces of attraction between a number of industrial sectors associated with the therapeutics sector. Table 6.6 and Figure 6.4 indicate that the therapeutics sector in particular has exercised a strong pull for new firms in other sectors, in particular in diagnostics and equipment sectors, to set up within the cluster. Entry of new firms is concentrated in four sectors—therapeutics, diagnostics, equipment, and agriculture—with these four sectors accounting for 88 per cent of the entrants over our period, 1979–90. There was much less entry into the other four sectors: chemicals, food, waste and energy. There has been some interaction between these four high-entry sectors, with therapeutics attracting equipment companies and equipment companies attracting therapeutics. The same two-way process applied between therapeutics and agriculture companies. Therapeutics strongly attracts diagnostic companies, but not the reverse.

It also appears that activity in one's own sector acts as a mild repellent to new firm entry. So the process of attraction between companies has been self-reinforcing within one group of sectors: companies entering are attracted by other companies entering except to their own sectors, but this feedback mechanism is limited to one group of sectors only in biotechnology. In particular, health care companies in therapeutics and diagnostics have benefited from positive feedbacks, and there has been specialization in the provision of equipment and research tools to service other sectors. Agricultural companies have also benefited both from spillovers from research centres and from the presence of therapeutics firms and to some extent chemicals firms.

Contrasting the results of the entry and growth models, several features are striking. The advantage to the incumbents' growth of locating in a cluster of similar firms is apparent in virtually all sectors. In other words whereas attraction to new entrants is confined to a group of sectors, the benefits to incumbent firms of being in a cluster exist in every sector. There is also a marked contrast between the negative effect of own sector strength on entry and its positive effect on growth. In other words, strength of employment in therapeutics at a cluster discourages other therapeutics firms from entering, perhaps for reasons of competition,

but encourages firms from related sectors, in particular from diagnostics and equipment sectors. However, the strength of employment in therapeutics benefits those therapeutics firms that are
already present in that cluster.

Entry and growth processes are also different in the effects of
the science base on them. The science base attracts entry of new
firms strongly in sectors where entry is prominent. However, the
effects of the science base on firm growth are negative in some
sectors and at best much more weakly positive in other sectors. As
with computing, this suggests that incumbents and entrants have
fundamentally different capabilities in absorbing spillovers in
their proximity: incumbents absorb the benefits of being in cluster
which occur within their own sector, but are not good at absorbing spillovers from the science base or from interrelated sectors.
New entrants on the other hand are effective at absorbing spillovers, and in some cases are created because of the opportunities
that arise from the science base and from the presence of certain
key sectors.

Another distinction between the two processes, as mentioned
above, is the spreading across all sectors of the benefits of clustering for the growth of incumbents. By contrast, the entry benefits
are confined to one block of sectors. They do not extend to the
chemicals, food, waste, and energy sectors. Several explanations
for this are possible. The non-entry sectors are either dominated
by large companies or are as yet underdeveloped novel sectors in
waste and environmental applications. One question which arises
with regard to the sectors where no entry has occurred and which
are dominated by large companies is whether these large companies absorb local spillovers and, in the process, deter entry by
potential competitiors. Moreover, large companies do not need to
locate close to research centres in order to absorb these spillovers,
and we explore this further in part 2. It is also argued in part 2 that
scientific research within the science base is less central to the
chemical and food companies than is their own in-house research,
which itself is geared to more downstream processes and marketing. This makes proximity to the science base and to other companies engaging in research less essential for the companies in these
sectors.

Another difference between the food, chemical, and energy
companies on the one hand and pharmaceutical companies on the

other is that the latter have needed collaboration with new companies in order to transform their own increasingly costly research processes. There have been more alliances in the pharmaceuticals area than in chemicals or food, based on symbiosis between therapeutics and diagnostics firms and pharmaceutical companies. The same types of relationships have not existed to the same extent in the chemicals, food, or energy sectors (Prevezer and Toker 1996). Possible explanations for the absence of such symbiosis between large and small companies in the latter sectors may be a perception that their core competencies and skills are challenged or destroyed by the new technologies, whereas in pharmaceuticals it is perceived that the new technologies enhance existing competencies. It might also be argued that pharmaceutical companies have greater absorptive capacity (Cohen and Levinthal 1990), being more outward looking and geared towards taking in external research, whereas chemical, energy, and food companies have preferred to rely on their own in-house research.

Our models have dealt separately with the forces influencing the entry of new companies into a cluster and the benefits to the growth of incumbent firms of being in a cluster. The entry models identified the science base and some interaction between a few sectors—therapeutics, diagnostics, equipment, and agriculture—as key attractors to the entry of new firms to a cluster. New entry was not attracted by strength in the firm's own sector. By contrast the growth of incumbent firms benefited most from the presence of other firms in the cluster in its own sector, but gained nothing from being near firms from other sectors nor from the science base.

PART 2: THE HISTORY OF THE BIOTECHNOLOGY INDUSTRY

INTRODUCTION

We shall now look in more detail at why new entrant companies differ from large established firms in their needs and in their interactions with surrounding companies and with the science base. We shall examine the forces that lead to the concentration of industry under the three main headings identified in part 1: specialized labour, specialized inputs, and specialized knowledge (knowledge spillovers).

Specialized labour includes the particular skills that academic entrepreneurs combined in being anchored firmly within the science base, yet seeing the commercial potential of their scientific achievements. However, these skills alone were not sufficient to set up new companies. They required the presence of experienced venture capitalists to raise finance, organize business plans and oversee the initial setting up and managerial needs of the scientific company. Specialized labour also includes an adequate supply of scientific staff trained in a variety of disciplines to postdoctoral level to employ the specific combination of scientific research skills needed in each case. It also includes access to the range and depth of expertise available only in the science base in particular places relating to the uses of the technologies being developed by the company. Scientists would be employed by the company on advisory boards and also in a more casual capacity, forming networks whereby scientists within the company would keep abreast of developments in their own and related fields in the scientific community.

Specialized inputs include the development of new tools and equipment for new uses in the industry. These new needs have included supplies of reagents and speciality chemicals and enzymes which have served as raw materials in DNA research. This industry has also given rise to the development of new measuring equipment and a variety of high-technology advances in this field such as spectroscopy equipment, nuclear magnetic resonance machines, and advances in biosensors and bioseparation equipment. In addition there have developed automatic sequencing machines to speed up and replace the lengthy procedures of postdoctoral labour. This variety of inputs has developed in the first instance around the key research firms and close to the science base which have constituted a significant part of their market and have been key to innovation in this sector. As the industry has matured and these inputs themselves have become standardized, the need for propinquity has lessened and we have seen the gradual dispersion of these firms across the country. But the initial development and needs of the new industry contributed to the clustering impetus for such new 'input' firms to locate close to other new research firms and to key research centres.

The third generic reason for clustering is the presence of knowledge spillovers which is particularly germane in this knowledge-based industry. Knowledge spillovers have been created in the form of scientific knowledge in the science base and research firms, and as technical knowledge and know-how about the processes of genetic sequencing, scaling up, the transferability of techniques from one organism to another, and from one organ to another. Such knowledge has often been tacit and uncodified and has required access to people known to be expert in the variety of fields which the new advances have touched on. One interesting feature of this industry has been the continuing need to have access to a variety of scientific expertise, as new technologies have continued to be developed out of new scientific advances. This interactive process has meant that even though early tacit knowledge has become publicly available and accessible, there has been a continuous process of generation of new tacit knowledge which companies forming on the basis of newer technologies have required.

In what follows, section 6.6 looks at the origins of the industry in the science base and at the development and concentration of the science on both west and east coasts that established California and Massachusetts as the prime early locations for the new industry. Academic excellence and scientific breakthroughs at universities in these states certainly played an important role in focusing attention on the science at these locations. However, the science by itself was not the only factor that allowed these states to achieve this outcome. The ability to collaborate between scientists and across disciplines and departments was a critical factor, coupled with a concentration of multidisciplinary scientists, as such collaboration required proximity. California in particular had such a concentration of scientists as well as a culture of networking which played a part here, in creating a climate of communication within the scientific community and between the scientific and industrial/entrepreneurial communities. And there were several other factors which also favoured location within the culture and infrastructure of the state.

In section 6.7, we look at the entry of new companies, their origins, the part played in the development of the industry by some key 'star' scientists and entrepreneurs, and why they chose to locate their companies near the science base rather than close to their customer or user companies. We examine in more detail the uses made of the science base and why locating near the science base has mattered to entrant companies. The variety of needs for different inputs that new companies have over the early stages of their life cycles is contrasted with the needs of established incumbents which are more often met internally or are not geographically constrained. We look at the interactions in alliances between entrant firms in different sectors which are more dependent on proximity than those between entrant and incumbent firms. We also look at some of the characteristics of networks of alliances and distinguish between features that are local that meet the needs of small new entrants and features that are not local and show the dominance of incumbents in the networks.

In section 6.8 we describe the structure of the biotechnology industry and how that has affected the impetus to cluster between different industrial sectors and between the sectors and the science base. The industry has developed into sectors with applications and technologies useful to established companies based in existing industrial sectors; we look at the data and classification in more detail. The early technological similarity between different sectors of the biotechnology industry contrasts with the division into sectors along technological lines of the computing industry. Where there is not much technological interaction between sectors, as in biotechnology, one type of clustering force that works by technological complementarity is weak. However, there has been some industrial specialization within biotechnology with the growth of an equipment and instruments sector which has provided new tools to the research base and to particular sectors of the industry. There has also been some transfer of technologies between fields. We ask whether this will continue. For some biotechnology applications, innovation started upstream in research, boosted by spillovers of knowledge from the science base. In others, where research in the science base is not so important, clusters have not developed.

In section 6.9, we look at the migration of clusters and regional policies to foster clusters in particular states. We look at how states have tried to define particular niches in which that location has strengths and also at the competition between clusters that exists in the form of states luring companies and other resources into their area. We see that policy has played an important role even in the early clusters and its role in stimulating the provision of infrastructure should not be underestimated. We look at the benefits of clustering in particular states and cities within the United States in terms of the availability and cost of the main inputs needed, in relation to the maturity of the industry in that state, and the degree to which the need for access to research and skilled labour dominates the need for access to more standardized and cheaper tools, processes, and land. As we shall see, this turns on whether that location specializes in small-scale research-intensive activity or more downstream processes; and that depends, in part, on the industrial sector of application that is being developed.

6.6 EARLY DAYS: SCIENTIFIC BREAKTHROUGHS AND INITIAL CONDITIONS, THE RACE BETWEEN WEST AND EAST COASTS

The roots of the biotechnology industry lie in what were the essential conditions for the commercialization of scientific breakthroughs. These conditions were the creation of a research-based company that combined the highest-quality, leading-edge research in the field of molecular biology; the scientific collaboration between several research institutes in the area; and their linkages with the new company, through key scientists being lured into the company, while maintaining their academic contacts. The conditions also included the complementary backing of an established pharmaceutical company with sharp commercial goals and downstream expertise, and the involvement of hands-on financial venture capitalist expertise which was intricately concerned with the running of the company and knew how to publicize its achievements, and which created access for the company to the public market. These initial ingredients, which were brought together in the creation of Genentech, set a model for others in the founding of new companies to commercialize their science.

We can separate the impetus to the creation of the industry into initial conditions and infrastructure which were conducive to the creation of small entrepreneurial high-technology firms in general, and conditions which were specific to the biotechnology industry. Infrastructure included venture capital which combined access to finance and venture capitalists who took an active role in creating new companies (Larsen and Rogers 1984), access to managerial experience in setting up entrepreneurial firms, and the existence of flexible networks in California with a culture of high job mobility, ease of communication, and technological transfer between firms and between the science base and firms (Saxenian 1994).

Factors specific to the biotechnology industry included the centres of scientific excellence in the relevant disciplines in the forefront of research in molecular biology and other relevant disciplines. This provided the pool of specialized labour at postdoctoral level on a scale necessary to entice sufficient numbers of people out of the science base and into new firms. Stanford and the University of California at San Francisco (UCSF) were also at the centre of those research breakthroughs which formed the backbone of the initial technology in recombinant DNA. Stanford had also developed expertise in achieving ownership of these scientific breakthroughs in knowledge and acquiring ownership through patenting of these lucrative technologies. This was something that Cambridge University, UK, failed to do with the hybridoma technology and the creation of monoclonal antibodies, which provided the other basic technological prong to the creation of this industry. There was also an easier regulatory climate for genetic engineering in California compared with the public outcry that genetic engineering experiments caused in Cambridge, Massachusetts. Fears of the dangers of genetic engineering led to public meetings in Cambridge with slogans such as 'No Recombination Without Representation', and the construction of a new P3 laboratory at Harvard for genetic engineering became a controversial matter (Hall 1987: 41–5).

The two scientific techniques that formed the basis for much of early biotechnology were the use of recombinant DNA, pioneered by Boyer of UCSF and Cohen at Stanford University in 1973, and the use of hybridoma technology or cell fusion techniques which created monoclonal antibodies, developed by Milstein and Kohler in 1975 at the Laboratory of Molecular Biology in Cambridge, UK. Recombining DNA or genetic engineering involves splicing a foreign gene into the DNA of another organism such that the properties of the foreign gene, its production of a particular protein for instance, are incorporated into the genetic structure of the other organism. Hybridoma technology is the fusion of a cell producing one specific, monoclonal as opposed to polyclonal, antibody with myeloma or cancer cells which confer a sort of immortality on the fused combination and enable the production of large quantities of that specific monoclonal antibody. However, both technologies were in fact an amalgam of distinct scientific breakthroughs involving many scientists at different institutions, requiring them to collaborate to put the various steps in the procedures together. Genetic engineering required a series of techniques including cutting DNA with restriction enzymes developed by Boyer on an enzyme from E coli, pasting fragments with ligases, and inserting the DNA into a bacteria cell, gene splicing techniques developed by Cohen, rapid sequencing pioneered by Walter Gilbert at Harvard, and techniques to produce particular proteins such as insulin and human growth hormone and then to induce the production of those valuable proteins on a scale large enough to make commercialization viable.

> The other factor specific to the biotechnology industry in the impetus to create a company to profit from these scientific techniques was the involvement and interest of large established companies, with complementary assets necessary for the commercialization of products of the new technologies. Hall (1987) dates the spring of 1976 and the insulin symposium in Indianapolis, sponsored by Eli Lilly, as a key spur to the creation of the biotechnology industry. Eli Lilly, one of the main suppliers of insulin for the diabetics market, noting the rising trend in the incidence of diabetes and the shrinkage in the consumption of pork, were concerned that a shortage of pig pancreases would develop towards the end of the century, threatening their main source of supply of insulin. The symposium was designed to bring together workers in the field of insulin research and the (newly developing) recombinants research. This latter field of research was into the recombining of genes in order to create DNA that would produce proteins such as somatostatin or insulin in large quantities. Eli Lilly encouraged a collaboration between William Rutter's research team at USCF, specializing in insulin research, and that of Howard Goodman who was at the leading edge of recombinant research. The objective was to make human insulin. Similar interest was taken in Genentech by the Swedish

firm Kabi Vitrum which was the leading producer of human growth hormone, reliant on extracting the hormone from cadavers and wanting the new genetic engineering techniques to be applied to producing hgH genetically. Kabi therefore also funded Genentech's scientific research to apply genetic engineering to producing hgH (McKelvey 1994).

Although some of the basic breakthroughs in recombination had been achieved, the process of turning the science into usable technology was just beginning, and the race between west and east coast laboratories in methods of cloning the insulin gene illustrates the interaction between the competitive process and iterative advance in the technology. The race was between different methods of producing human insulin: between Walter Gilbert's laboratory in Harvard to clone the insulin gene using rDNA and the Rutter–Goodman laboratories at UCSF to use synthetic DNA chemistry to produce insulin (Hall 1987). The west coast laboratories won this race, in some part because recombinant work with human genetic material had to be done in a P4 laboratory, which necessitated the Harvard team transferring to military laboratories at Porton Down (UK) with considerable delay. They had not believed the synthetic route to be possible. Meanwhile the west coast team, including the UCSF laboratories and a group from the City of Hope Memorial Hospital, pushed ahead using man-made DNA produced by synthetic chemistry, unimpeded by regulation of human genetic material.

The involvement of teams of scientists in different laboratories illustrates both the collaboration between the scientists and also the competition between them in the race to clone and express insulin and human growth hormone. The concentration of scientists in California might also have given this area an advantage over the east coast. The leading scientists included the two laboratories at UCSF mentioned above, backed by Eli Lilly—William Rutter's and Howard Goodman's, employing scientists such as Axel Ullrich, Peter Seeburg, and John Shine, as well as the expertise of medical doctor John Baxter, also at UCSF. There was another UCSF group which was linked to the City of Hope group with the collaboration of Genentech and Eli Lilly. This UCSF group was the laboratory of Herbert Boyer. The team at City of Hope including Arthur Riggs, Keiichi Itakura, and Roberto Crea, and the Genentech team of Robert Swanson, Dennis Kleid, David

Goeddel, and others. These teams were in competition with each other and with the Gilbert group linked to Biogen.

Kleid had had a postdoctoral post at MIT, had gone to Stanford Research Institute, and had started a laboratory. He had hired Goeddel, another postdoctoral researcher with specialisms in synthetic nucleotides; and they had both been recruited to Genentech by Boyer and Swanson to work with the City of Hope team on insulin (McKelvey 1994: 72, 94–5). The distances between the scientists in the science base and those based in the early companies were very small, with well-established links and common backgrounds. This, as we shall see, has remained a feature of later research-based firms, which have chosen to locate close to the science base.

However, it was not just that the west coast won the scientific race. The Bay area had accumulated considerable expertise in venture capital interested in founding new technology ventures. These venture capitalists were entrepreneurial and yet were open to the language of scientific or technological advance. Genentech was founded in 1976 out of an alliance between venture capitalist Robert Swanson from Kleiner Perkins, and Boyer at UCSF, drawing on the skills of teams of scientists such as Riggs, Crea, and Itakura from City of Hope, Rosenberg and Dickerson from CalTech, and Goodman, Shine, and Heynecker at UCSF. This combination of different laboratories with their own specialisms was fused into a company by the entrepreneurial Swanson. This was a new type of company, based on research strengths and attractive to academic scientists but with commercial backing and links with the financial community and large pharmaceutical companies. The involvement of Eli Lilly and the commercial impetus meant that techniques which were scientifically interesting were tried out in making somatostatin and then transferred to the commercially interesting insulin. A similar commercial prototype was created in 1978 on the east coast in the form of Biogen, with Walter Gilbert in the equivalent position of Boyer and Novo, Lilly's competitor in insulin, backing Biogen. It is clear that it was more important for these small companies to be set up close to the science base than for them to be located near their large-company sponsors. The backing of Eli Lilly, Kabi Vitrum, and Novo illustrates the ability of the large pharmaceutical companies to foster alliances globally, with no necessity either to encourage the small companies to locate near them, nor to be located themselves in the centre of scientific activity. We return to this in the next section.

Experienced venture capitalists were to be found on both west and east coasts and were concentrated in California and Massachusetts. More peculiar to the west coast was a history of having grown the computing industry. This established a culture of small entrepreneurial start-ups, where risk-taking was the norm and people moved easily between jobs. The creation of fluid networks in computing in California is described vividly by Saxenian (1994). She looks at what she calls local industrial systems in the computing industry in California and Massachusetts and finds a distinct contrast between them.

Silicon Valley has a regional network-based industrial system that promotes collective learning and flexible adjustment among specialist producers of a complex of related technologies. The region's dense social networks and open labour markets encourage experimentation and entrepreneurship. Companies compete intensely while at the same time learning from one another about changing markets and technologies through informal communication and collaborative practices; and loosely linked team structures encourage horizontal communication among firm divisions and with outside suppliers and customers. 'The functional boundaries within firms are porous in a network system, as are the boundaries between firms themselves and between firms and local institutions such as trade associations and universities' (Saxenian 1994: 3–4). Saxenian contrasts those Silicon Valley firms in the computing industry with firms on Route 128 which were dominated by a small number of integrated corporations, with more internalized and secretive procedures and a culture of self-reliance rather than of networking.

Massachusetts and California are more similar in the type of biotechnology company formed. The east coast also fostered small scientific companies, such as Biogen or Genetics Institute, under similar sorts of conditions as in California with venture capital backing (Teitelman 1989). However, it is probably true that biotechnology benefited from the cultural networks that had grown up on the west coast. In biotechnology the networks that were most significant were those that linked parts of the science base together and those linking scientists with the commercial community in its various parts: other small firms, venture capital, and large user companies. The ability to build informal networks through trade associations, personal ties, scientific conferences, and venture capital was state of the art in California. The process was self-reinforcing: job mobility was higher because easier in an area densely populated by all types of firm within a high-technology industry. The region's culture encouraged risk and accepted failure. Highest regard was given to those who started firms and their technological achievement. The role of networking in the success of the northern Californian cluster was recognized and copied in the formation of a more formal networking mechanism in southern California, by the University of California at San Diego. It created its CONNECT network in 1985 as a university–private sector partnership to serve the needs of high-technology entrepreneurs by linking them with the technical, managerial, and financial resources they needed.

Firms such as Genentech that were set up in California in the early days espoused a culture that was informal and relied on self-motivation. Openness and communication was cultivated in the realization that such firms relied on attracting the highest calibre of scientific talent from the academic science base. Creating conditions that were similar to those in academic life was felt to be important in order to attract the sort of scientist who would be at the leading edge of his or her discipline and would create scientific breakthroughs within the firm, on which these new research-based firms relied. Employees were encouraged to maintain their links with the science base, to continue to publish papers, to attend conferences, and to retain their status as academics as far as possible. Features such as informal dress and keeping firms open day and night to enable flexible working times were designed to mimic academic laboratory life and be attractive to the best scientific minds (Teitelman 1989: 25).

Finally, the financial precedent set by Genentech with the success of its spectacular public offering in 1980 made the achievements of the biotechnology industry public knowledge in the USA and made it easier for other firms based elsewhere to follow in its footsteps. But it also established California firmly as the main cultural centre of biotechnology in the eyes of the world.

6.7 COMPANY CHARACTERISTICS AND LOCALNESS

We turn now to two particular issues of importance: first, the different uses made of the science base in this industry and why proximity to the science base for companies has mattered; and second, the interactions between companies of different types—specifically, new dedicated biotechnology firms (DBFs) and larger established incumbent firms related to this industry. We shall discover whether propinquity has been important. Local linkages between companies and the science base have been significant to the development of the industry. Interactions between DBFs have tended to require more proximity than those between incumbents and DBFs. We examine the reasons for these differences.

As we saw in the previous section, the early companies in biotechnology came out of the science base. Many were founded by academic entrepreneurs, choosing to set up new companies to commercialize their research findings. These companies were formed close to the research centres of the responsible academics. If we take a handful of the leading firms created in the late 1970s and early 1980s, we can associate a leading scientist with the creation of each one of them—Herbert Boyer from UCSF with Genentech (Calif.), Walter Gilbert of Harvard with Biogen (Mass.), Ivor Royston of UCSD with Hybritech (Calif.), Mark Ptashne of Harvard with Genetics Institute (Mass.), and William Rutter of UCSF with Chiron (Calif.). All the principal early companies were centred around the activities of prominent scientists and their laboratories or departments. These scientists retained their university posts as well as being involved with the companies; indeed their connection with academic research and scientific networks was what was valuable to the company. This association of leading academic scientists with the founding of scientific companies continued throughout the 1980s. For instance David Baltimore of MIT, a Nobel prize winner in 1975, was a co-founder of SyStemix; Malcolm L. Gefter of MIT founded ImmuLogic; Robert M. Bell of Duke University helped found Sphinx; and Jonas Salk of the Salk Institute for Biological Studies founded Immune Response (Stephan 1994). David Goldenberg of the University of Kentucky set up Immunomedics in 1983 to commercialize his work, which the university had felt was not worth patenting. John Stephenson of the University of Toronto and the US National Cancer Institute started Oncogene Sciences in 1983, taking NIH intellectual property and scientists with him. He later started Santa Cruz Biotech in 1991.

In a study of the birth of US biotechnology enterprises and the role of intellectual capital, Zucker et al. (1994) determine that it was the presence of key 'star' scientists that influenced the timing of the creation and location of new biotechnology firms. Such key scientists were the scarce immobile factors, who could recoup economic rents from commercializing their knowledge. Stephan (1994) also finds that the reputations of the scientists positively affected the market value of biotechnology firms going public, especially those scientists with Nobel prizes. The idea that knowledge spillovers were important in influencing the entry of new firms into this industry is supported by work by Jaffe (1989), and Jaffe et al. (1993), that finds that there is a limited geographical area where knowledge from universities and other research is translated into patentable innovations. In short, knowledge spills over from university research into the geographical area that is close to the university.

However, being a founder has not been the only type of tie between the scientist and the firm. Scientists have also been members of scientific advisory boards and research scientists within firms. Founders and members of scientific advisory boards generally retain links with their universities. There are also scientists engaged more loosely as reviewers of research and to boost the reputation of the firm to both scientific and investment communities (Stephan 1994). Audretsch and Stephan (1995) distinguish between the role played by scientists as founders and their role as members of scientific advisory boards. They discover that proximity has mattered more when scientists created the start-up than when they were involved in an advisory capacity.

Another key feature in the process of the creation of new companies has been the combining of both scientific and entrepreneurial skills, either through particular individuals who had both scientific and entrepreneurial flair or through collaboration between scientists and entrepreneurs. From the early days of the industry, certain individuals stood out for their activities in creating several companies, specializing in the process of creating new start-up companies out of scientific ideas. These scientist-entrepreneurs often combined expertise in large established companies with accumulated experience in creating new companies. For instance, Roberto Crea was involved at the start in Genentech in 1977; he directed DNA synthesis at Genentech and wanted to set up a company to support other new companies by doing DNA synthesis for them. He formed Creative BioMolecules (Mass.) in 1981 with Charles Cohen and Fred Graves, with two laboratories at first on the east and west coasts but refocusing on recombinant protein products and consolidating in Hopkinton, Mass., in 1985. In 1991 he founded Creagen. Graves moved from Creative BioMolecules to head Codon (Calif.) and then Berlex Biosciences (Calif.), a merger between Titon Biosciences and Codon. Cohen had come from NYU Medical School and the University of Virginia, and had then worked at a subsidiary of Millipore which was making automated equipment for gene and protein synthesis and sequencing. This took him to work with Crea on a gene machine for Genentech which developed into co-founding Creative BioMolecules.

Patrick King from MIT, Du Pont, and Johnson & Johnson went to Centocor in 1982 as vice-president of research. He left to start T Cell Sciences and discovered the Ortho King T cell monoclonal antibody in 1986. He wanted to straddle both the academic and industrial worlds in this industry and enjoyed building companies from early stages. He had found Du Pont and Johnson & Johnson too big but had learned about the commercialization process from working for them. Others included Leslie Glick, chief executive of Genex from 1977 until 1987, who then moved to Bionix Corporation (Md.), David Hale, president of Hybritech from 1983 to 1987 and then president of Gensia and Viagene (Calif.). Others came from established incumbent firms. Ted Greene was one of a number of key entrepreneurs to come from Baxter Travenol which spawned a generation of executives for biotechnology companies. Greene founded Hybritech and two spin-off companies—Gen Probe and IDEC—and helped found Cytel and Amylin and was on the boards of Neurex and Vical.

Dibner has established that the process of biotechnology company creation shifted during the 1980s, as the industry became established and was able to attract more experienced managers. In a study of the background of the founders of new biotechnology companies, he uncovered several features. Companies were founded by up to six people, on average by three. The academic/industry mix of background changed between the late 1970s and the mid-1980s. In the late 1970s over half of the founders came from universities. By the mid-1980s this proportion had dropped to a fifth. The proportion of founders from industry rose from a quarter in the 1970s to two-thirds by the mid-1980s.

The new biotechnology companies had close ties with existing industries and the existing industrial structure. The new technologies were applied to the existing industrial specialization. Thus applications of these technologies were made for an existing set of industries: pharmaceuticals, diagnostics, agricultural, chemical, food processing. This closeness of application to incumbent industries created opportunities for managers within large pharmaceutical and chemical companies to break away and help found a start-up in a related area. The movement of individuals from large companies to help build up new companies did not depend on the proximity of the large company to a cluster. Baxter Travenol, based in Illinois, spawned a generation of executives for biotechnology companies, as IBM had supplied the computer industry. Ted Greene went to Hybritech (Calif.), Henry Termeer to Genzyme (Mass.), Stephen Chubb to Cytogen (NJ), James Glam to Genetic Systems (Wash.), Gabriel Schmergel to Genetics Institute (Mass.), and Robert Carpenter to Integrated Genetics. George Rathmann left Abbot in Illinois to go to Amgen in California. G. Kirk Raab left G. D. Searle in Illinois to go to Genentech in California. Fildes, chief executive of Cetus, came from Glaxo and Bristol Myers and Biogen. Stephen Mendell, chief executive of Xoma, came from Becton Dickinson. The challenge of breaking away from a large company to help a small new company to grow increased in appeal to those with experience in the relevant industries. Whereas the movement of academics to found a new company required that the company locate close to the founder's academic base, industrialists tended to leave the location of the large company and move to the existing clusters where the industry was forming.

There was another type of person who played a key part in the creation of this industry. This was the individual who helped to form the links and networks between scientist and entrepreneurs.

Such people came in a variety of guises. Venture capitalists such as Robert Swanson and Brook Byers of Kleiner Perkins Caulfield and Byers were important (Swanson was instrumental in the setting up of Genentech and was the first chief executive of the company; KPCB had investments in Genentech, Athena Neurosciences, and Glycomed. Byers was president of Hybritech, IDEC, Insite Vision, and Progenex and was involved with eighteen companies). Others were lawyers and analysts such as Peter Drake of Vector Securities, Stephen Burrill of Ernst & Young, Bruce Mackler of the Association of Biotech Companies, who was a lawyer, scientist, and industrialist, and Leslie Misrock, a lawyer specializing in patent law in this area. Other individuals who can be singled out as brokers of the burgeoning industry are Joseph Perpich, a lawyer involved in Grants and Programmes at the Howard Hughes Medical Institute, and James Watson, who continued to be involved with the industry through the Office of Human Genome Research at the NIH and through his Cold Spring Harbor Laboratory. Venture capital tended to be concentrated on the east and west coasts. Of fifty-nine venture-backed companies between 1980 and 1982, twenty-five were in California and eight in Massachusetts and in no other state were there more than three. These financiers, lawyers, and analysts were important in recognizing the commercial potential of the new biosciences and promoting and publicizing it and also tended to be concentrated within the central clusters of the industry.

There has been a difference between the entrants, the DBFs, and the incumbent companies (the large pharmaceutical and agrochemical companies) in the nature of their reliance upon local linkages. The key difference has been the need and ability of entrants to have access to all three inputs—labour, tools, and knowledge—outside their own firm boundaries, but within a certain geographical vicinity. In general, the entrants are extrovert firms: they are formed, and they survive, because they can ferret out and absorb the maximum possible from the surrounding atmosphere. To exploit this talent, they need to locate in a nourishing atmosphere, with the right mix and variety of constituent ingredients. They benefited from a measure of competition from other firms in their own sector, but preferred to have an element of monopoly within their own product niche. They were not positively attracted by the presence of other firms within their own area of operation.

Incumbent firms on the other hand have tended to be larger, being older and further on in their life cycles, and such firms are more insular by constitution. They have tended to become more introverted, preferring to access scientific expertise and to create company-specific management skills *within* the company. Their financing needs are dealt with internally by their treasury departments. This variety of internal skills means that geography ceased to be a constraint.

They too needed access to the new technologies, to a wider spectrum of scientific expertise than that available within the company, and to finance. However, they could transcend geographical boundaries to do this. They are adept at creating alliances which are worldwide, at employing people from much further afield, and at participating on the public stock markets to raise finance. Having much more rigid internal procedures and portfolios, they are less adept at scouring the immediate vicinity for contacts and collaborations which are outside their own field of technical expertise. They would overlook spillovers that happened to be created within their locality but outside their own sector, in favour of absorbing those requirements through more formal contacts worldwide. They would be much more attuned to local competition and developments within their own sector, and more likely to absorb any local spillovers akin to their own scientific and technical trajectories.

Inter-firm collaboration increased markedly particularly during the 1980s, and alliances between companies have been a prominent feature of the biotechnology industry. Hagedoorn and Schakenraad collected over 1,200 cases of inter-firm cooperative agreements in biotechnology in their MERIT-CATI databank, 90 per cent of which occurred in the 1980s, 60 per cent since 1985 (Hagedoorn and Schakenraad 1990). Within a sample of biotechnology alliances between USA companies between 1988 and 1991, of 374 alliances, 52 per cent were between two DBFs and just under half involved incumbent firms, almost all in alliance with the DBFs (Dibner 1991). Such alliances have served various functions: to bring together complementary assets between different types of company; and to learn about and absorb new technologies outside the core competencies of the established companies (Arora and Gambardella 1993). 'External linkages are . . . *both* a means of gaining fast access to knowledge and resources that cannot be secured internally *and* a test of internal expertise and learning capabilities' (Powell and Brantley 1992: 371). In particular those alliances between entrants and incumbents have been based on complementarities between DBFs specializing in developing new technologies and established companies within an industrial sector whose downstream facilities have been necessary for the commercialization of new products or processes, or for whom the new technologies were useful in transforming internal research or development procedures (Dodgson 1991*b*: 116). Similar symbioses have existed between DBFs specializing in different technologies.

Alliances may act as a reinforcing characteristic of clusters, with alliances forming more easily between firms in close proximity within the same state; or they may act as an alternative mechanism of forming linkages between companies without requiring the proximity of clustering. Evidence on whether or not alliances reinforce clusters rests partly on determining whether they have been predominantly local in character, between firms in the same state, or whether distance has been no object and the two firms in an alliance are based in different states within the USA or different countries. There is some evidence that entrants or DBFs, and incumbents or large multinational companies, operate differently in this respect. Alliances between entrants have tended to be more local than those between entrants and incumbents, in part because incumbents have not tended to be situated within the areas where the new firms have settled and grown up. Clusters have not grown up around the incumbent companies but rather around areas of particular scientific expertise in the research base, as discussed above.

The established pharmaceutical and chemical companies have been located in the older industrial states such as New Jersey, New York, Illinois, Michigan, or Delaware as well as abroad, in contrast to the new companies based in California, Massachusetts, Maryland, North Carolina. In addition in a study of the networks of alliances in California and Massachusetts between 1988 and 1991, it was found that DBFs based within the state were most central to their respective networks: they had the greatest number of ties (higher 'degree centrality'), were more tied together into indirect as well as direct links in alliances (higher 'betweenness centrality') and were 'closer' to other firms in the network (higher 'closeness centrality') than were the large multinationals involved in the network. It was noticeable that the multinationals tended to be based in other states or abroad, in contrast to the DBFs (Prevezer and Lomi 1995). It seems therefore that entrants or DBFs have tended to form alliances within their own states to a greater extent than have incumbents, and this would have tended to reinforce the clustering tendency of entrants to seek information and complementarities more locally than do incumbents.

However, it is also clear that incumbent companies have not felt entirely self-sufficient, in isolation away from the centres of clusters of these industries. During the 1980s some established companies chose to locate biotechnology subsidiaries within clusters. For instance Baxter Healthcare Hyland Biotechnology (Calif.), Abbot Biotech (Mass.), Ciba-Corning Diagnostic Corp. (Mass.), Lubrizol Agrigenetics (Calif.) have all been established as branches to their parent companies, locating within the clusters in California or Massachusetts. Glaxo and Burroughs Wellcome have established research bases in North Carolina, at Research Triangle Park, in order to benefit from the cluster of research expertise and other biotechnology-related facilities that they see growing up there. Other European and Japanese companies have done the same: BASF Bioresearch Corporation in both Cambridge and Worcester, Mass., Hitachi Chemical Research Center in California on the grounds of the University of California at Irvine, wanting access to the university resources. Incumbents have acquired small firms located within clusters: for instance Tanabe Seiyaku acquired the R & D laboratories of Immunetech in San Diego forming Tanabe Research Laboratories; Berlex Laboratories, a subsidiary of Schering, have been set up on the site which was formerly Codon Corporation in California. In a comparison of European and Japanese company practices in establishing these sites, it was noted that the European sites have tended to be larger and more integrated with the local universities with more collaboration between European sites and US universities than between Japanese sites and US locals, illustrating the explicit aim on the part of the European companies at least to establish an

R & D foothold at those locations and benefit from the local connections (*Bio/Technology*, Dec. 1992).

To summarize, the establishment of this industry in clusters has in the early days been driven by the creation of new companies, entrants into the industry, close to centres of scientific excellence. This was facilitated, at first, by the close association of academics with new start-up companies; but increasingly, as the industry matured during the 1980s, the entrepreneurs came from the established industrial base, involving scientists as co-founders or advisers. Key individuals combining scientific and entrepreneurial flair have been prominent in the founding and establishment of several companies, specializing in the building of companies in their early stages. Also important have been the venture capitalists, analysts, and lawyers for their involvement in assessing companies, forming linkages, and providing access to the managerial and financial expertise that young companies require. These 'infrastructural' skills have been more available at the centres of these new industries, in California and Massachusetts, although it is not clear from econometric evidence how strong a pull these factors have exerted in the location decisions of new firms. Clearer evidence has established the pull of the science base, and in particular the role of key 'star' scientists who have been particularly keen to form linkages through collaborating with new firms, as a critical factor in attracting new firms to particular clusters.

Those companies particularly based in sectors heavily reliant on innovation in research areas, namely therapeutics, diagnostics, and agriculture, have needed to be nearer the science base and close to other entrants rather than close to other established companies. This is in spite of the fact that the involvement of the incumbents in the development of this industry, through the complementary assets that have established their competitive advantage in downstream processing, has been substantial right from the early days of the industry. However, the incumbents in older established pharmaceutical and chemical industries have been geographically more dispersed and their involvement has been achieved through strategic alliances of many sorts, which have not required that the company headquarters be located in the middle of a cluster. None the less, it is clear that the science base has also exerted some pull for incumbent firms—multinationals, established outside clusters in the US and abroad—to set up research branches within growing clusters, where the absorption of new research ideas is particularly relevant and important to its success. Proximity has been necessary for such links with university research, in particular, to supplement the more formal ties that are established through strategic alliances with new firms, where geographical closeness has not been important.

6.8 THE STRUCTURE OF THE BIOTECHNOLOGY INDUSTRY AND THE IMPLICATIONS FOR CLUSTERING

We turn now to the structure of the biotechnology industry and how that has affected the impetus to cluster within its different industrial sectors. In particular we build on the results established in the first part of this chapter which suggest that, in biotechnology, links *within* sectors have been more important than those *across* sectors. The case of the equipment and instruments sector is something of an exception to this, with cross-sectoral links being quite important. But for the other sectors, linkages have tended to be formed within the therapeutics or diagnostics sectors or within the chemicals and food sectors, rather than between them. We look at the lack of technological complementarity between sectors in this context: at the similarity of biotechnologies used between different industrial sectors with complementarities occurring within sectors upstream and downstream rather than between sectors. This applies in particular to the early technologies and we look to see the extent to which subsequent technologies have tended to develop their own within-sector trajectories or whether there has been a continuation in the applicability across sectors of new technologies. We find that even with more recent technologies—of the late 1980s and 1990s—there are indications that these are being applied across sectors, and are not contained exclusively within one sector, although it takes time for such diffusion of technologies between sectors to occur. We deal separately with instrument and equipment technologies, which form a distinct industrial sector within the biotechnology industry, because there are some cross-sectoral links between the equipment and instrumentation sector and other sectors and between it and the science base.

This tendency for many sectors not to have structural, technological complementarities with other sectors has had implications for the clustering process in this industry. Why is clustering concentrated in some sectors and not in others? The answer is to be found again in the distinction between entrants and incumbents, with some sectors based on new firms, and others dominated by incumbents. This is due to the importance of upstream research differing between sectors, with innovation in some sectors such as therapeutics, diagnostics, and agriculture deriving from breakthroughs in the research area, whereas research is less important in overall profitability for sectors such as chemicals, food, and energy where downstream processes add more of the value. Whereas a mix between the science base, research-based sectors, and new instruments has helped clusters of companies to grow in certain sectors, other sectors such as chemicals and food have been more self-sufficient, more dominated by incumbents, and growth has been faster for incumbents in the presence of other firms within their own sector rather than with a mix of sectors at that location.

The biotechnology industry as a whole can be divided, and datasources and commentators have made this classification, into sectors of the industry according to type of industrial application that the sector develops (Dibner 1991; Coombs and Alston 1993; Orsenigo 1989). Thus there is a therapeutics 'sector' which focuses on developing therapeutic applications of the new technologies; a diagnostics sector making diagnostic applications; an agricultural sector, including plant and animal agriculture with new technologies being applied to seeds, plants, and animal characteristics. Classifications also commonly identify a chemicals sector with applications creating new speciality chemicals, and new products such as biopesticides and new insecticides and herbicides that have traditionally been made chemically within the chemicals sector; a food and cosmetics sector is also identified, where the applications are new enzymes and flavours to traditional processes; an environmental sector, or applications that deal with waste products; and an energy sector where the new technologies can potentially be applied to create new sources of biomass energy instead of petroleum-based energy. We are taking pains to describe the classification of the industry in this way, with the understanding that it is a classification that has been adopted by most commentators, because it stands in quite sharp distinction to the division into sectors most commonly used for the computing industry (see Chapter 8) and has distinct implications for the tendency of companies in different sectors so classified to cluster together. We are tentative about it, because although commonly adopted, there is no law which applies to this industry which distinguishes so clearly between a firm employing a new technology to create a new therapeutic product and one employing the same technology to alter the characteristics of a plant. Our conclusions about the tendency for firms within this industry, but in different sectors of it, to cluster together depend heavily therefore on this initial classification of firms into these distinct industrial sectors.

However, we are content to follow such precedents and classify the industry into such industrial sectors. Dibner also identifies the technologies most commonly used by the companies, and it is clear that for the first generation of companies, there were a few new technologies which were adopted by firms within most industrial sectors. These were recombinant DNA technologies, hybridoma or monoclonal antibody technologies, and various forms of cell or tissue culture, protein engineering, and purifying and separation technologies. The first two technologies formed the backbone in their various parts, both being sequences of highly complex technologies, of the scientific breakthroughs that created the inital impetuses to the foundation of the industry (see section 6.6). The purifying and separation technologies along with a series of other technologies—sequencing, bioreactors, analytical instruments such as nuclear magnetic resonance and mass spectroscopy—are technologies developed more distinctly by companies which specialize in equipment and instruments and have been classified into a separate sector. There has been technological complementarity between the instrument sector and other sectors, by which we mean that the technologies developed within that sector are not developed within other sectors but can be used by and complement the technologies of those other sectors. Both the science base and all sectors of the industry have been users of the new instruments and equipment developed within that sector.

In sectors other than instrumentation, the early technologies—recombinant DNA, hybridoma technology, and tissue culture—were used across all the industrial sectors. For instance the above technologies have been those used for plants as they have been in health care. In a National Science Foundation Survey, a breakdown of techniques in a sample of fifty-four companies in R & D was analysed. The recombinant DNA/RNA techniques occupied about half of the expenditure on R & D. The breakdown is given in Table 6.8. The therapeutics sector has heavily dominated R & D in this industry and this has been increasing during the 1980s. Plant agriculture has also been growing in importance in R & D expenditure, but only a quarter of that spent on therapeutics R & D was spent in this area in 1987. The use of DNA technologies increased in the 1980s whereas use of hybridoma technologies

Table 6.8 *Breakdown of R & D expenditure by technique and application, for sample of companies ($m)*

	1984	1985	1986	1987
Total industry R & D	900	1100	1300	1400
In sample	458	549	634	710
DNA/RNA	224	270	313	359
Hybridoma	47	63	63	62
New bioprocess	86	102	115	130
Old bioprocess	63	65	70	64
Other	40	48	73	95
By major applications				
In sample	458	549	634	710
Healthcare	301	368	425	487
O/w therapeutics	n.a.	294	345	405
diagnostics	n.a.	66	70	77
Plant	62	76	88	93
Animal	37	42	48	54
Chemical/food	40	43	42	39
Energy/environment	4	4	5	8
Other	14	16	27	29

Source: National Science Foundation Survey, in *Genetic Engineering News* (May 1988).

was static. Other newer technologies increased in importance in the late 1980s and 1990s (see below) and new bioprocess technologies also grew in importance.

Companies were founded on the basis of the application of a technology within a particular industrial sector. The early new products consisted of proteins that already existed but had not been available in great amounts and the new technologies introduced new ways of producing them more cheaply and in large quantities. For instance the early products were such proteins as the interferons, interleukins, human growth hormone, human insulin, factor VIII, rennin, erythroprotein, tissue plasminogen activator. All were produced by various methods using recombinant DNA technologies. Similarly hybridoma technology produced many outputs in the form of different monoclonal antibodies, over 600 of which had been created by 1984, with a variety of uses. Protein engineering involved the design and production of novel proteins making them more stable, specific, and efficient; hybrid proteins were made using recombinant techniques or synthetic chemistry techniques for novel proteins. So within these broad categories of a technology such as recombining DNA or protein engineering, there existed many different methods and routes to obtain similar end-products.

Subsequent 'generations' of the early technologies have been evolving during the 1980s and 1990s. These have included polymerase chain reaction (PCR) technologies in the mid-1980s, liposome technologies in the late 1980s, rational drug design, antisense technologies, transgenics, gene therapy, and chirality technologies to name the most prominent. These in turn have not been single technologies but have developed their own trajectories of their related technologies. Alternative amplification of DNA and RNA technologies to PCR have been developed, in part owing to the restricted access to PCR technology. These have included ligase chain reaction technology, repair chain reaction, ligation activated transcription, or strand displacement activation, all technologies stemming from the initial PCR breakthroughs. Rational drug design involves defining protein structures with the use of computers, bringing together leading edge software with screening technologies (see Chapter 8). Antisense technologies make antisense compounds to block gene expression; transgenics involves transferring genes across species; and gene therapy corrects genetic malformations on somatic cells. Most of these have evolved in the context of a particular sector—indeed mostly out of applications relating to health care in the first instance. However, they too are general technologies which can be applied across sectors for a variety of applications, and this has slowly been occurring. For instance, antisense technology evolved in the first instance looking at the functioning of genes in human diseases. It has already been applied by Calgene to its tomato to improve its ripening and softening qualities. It applies to cancer, cell biology, animal and plant development, viruses, and can enhance flavours and improve yields. Similarly transgenics, transferring genes across species, was developed through its application in health care, using animals as factories for such proteins as factor VIII. It can be used to improve animal models of human diseases but also in other sectors such as enhancing or deleting characteristics of farm animals—making them disease resistant, for instance. The speed at which these technologies will diffuse across sectors will depend, however, on a number of factors such as the acceptability of altering foods in this way. Another new area of technologies in the 1990s has been the development from protein engineering to a better understanding of the more complex compounds that are carbohydrates and their roles in determining cellular functions. New companies have been spawned based on commercializing this new area such as Cytel Corp., Glycomed, Biocarb, or Oxford Glycosystems.

To summarize, although it appears at first that the subsequent generations of technologies may apply more specifically to one sector than another and that trajectories of technologies develop within one sector, there are indications that these later technologies, as in the case of the early ones, will similarly be applicable and indeed will be taken up across a range of industrial sectors, although the speed at which this will happen will vary.

The importance of scientific research in the science base to biotechnology innovation differs between industrial sectors of application. Dibner looked at the ratios of science weight to business weight in a sample of firms, dividing the industry into three broad sectors of therapeutics, diagnostics, and agricultural, and looking at small, medium, and large companies. He found that, by sector, therapeutics had the highest science to business ratio, and agricultural biotechnology the lowest. Smaller newer firms tended to be more focused on the science and their business part grew as the firm matured (*Bio/Technology* 1988). Across a wider spectrum of sectors, scientific research is more significant as a source of value-added and innovation for therapeutics, diagnostics, and agricultural biotechnology than it is for chemicals, food processing, or energy. In the latter three sectors, innovations in processing or other downstream activities such as marketing assume a larger role in the creation of profit.

Biotechnology's impact on the chemical industry is far-reaching, affecting a range of substances used by the industry— amino acids, enzymes, oils and lipids, aromatic compounds, biopolymers, catalysts and dyes for uses in feed, detergents, dietary, pharmaceuticals, agricultural, pesticides, flocculants, and thickeners. The potential is to replace synthetic chemicals with naturally occurring bioconversions, particularly in the area of speciality, organic chemicals. The role of bioprocessing technologies in these fields is important. The greatest contribution of biotechnology here is in the field of biocatalysis where chemical catalysts with enzyme-like characteristics or stabilized enzyme catalysts play a large role. But there are greater problems of biocatalyst instability in the presence of many chemical reactants and organic solvents than when used in the formation of molecules such as antibiotics. There is also a high degree of process development and integration in the organic chemical sector which makes the introduction of new biocatalysis techniques more difficult (Dunnill and Rudd 1984: 18). There is greater reliance on new instruments, such as bioreactors and biosensors, which are designed to cope with the scale-up problems encountered when moving from small-scale research procedures, often using easily cultured bacteria, to the use of unstable biological materials on a larger scale.

In food processing, biological technology, which includes fermentation, has been used for thousands of years. However, the new biotechnologies are much slower to be introduced for reasons connected with food consumption patterns, and the caution with which new food ingredients need to be introduced. As in the chemicals industry, biocatalysis is important in this industry in the production of new enzymes and other catalysts to alter the properties of reactions; recombinant DNA techniques are also being applied in producing enzymes. In this area there is potential for use of new instruments and diagnostic tests to measure and analyse food quality.

There is a difference between industrial sectors in how much of the introduction of new technologies is done, on the one hand, by companies specializing in the new technologies, along the lines of what Arora and Gambardella (1993) have called 'changing patterns of specialization in inventive activity', or on the other hand has been developed in-house within companies. The health care area has seen the greatest degree of specialist companies, building on research, providing services, licensing new technologies, or selling products to the user pharmaceutical companies. Health care users such as hospitals have also been important in this context, with many new technologies for the *in vitro* diagnostic medical market, such as diagnostic probes, being initiated and developed by hospitals, which bring together the variety of disciplines—chemistry, microbiology, haematology, histology/cytology, and immunology—involved (*Genetic Engineering News*, June 1992). Specialization has also extended to research activity, with the growth of contract research organizations taking an increasing slice of R & D spending, concentrating on conducting trials and managing clinical data. They provide a service to the therapeutics companies, exploiting the generic nature of clinical trials, with multiple trials in cardiovascular, infections, or neurology for instance being performed by one specialist company. Non-health care sectors have not seen such specialization of research activities. As mentioned, they have been more reliant on bioprocess technologies, which have not necessarily come from the academic science base but have been more likely to evolve from engineering and biological scientists employed within companies out of the need to lower separation and purification costs. An example of this was the automated membrane affinity separation system developed in-house by NY Gene Corporation (*Genetic Engineering News*, Apr. 1990).

The move from scientific research-scale activities to industrial-scale commercialization could not have been accomplished at the speed it was in the 1980s without the enormous advances in a whole range of instruments which automated procedures and created much more sensitive machines with which to work. Expensive, highly skilled procedures which could be done only by postdoctoral scientists, were automated with sequencer and synthesizer machines and became possible to do much more cheaply and on a large scale inside industry. The technologies developed for these purposes have included new separations and purifying technologies, and bioreactors and biosensors for growing and monitoring the growth of biological materials. The evolution of such instruments and analysis technologies, which has formed a large part of the development of the industry, has been done both by new specialist companies in particular niche markets, by established older equipment companies, and by companies adapting equipment in-house to their own specialist needs. In some cases scaling-up difficulties have meant that equipment suppliers and customers either have to work closely together or companies will purchase equipment and adapt it in-house in order to keep the proprietary edge.

We may divide the instrument technologies into five broad categories: separation technologies such as electrophoresis, chromatography, filtration, membranes, ultracentrifugation; sequencers and synthesizers; bioreactors for growing cells and fermenters; analytical instruments such as nuclear magnetic resonance and spectroscopy instruments; and biosensors, bioassays, and monoclonal antibodies for assessing bioactivity. Also extremely significant has been the development of computers for a variety of uses such as data analysis, molecular modelling, computer-aided design; these developments are dealt with in more detail in chapter 8 looking at the convergence of the computing and biotechnology industries. Customers for these instruments have been research laboratories in government, industry, and universities as well as later stage bioprocessing within industry, these technologies affecting both research processes and downstream manufacturing processes.

Fifteen per cent of the equipment market was in DNA sequencers and synthesisers in 1992. Sequencing technologies have massively speeded up the process from a hand-done, highly skilled one of chopping DNA into fragments, reacting with molecules, labelling them, separating them, analysing them, into an automated, relatively unskilled process. In 1980, it took one postdoc one week to add one nucleotide to a growing nucleotide chain. By 1985 the average time for a base addition was ten minutes and the operator did not need to understand anything about chemistry. Increasingly there has been integration of synthesizers with other new technologies such as PCR and antisense, with the development of synthesizers for use with these specific technologies. Some of these gene mapping and sequencing techniques have companies based on them which are closely located to the main clusters of companies: such as Applied Biosystems (Calif.), Affymax (Calif.), MacConnell Research (Calif.), Clontech Laboratories (Calif.) supplying services and equipment to companies or Human Genome Sciences (Md.), Transkaryotic Therapies Inc. (Mass.), and Collaborative Research (Mass.) which focus on gene mapping. The Human Genome Project, based in Maryland, has given a particular boost to the development of purification and analysis instruments, and to the use of robotics and the automation of sequencing instruments (*Genetic Engineering News*, Oct. 1992).

Other areas of research and particular research institutions have in a similar way given rise to new instruments and companies based on them in that locality to further the development of the research. For example the National Bureau of Standards in Maryland has spawned new sensing methods to monitor biochemical reactor parameters and has fostered new concepts and data for process design and scale-up. The Center for Chemical Engineering has produced advances in protein separation techniques and facilities to produce cell cultures and cell products on a mass scale. The new carbohydrate technologies mentioned above have also spurred the development of new instruments and companies making them to characterize glycoproteins for instance, which have tended to be near areas of research in that technology. These include Finnigan MAT (Calif.) with mass spectroscopy instruments for glycochemists, Varian (Calif.) for NMR, Dionex (Calif.) and BioRad (Calif.) and Waters (Mass.) with chromatography products, BioCarb (Md.), Dionex (Calif.), Genzyme (Mass.), and Oxford Glycosystems (UK) for reagents, enzymes, and chemicals for carbohydrate analysis, or the CarbBank database and NMR facility at the Complex Carbohydrate Research Center at the University of Georgia.

Separations technologies—techniques of manipulating biological and chemical processes at the molecular level—take the new molecular technologies from the laboratory to final downstream processing across industrial sectors. Scale-up is very difficult, with large quantities of pure substances needed, unlike growing bacteria at the research stage which is relatively straightforward. This separations segment of instrumentation has been dominated by a relatively small number of large companies such as Millipore (Mass.), Pharmacia (NJ), Applied Biosystems (Calif.), Dionex, Grace, Du Pont (Del.), Rohm and Haas, Monsanto, Kodak, and Cyanamid, Hewlett Packard (Calif.), and Perkin Elmer. These sell membranes, resins, and reagents to the research end of the spectrum and scaled-up detoxification and bioprocessing systems further downstream, with varied degrees of integration with their customers. The electrophoresis apparatus and reagents part of separations has also been dominated by a few companies: Beckman Instruments (Calif), Corning Medical (NY) and Helena Labs (Tex.), Bio-Rad Labs (Calif.), LKB (Md.), and Pharmacia (NJ). There have also grown up many specialist small companies producing purity reagents, enzymes, tissue cultures, and DNA probes, with applications across diagnostics, food, and water industries in particular.

New instruments have therefore been both close to the research end of the spectrum with new sensing methods to monitor biochemical reactor parameters, new concepts, and data for process design and scale-up, new sequencers, synthesizers, and probes, and they have been important for downstream processes with facilities to mass-produce cell cultures and cell products. This helps to explain the position in the entry models of the equipment sector, which is quite strongly connected to the science base and to the therapeutics sector in particular within clusters but is not very close to other sectors of the industry. Specialist equipment and instrument companies have entered the industry close to centres of research and to research-based companies based in clusters, to provide specialist services and to enable the development and adaptation of equipment which firms need. Something like this process has been operating around some of the gene mapping and sequencing activities of the Human Genome Project for instance, or close to the research bases and companies developing the new carbohydrate technologies. However, a large part of this sector is still dominated by the older established equipment companies, which have not been based within these newer clusters but continue to operate from their existing locations, not necessarily close to research-based clusters. In addition the sequencing or synthesizing equipment or reagents produced by some of these companies became, during the 1980s, relatively standard and widely spread tools of the industry, marketed and sold globally and without need for proximity to any particular user-companies.

6.9 THE MIGRATION OF CLUSTERS AND REGIONAL POLICY

The role of policy in stimulating clusters to develop in other states than those in which the industry took root when it came into being is an intriguing one. It is interesting for the lessons that may be learned more generally about the conditions which are necessary for state policy to be effective in encouraging entry of new firms, and of established companies to come to that state and engage with the local communities of researchers and manufacturers and enable a new industrial network to emerge. These policy issues will be examined more generally in Chapter 9. Here we look specifically at biotechnology initiatives that have been tried by particular states in the USA to cause clusters to migrate and develop. We analyse them in terms of their specialization in particular biotechnology niches and whether local conditions are propitious for that concentration.

One of our main findings has been that the biotechnology industry, in its constituent sectors, is linked more closely to those user industrial sectors where the technologies are applied than to other sectors within the biotechnology industry. The impetus for innovation lies in different parts of the production process in different industrial sectors. Thus research is particularly central to innovation in therapeutics and diagnostics, production processes and manufacturing in chemicals and food processing, and the role of users in instrumentation and diagnostics as well. The success of policy initiatives hinges on focusing on initial conditions needed to foster particular sectors or niches that are appropriate to those sectors. We would expect therefore that research conditions—its quality and concentration, the conditions for transferability into the industrial sector, the availability of skilled research labour, complementarity of research interests between the science base and pharmaceutical companies—would be particularly critical to encouraging clusters in therapeutics to develop. Or the strength and accessibility of the user community, in the form of users of new instruments, medical technology, and new diagnostics, would be critical for the development of firms specializing in those sectors.

The cost of labour and other inputs varies across states. The importance of these cost variations for location depends on whether the area or state is specializing in upstream research or in downstream processing and manufacturing, as outlined in section 6.8. A league table of operating costs for this industry, including labour costs, utilities, occupancy, and transport placed Boston, San Francisco, and San Diego at the top of the league, having the highest costs and in particular labour costs and utilities. This has not been a deterrent for those companies reliant on the science base and with a need for access to top-class research scientists. However, if manufacturing facilities are being considered, then locating them away from the science bases and nearer other manufacturing facilities has advantages. For instance Genetics Institute built its development and clinical bulk materials production unit in Andover, Mass., near its manufacturing facility to interact with downstream functions (Dibner et al., *Bio/Technology*, Oct. 1990).

We turn now to examining the intiatives that have been put in place across the USA in biotechnology, mainly in the form of biotechnology centres located in particular states as part of local government policy. These centres vary enormously in their aims and focuses, but they have a number of common types of policy. Features are:

1. encouraging the particular specialisms of that area and enhancing and making use of local expertise, for instance, strength in particular disciplines or industrial sectors, in research such as Research Triangle Park, in health regulation such as the area near the National Institutes of Health;
2. tax breaks or other fiscal inducements to entry of new companies; financing inducements;
3. creation of infrastructure that can be shared between small companies that would otherwise not have access to such

facilities. Examples are research parks, incubator buildings, pilot plant facilities, DNA libraries, and gene banks.

It is difficult to determine the precise results of these policies in numbers of companies thereby brought into an area or state. We shall try to assess the success of these policies in particular states according to their appropriateness to local conditions and strengths, and whether the biotechnology industry is in fact developing in that state.

In a survey of Biotechnology Centre Strategies by Dibner and Hamner, it was found that in 1991 there were 75 centres in 33 states. They had increased in number and in dispersion, from 36 centres in 23 states in 1987. Sixty per cent of those in 1991 were based at single universities and focused on the 'home' institutions available through the university. A quarter were not aligned with a particular university and covered the whole state, and 15 per cent were for general technological development and not just for biotechnology. Most of them received their funding from the state or from the state universities. In terms of dispersion, in 1991 there were seven centres in California, ten in Maryland, three in Massachusetts, one in North Carolina, three in New Jersey, two in New York, three in Ohio, and three in Pennsylvania and their functions included industrial development, public education, promoting scientific research and use of resources, and fostering local industry (*Genetic Engineering News*, Jan. 1992).

We look first at the clusters that have been at the core of the development of the industry, and the policies associated with them. These might be called the successful clusters, in terms of activity generated in both research and companies starting up or settling in the state. The most important and earliest clusters have been clearly in California, which has two distinct clusters of companies and research activity—around San Francisco and San Diego, and in Massachusetts. What one might call the second generation of clusters, also extremely important in the growth of the industry, has been located in a mix of 'newer' industrial areas in Maryland and North Carolina, as well as in the 'older' industrial states of New Jersey, New York, and Illinois. The 'outer' group of states, where some activity has been occurring more recently, include Washington, Idaho, and Tennessee on the west coast, and Texas, Michigan, and Delaware. This third group has focused more on agriculture, chemicals, and bioprocesses, as well as on health care, where there are particular health care resources. This does not cover all biotechnology activities and policies that are in place all over the USA; but it does provide us with examples of how particular states are making use of their local strengths, and the types of policies that are being employed in each case. Finally we compare these activities in the USA briefly with the models of development and types of policies that are being used by other countries in Europe and in Japan. We suggest why clusters have been much slower to develop outside the USA and what type of policies are needed to understand and forge the linkages that are necessary for clustering to take off.

The original areas for the creation of this industry were in northern California, in the Bay area, and in Massachusetts. The main attraction there was the concentration of leading-edge research that was happening in the late 1970s, which we have described in some detail earlier. Despite these areas having the highest labour costs, companies setting up needed access to top-class research scientists and the added expense of labour was not a deterrent. This again is substantiated by the emphasis that has been shown to have been placed on key 'star' scientists in the setting up of the companies close to the main research centres in this field. High-calibre scientists, on which this industry has been built, were not going to be attracted off the beaten academic track, especially if access to research was a continuing need for the growth of the company. Manufacturing facilities on the other hand were located further away from the science base.

In southern California, again there has been a mix of concentration of research strengths and other types of infrastructure. The infrastructure in southern California has been advantageous in the form of banks, venture capital, marketing gurus, and academic scientists, with diverse constitutions: public and private, finance and science, academic and business credentials. There are many research centres concentrated in this area: the Scripps Institute, Salk Institute, La Jolla Cancer Research Foundation, Whither Institute for Diabetes and Endocrinology, La Jolla Institute for Allergy and Immunology, University of California at San Diego, Center for Molecular Genetics. The Universities of California in the South include Irvine, Riverside, San Diego, Los Angeles and there are private universities as well as the California State Universities and community colleges. Some of these research institutes are particularly renowned and well endowed: the Salk Institute has over 500 scientists, as does the Scripps Research Institute. In the Los Angeles area there are the Citrus Research Center and Agricultural Export Station, the Center for Neurobiology of Hearing and Memory, and various others in the biotechnology and medical fields. There have also been in place specific programmes such as CONNECT to create linkages between institutions. CONNECT has been a UCSD programme in Technology and Entrepreneurship which has nurtured high-technology development, networking, and educational and practical linkages.

California's two main clusters have been built on diverse, decentralized planning which has taken advantage of local strengths. There have been industrial intitiatives in both California and Massachusetts as well. In California the Harbor Bay Business Park near San Francisco and Orange County Bioscience Park have focused industrial attention on those locations. Stanford's Office of Technology Licensing ran a policy of a fixed royalty rate or membership fee to gain access to a pool of licences for the use of basic biotechnology patents (*Bio/Technology*, May 1983). This has had the advantage of speeding the transfer of technology, giving wider access to the licences of participating universities. The Office has engaged in the more thorough prosecution of patent violators, has given faster access to a range of tools, and has ensured more uniform licensing policies. The advantages to the universities have been to insulate them to some degree from the corporations and to lower the costs of negotiation and administration of patenting and licensing. It has meant that individuals within universities have lost some control over the negotiation, and revenues have been less likely to return to the inventor or individual's laboratory.

In Massachusetts, the centre in Worcester has been particularly important in fostering activity in the state. Its aim was to imitate MIT's encouragement of the growth of Route 128. It has been based around a cluster of research bases—Worcester Polytechnic Institute, Clark University, and the University of Massachusetts Medical Center. It has been close enough to Boston and yet has promoted its own resource base. It has had links to the Massachusetts Biotechnology Research Institute with its incubation facility, shared instrumentation including computer equipment and

Martha Prevezer

fermentation pilot plant, NMR facility, downstream processing equipment, biotechnology library, conference centre, and training facilities. Genetics Insitute was one company attracted by the pilot plant facilities. The Worcester centre has found itself to have been an attractive location when companies needed to expand whilst still maintaining access to the universities at the epicentre of research in Cambridge. Its tenants have included Alpha-Beta Technology, TSI Corp., Hybridon Inc., Ecoscience Corp. as well as BASF Bioresearch, Cambridge Biotech, E-Z-EM, and Genica Pharms. In all in 1991 there were fifteen biotechnology companies located there alongside five research institutes.

It would be wrong, therefore, to think of the initial clusters in California and Massachusetts as having grown up in the absence of policy initiatives and inducements and being entirely 'market-driven'. Both states have cultivated a range of policies, and several of the biotechnology centres were located in those states and helped to create the type of infrastructure that has encouraged start-up companies, especially in high-technology areas.

The 'newer' industrial states which have grown in importance in this industry have been North Carolina and Maryland. The clusters there have been based on particular strengths in each state: in research in North Carolina, and in medical regulation and standard setting in Maryland. In North Carolina there has been a concerted effort to concentrate academic resources around Research Triangle Park and to attract industrial interest in research. It has been built on academic strength and promoted as a research-oriented park, with the promise of an academic campus-like atmosphere. It is located between Duke University, Durham, North Carolina State, Raleigh, and the University of North Carolina in Chapel Hill and was founded 1981. Its focus has been multi-institute research and policies have encouraged multidisciplinarity, education, and business development. It has also housed the largest incubator facility in the USA. The climate is thought to have been helped by clear regulation under the Genetic Engineering Organisms Act. The Park has been successful in attracting start-ups as well as the biotechnology units of Glaxo and Ciba Geigy, research laboratories of Burroughs Wellcome, IBM, and General Electric as well as subsidiaries of Data General, Monsanto, Becton Dickinson, the National Institute of Environmental Health Sciences, and NASA. In 1985 North Carolina had 110 small companies. In addition the North Carolina Biotechnology Center was established in 1984. The centre has helped to fund twenty-nine biotechnology companies of which two, Embrex and Sphinx, went public in 1991. It is estimated by Burrill and Roberts (*Bio/Technology*, June 1992) that the centre has helped to spawn thirty-eight biotechnology companies in North Carolina.

Maryland has become a centre of biological science and medical technology and specialist industrial development. After California and Massachusetts, Maryland had the third largest concentration of organizations and scientists in biotechnology in the early 1980s. In 1985 a quarter of the biotechnology industry was located there (*Genetic Engineering News*, Feb. 1985) and the state was estimated to have the highest annual expenditure in health-related R & D. The concentration of scientists was based in part on the location of the National Institutes of Health and the National Bureau of Standards there, as well as other research institutes, such as the Gillette Research Institute. The Center for Advanced Research in Biotechnology was established under the impetus of the University of Maryland, and this has been linked to the National Bureau of Standards for the development of standardized measurement and techniques. This centre has been at the core of much of the work in protein engineering analysis and the development of equipment for rational drug design. The Shady Grove Life Science Center in Montgomery County has provided a concentrated area for many firms to locate, close to research institutes and other companies. The Centre was located there to exploit access to NIH scientists, to be near the National Bureau of Standards and close to information sources such as the National Library of Medicine. It was decided to build a subway to connect the centre directly to Washington, DC, and form part of the Baltimore–Washington corridor with access to government resources, the NIH, NBS, FDA, and National Naval Medical Centre. In the mid-1980s Montgomery County already had a high concentration of people in computing occupations and in 1984 it was home to 250 bioscience firms (*Genetic Engineering News*, Jan. 1984). Amongst the firms that settled in the cluster were Genex, Litton Bionetics, Microbiology Associates, Bethesda Research Labs, Hazleton Labs, as well as subsidiaries of larger companies such as Boehringer Mannheim and the first Japanese research facility in biotechnology in the USA, Otsuka Pharmaceuticals. By 1987 it was estimated that there were over 400 high-technology companies in the area.

The 'older' industrial states such as New Jersey, New York, and Illinois have also had policies to foster high-technology industries in their states, focusing on both their academic research prowess and the presence of high-quality research centres and hospitals and on their established industrial companies in pharmaceuticals, especially in New Jersey. The New York Science and Technology Foundation established four centres for advanced technology, two of which have been devoted to biotechnology. One has been based at Cornell University, specializing in agricultural applications, and the other at the State University of New York at Stony Brook, specializing in diagnostics. In Illinois there has been a range of programmes to attract inward investment especially from large corporations, based on their five major universities and three large pharmaceutical companies (Abbott, Searle, and Baxter Travenol) there. Inducements have included a research park, incubator building, financing programmes with tax exemptions for firms creating new facilities, as well as urban renewal projects to try to encourage local high-technology industry to settle in older industrial areas.

The most recent spread of the industry has been towards the west coast, with a sizeable cluster of companies in Washington state by the early 1990s, focusing on the Washington State University Research and Technology Park, the Tennessee Technology Corridor, and the University of Utah Park in Salt Lake City. Industrial focus has been on agriculture in Washington state, Idaho, and Utah and biomedical research in Tennessee. The state of Michigan has also targeted agriculture and plant biology, building on its agricultural resources at Michigan State University and the presence of large companies such as Upjohn, Kellogg, and Dow Chemical, with these large companies contributing towards the budget of the Michigan Biotechnology Institute in East Lansing. As with other older states, the policy has been to try to diversify away from the state's former concentration on automobiles, and towards high-technology industry. In a similar spirit, Delaware has concentrated its technology efforts on agricultural and industrial chemical applications and on health care, to build on existing strengths in these areas as well as on the presence of

Du Pont. The involvement of Du Pont in building a new life science research station is hoped to act as a magnet to other companies to the state. Texas is another state which has fostered a significant number of new companies in biotechnology, helped by a series of state policies and promoted actively in particular by Mayor Cisneros of San Antonio. The policies have focused on the potential of the University of Texas Health Science Centre in Dallas, and a task force was formed, combining local businesses, Batelle Columbus, investment firms, and banks. The Dallas Biotechnology Development Corporation was formed, the first private investment fund for biotechnology, to fund the gap between basic research and commercial exploitation. It has created general patent licensing programmes at the universities, industrial affiliates programmes, centres of excellence, and for-profit companies with links to the universities, with the Corporation taking a share of the profits. The scientific committee of the Corporation has had the functions of evaluating projects, screening research, and assessing competition and market potential, costs and patentability.

All this gives some flavour of the range and number of policies and programmes that have been put in place at the state level, and by many states in the USA, in order to attract companies and to create links between the research specialisms that were present in the state and company activity, whether by start-ups or by subsidiaries of large corporations. The involvement of the spectrum of companies and research institutes—as well as the creation of linkage and transfer institutions which have helped with pilot plant and incubator facilities, licensing and patenting activities, assessment of commercial potential—have been critical in helping these distinct clusters to grow. The element of competition between states to attract activity, with decentralized funding at the state level, alongside the searching for niches and specialisms that are based on the particular strengths of the area, has also been helpful in diversifying activity both geographically and across industrial sectors.

Finally let us look briefly at the models of development in this industry that other countries have employed. Industries are typically being built around the different and distinct strengths and expertise of each country. The Japanese biotechnology industry focuses on processes and has had very few start-up companies

although over 300 Japanese companies are thought to be working
with biotechnology in the 1990s. There has been no venture capital and there has been more emphasis on central government
funding (Burrill and Roberts in *Bio/Technology*, June 1992). In Germany the chemicals industry provides the foundation for 80 per
cent of biotechnology. There are over 1,000 research institutes and
five gene centres (at Hamburg, Cologne, Heidelberg, Munich,
and Berlin) which aim to coordinate universities, government,
and industry. However, there is a sharper separation of universities from industry than in the USA and the regulatory uncertainty
has not assisted the climate for commercializing research.
France's resources focus on agricultural biotechnology as well
as on medicine. It has a strong research base, especially in the
Rhône-Alpes region and leading research centres include
the Centre des Études Atomiques, Centre National de Recherche
Scientifique, Institut National pour Recherche Agronomique,
Institut National de la Santé de la Recherche Médical, and the
Institut Pasteur. It has important pharmaceutical companies in
Rhône Poulenc and Pasteur Merieux and attention is being concentrated on the Lyons area with a protein engineering institute
being built in Grenoble near the European Synchotron Facility. In
particular regions, similar initiatives to those in the USA are being
tried, but with more centralized planning and funding behind
them than in the USA. The UK's model of development of biotechnology is, if anything, closest to that in the USA, but on a
much smaller scale, and without the scale and scope of regional
state-level programmes that are in place in the USA. The UK
industry is assessed in the following chapter. In particular it is
pointed out by Zucker and Darby (1995) that, given the strengths
of the science base in the UK, France, and Germany, the science-
industry linkages and active commercial involvement by scientists are much weaker than in the USA, and that this type of
linkage has been a critical factor in the growth of the US industry.
In the absence of policies to go some way to remedy this, the
industries in Europe will not achieve the commercialization of
bioscience in the way that we have seen in the USA.

   To conclude, the role of policy in the USA in helping the industry to migrate and clusters of concentrated activity to form should
not be underestimated, even for the earliest clusters in California
and Massachusetts. The creation of all sorts of infrastructure—

skills, licensing and patenting facilities, financing programmes, incubators and pilot plants, and DNA libraries—have all played their part in helping companies to form and in luring established companies to locate in particular states. Also critical have been the people and institutions that link together the research disciplines and companies with different specialisms, and that mobilize the local customers or users of the new technologies such as hospitals and large companies. The scale of these resources and their range is only beginning to be recognized by European policy-makers in their attempts to create similar dynamics for clustering.

7

Clustering and UK Biotechnology

SIMON SHOHET

INTRODUCTION

The UK biotechnology 'industry' comprises two historically distinct industrial strands. The first—the traditional chemical and pharmaceutical industry—has long established roots traceable to the late nineteenth and early twentieth centuries when firms such as Glaxo, Wellcome, and ICI were founded. A number of US and continental European firms with UK subsidiaries also fall into this category. In some cases these were established before the Second World War and have since developed significant R & D and manufacturing operations in the UK. The second strand of firms has more recent roots and emerged from the new cell and gene discoveries of the mid and late 1970s. These start-up firms, the dedicated biotechnology firms (DBFs), are making an important contribution to growth of the sector, and represent the largest grouping of such firms in Europe, though smaller and compositionally different from the US sector discussed in Chapter 6.

This chapter has two parts—one historical and one analytical. In sections 7.1 to 7.6, we sketch the industrial history of UK biotechnology and the respective roles of established multinational firms, on the one hand, and the more recent new entrants (DBFs), on the other. From section 7.7 onward, we use the available data to test for the presence and the importance of attractors—particularly the presence of other firms and a science base—that may lead to regional agglomerations and clusters, concentrating mainly upon the role of DBFs in this process.

7.1 HISTORY AND BACKGROUND: THE PHARMACEUTICAL INDUSTRY AND ITS CLUSTERS

The discoveries underpinning modern biotechnology have led to the formation of a range of new linkages, both between firms of different sizes and between firms and public sector organizations such as medical schools, universities, and research institutes. However, the strength and nature of these linkages—and the subsequent development of regional clusters and agglomerations—appear to have evolved differently in the UK than in the USA. The following section discusses, within a historical context, the role of UK-based large firms in these agglomeration processes.

Corporate logistics—rather than advantages gained by sourcing local knowledge, specialized labour, and suppliers—seems to have been the key factor influencing the location of the large multinationals' manufacturing, R & D, and administrative functions in the UK. In many cases the siting of operations can be directly traced back to the founding of firms and the first establishment of research centres. While this has resulted in local concentrations of R & D and operational activities, there is little evidence of the intensity of linkages in the UK that is to be found in parts of California and Massachusetts as described in Chapter 6. However, there are well-known and distinct areas of concentration of the pharmaceutical industry in the south-east counties of England such as Hertfordshire and Surrey; and in north-west England, notably Cheshire, and it is these local concentrations, and the firms that have developed within them, that will be discussed in the following section.

Three general features stand out. First, as we have suggested above, R & D has been relatively immobile in the UK—firms have tended to stay in the locality at which R & D functions were first established, and where new R & D facilities have been built they have tended to be close to the original sites. Second, R & D and corporate administrative functions are often to be found close together. Third, the R & D activities have tended to be separated from production and manufacturing (see for example Howells 1990).

In relation to R & D immobility, the risks of losing key research staff by major relocation, as well as the tendency to add new

R & D activities close to existing sites to maintain effective communication, are important determining factors. There has been a strong tendency for pharmaceutical research to be located close to London-based headquarters in areas such as Hertfordshire and Surrey, allowing good flows of communication to corporate HQs. There are exceptions such as ICI's pharmaceutical research base in Cheshire, with its corporate headquarters in London. As we showed in Chapter 4, technology-based firms are strongly attracted to the south-east of England both for supply-side and demand-side reasons: namely, the highly developed infrastructure, the science base and the availability of highly qualified labour, the presence of UK markets, and the closeness to continental European markets.

In the USA, there is stronger evidence of the separation of corporate headquarters and R & D, where the latter have been located close to universities (Chapter 6). This may reflect the historical organization of firms along product division lines (M-form) versus more centralized governance structures found in UK firms. Communication and close cooperation between R & D and corporate administration would be expected in centralized firms which are strategically dependent on long-term research. Centralization and efficiencies through scope and scale economies have been a feature of R & D strategies of large pharmaceutical firms in recent years, particularly in south-east England (e.g. the mergers between SmithKline Beckman and Beecham and, more recently, Glaxo with Wellcome).

The bulk nature of pharmaceutical chemical precursors has meant that production activities, in contrast to R & D, are often located close to ports—examples include Glaxo sites in Montrose in Scotland and Speke in Liverpool, ICI at Billingham, Cleveland, as well as Wellcome at Dartford in Kent. Overall, the need for close coupling and communication between manufacturing and production and corporate headquarters would seem to be less important to these firms than coupling to R & D and headquarters. These observations point to internal logistics rather than external knowledge acquisition as the principal factor influencing location, and it explains the lack of intense UK clustering which is seen in the USA.

A good illustration of pharmaceutical industry agglomeration (rather than intense clustering) is the county of Hertfordshire, which probably contains the largest concentration of multinational pharmaceutical activities in the UK. Merck & Co.—the large US pharmaceutical company—set up its UK division in the area in 1948. The siting of Merck's UK operations follows the model described above: administrative and research activities close together, and production more widely dispersed. Roche Products Ltd., the UK subsidiary of the Swiss firm Hoffmann-La Roche, began operations in Hertfordshire in 1937, later moving its chemicals and vitamins production activities to Dalry in Glasgow in 1947. The R & D facilities were subsequently expanded and it is now a major international R & D site for Roche with around 800 staff (see Breheny et al. 1992).

SmithKline Beecham, formed from the merger of SmithKline Beckman and Beecham's Pharmaceuticals in 1989, has manufacturing and research sites in Surrey and Sussex and in Essex and Hertfordshire, all in close proximity to corporate headquarters in north-west London. In 1993 the company began a process of consolidating its R & D centres at a new site in Harlow, Essex (Green 1993). According to Breheny et al. (1992), Roche, Merck, SmithKline Beecham, and Glaxo employ 90 per cent of the pharmaceutical workforce in Hertfordshire—equivalent to around 5,500 employees. Few areas in the UK have a comparable concentration of pharmaceutical R & D personnel. One other may be Cheshire, where much of ICI and Zeneca's production and R & D activities are located.

As well as corporate logistics, other factors such as post-war planning policies have had an impact on large firm location behaviour. The towns of Stevenage, Welwyn Garden City, and Harlow, which are the centres of pharmaceutical R & D in Hertfordshire and neighbouring Essex, were built as overflows from London in the 1950s as a result of the 1946 New Towns Act, which began a publicly financed programme for the creation of centres of population and employment. Manufacturing firms in particular were attracted to these locations in line with the aim of creating local, self-contained economic development. Glaxo's decision to locate in its major R & D centre in Stevenage in 1993 was based on the availability of a large site with good access to road, rail, and air communications (Steadman 1993). Philpott (1989) notes that the town reversed earlier planning controls after the recession of the early 1980s in order to attract new industry. The location of

Box 1. *Wellcome plc*

> Wellcome plc was an important element of the pharmaceutical indus-
> try in south-east England (it merged with Glaxo in 1995). As far back
> as 1889 Wellcome operated a chemical works in Dartford, Kent, and
> this remains a major manufacturing plant. In 1922 the company estab-
> lished research laboratories in Beckenham, Kent, where vaccines and
> antisera were developed. During the 1940s Beckenham was a key
> production site for vaccines against diptheria (Wellcome 1980). Symp-
> tomatic of the consolidation of the industry and the gains from scale
> economies in R & D, operations at the Beckenham site are closing,
> following the merger between Glaxo and Wellcome in 1995, and
> activities are being centralized at Glaxo Wellcome's new site at
> Stevenage.

Stevenage close to a good transport infrastructure makes it highly attractive to new firms. However, there is also good access to the science base: R & D intensive firms based in Hertfordshire and Essex undoubtedly benefit from being at a triangulation point between academic centres in London to the south, Oxford to the west, and Cambridge to the east. The teaching hospitals of London also provide access to patients for clinical trials. While gaining access to technological opportunities arising from univer- sities and research institutes has been a key aim of these large firms the relatively small travelling distances compared with the USA have meant that, on the whole, co-location has not been necessary.

ICI has roots rather different from Wellcome's—many of its activities are based in Cheshire in north-west England—though it has also played a critical role in the development of the UK pharmaceutical industry, and heavily shaped regional devel- opment at its sites. The dyestuffs operations at Blackley in Man- chester provided ICI with organic chemistry expertise that enabled it to begin research into medicines, originally within the dyestuffs division. ICI established an experimental biology section in the late 1930s with scientists cooperating extensively with university laboratories at Edinburgh, Glasgow, and Oxford (which remain pre-eminent in life science research), with grants provided to these laboratories in the first two years as the ICI section was built up. It also carried out extensive cooperative

Box 2. *ICI and biotechnology*

> ICI was able to build on fermentation expertise developed from its penicillin manufacturing and to extend this to its agricultural operations for the manufacture of single cell protein (SCP) for use as animal feed. This began in the late 1960s, in collaboration with scientists at Sheffield University who had expertise in micro-organisms capable of growing on methane as a carbon source. In 1971 an SCP pilot plant at Billingham was built and later a large-scale plant in Teeside. However, the price of methanol rose dramatically after the 1973/4 oil shock, the process became uneconomic, and SCP markets collapsed (see Kennedy 1994). The experience provided the firm with important capabilities in biotechnology which it has been able to use in a number of new ventures: for example, the manufacturing of polymers derived from micro-organisms such as the biodegradable plastic Biopol; and of the fungal-derived meat substitute Quorn. ICI also moved rapidly to develop the genetic fingerprinting techniques invented by Alec Jefferies at Leicester University. Cellmark Diagnostics was established as an ICI subsidiary in 1987 to commercialize and market the technology. In 1993 ICI began a demerger process essentially separating its bioscience operations into a new firm, Zeneca plc, with ICI remaining as a chemicals and paints business.

research on the production of penicillin with H. W. Florey's team at Oxford, and set up a penicillin manufacturing plant at Trafford Park in Manchester. In 1957 a major pharmaceuticals research centre was established in Alderley Park in Cheshire, which remains a key centre for research for ICI and its demerged offshoot, Zeneca plc (ICI 1957).

7.2 DIFFUSION OF BIOTECHNOLOGY AND ITS IMPACT ON LARGE FIRM STRATEGY

Developments in biotechnology in the late 1970s and early 1980s spurred a number of multinational firms with agrochemical and food businesses to realign their activities strategically. They were concerned that the gene technologies might displace their major revenue-earning products. Pest-resistant crops and nitrogen-fixing cereals were then thought to be potential threats to the pesticide and fertilizer industries although the emergence of these products has, in fact, been slower than expected. In this sense, biotechnology was seen to be a 'competence destroying' technology (Tushman and Anderson 1986) and a spate of acquisitions of seed companies by larger agro-industrial firms occurred in the mid-1980s in the UK. Shell bought Nickerson Seeds, and in 1987 Unilever acquired the former Plant Breeding Institute in Cambridge—one of the first government research institutes to be privatized (Webster 1989). ICI also established a new seeds research facility at its agrochemicals research centre in Jealott's Hill, Berkshire.

As Sharp (1994) points out, the pharmaceutical industry, and to some extent the agrochemicals industry, have seen a shift in their technological dependencies: away from chemistry-based approaches and towards biological ones—though this is not entirely clear-cut and there is now a convergence of these strands in areas such as combinatorial chemistry which involves chemical synthesis of multiple combinations of biochemical precursors. The technological shift is most evident in a firm such as ICI which has demerged along technological and sectoral lines. It is less obvious in the case of a firm such as Wellcome which depended on its biological capabilities for vaccine manufacture as far back as the 1920s. Later its focus shifted to the discovery of new chemical entities in the period between the 1940s and mid-1970s and parts of its operations then refocused on gene and cell technologies when Wellcome Biotechnology Ltd. was established in the 1980s. However, attempts to create a small biotechnology company out of Wellcome were unsuccessful and the firm was later to sold to Murex Corporation.

While biotechnology has had most impact in pharmaceuticals, other UK sectors have at one time or other adopted or experimented with the possibilities. UK brewing and food firms invested in biotechnology process development in the beginning in the early 1980s. Bass Brewers, based in Burton-on-Trent, established Delta Biotechnology in 1984 in Nottingham to exploit the commercial possibilities of its yeast genetics expertise for the production of pharmaceuticals, though the firm was later sold to BOC plc—a maker of industrial gases. Grand Metropolitan plc also invested in biotechnology production but exited rapidly when the initial optimism about growth in the industry dampened. Diffusion of biotechnology methods into food and drink production has in general been limited in comparison to health and pharmaceutical areas. This is the case in the UK as well as in the rest of Europe and the USA. This is widely believed to be related to concerns over consumer perception, labelling requirements, and regulation, though firms with major organizational resources in these areas have successfully delivered products to the market. Zeneca Seeds (formerly ICI Seeds) has launched a tomato paste made from genetically modified tomatoes which have high solids and improved shelf life. Unilever has been active over fifteen years in using biotechnology across its product ranges: e.g. in tissue culture methods for oil palms, cereal breeding, enzymes for detergents, modification of edible oils, as well as the use of monoclonal antibodies in diagnostics. However, new entrants have been sparse. We estimated that less than 5 per cent of UK DBFs operated in the food and drink sector in 1993 (Shohet 1994).

To conclude this section, it appears that the role of large firms in the development of biotechnology in the UK has been different from what has been described for the USA. The large UK firms developed in-house expertise and established competences in areas such as fermentation and vaccines and outside health care, in areas such as plant tissue culture and industrial enzymes. While augmented by collaboration with universities, there is little to suggest that large UK firms have needed to be geographically close to the science base—the needs of corporate communications and historical 'lock-in' have been the dominating factors affecting location behaviour. We may speculate that large UK firms felt that their historical capabilities—built up in some cases before the Second World War—absolved them from the need to build extensive external collaborations when biotechnology first emerged in the mid-1970s. Clustering between large firms' R & D activities and the science base, or between large pharmaceutical firms and small biotechnology firms, is therefore only weak. The US story is different—early relationships were formed between large firms and the new academic start-up companies. Intricate local linkages have also formed between DBFs, catalysed to some extent by larger firms and venture capitalists, leading to the evolution of distinctive clusters (see Barley et al. 1992 and Chapter 6 above). In the following section, we turn to DBFs and the role they have played in the local and regional development of biotechnology in the UK.

7.3 THE EMERGENCE OF DEDICATED BIOTECHNOLOGY FIRMS IN THE UK

Because the development of a dynamic population of new UK companies arising from the science base and from existing firms occurred later, and on a smaller scale, than in the USA, the UK can be viewed as being at an earlier stage in the cluster life cycle. Concern at the lack of new entrants and the slow adoption of biotechnology in the UK was recognized in the Spinks Report of 1980 (ACARD 1979) which recommended that the funding agencies (the Research Councils) should increase their support for biotechnology; that coordination between government departments be strengthened; and that a programme of industrial research be initiated between various public and private agencies. The report also advocated direct state funding to help establish a dedicated biotechnology firm to exploit developments arising from the UK science base.

Key to the successful development of US biotechnology was the close collaboration between the main institutions—state and federal research agencies, scientists, universities, and venture capitalists—and the networking between key individuals (Orsenigo 1989; Kenney 1986; Chapter 6 above). This coupling was weaker in the UK, and, importantly, the venture capital market was virtually absent—in sharp contrast to the USA, where that market was well developed and receptive to high technology in part as a result of the success of the electronics industry. Again in contrast to the USA, incentives for UK academics to leave their university posts and set up biotechnology firms were limited—and only later did a small number become scientific advisers to new firms and to the nascent venture capital sector. Poor systems for allowing movement between industry and academia, fewer intermediaries acting at the interface, and higher exit costs, because of the difficulty of returning to an academic post after possible failure, may also have discouraged academic entrepreneurism in the UK.

The weak commercialization performance of UK bioscience

was highlighted when opportunities were missed to patent the discovery of monoclonal antibodies arising from the Medical Research Council (MRC) Laboratory of Molecular Biology at Cambridge. A combination of efforts by the National Enterprise Board and support by the Medical Research Council, backed by recommendations of the Spinks Report, provided the impetus for the formation of Celltech, a new company that would receive first right of refusal on biotechnology discoveries emerging from research by the MRC. Thus state intervention was deemed necessary to get the UK biotechnology industry off the ground, again in contrast to the USA which by this stage had nearly 100 dedicated firms.

The siting of Celltech was seen as important by its founders. The initial aim was to locate this company in Cambridge, presumably because of the proximity to the Laboratory of Molecular Biology, and the potential research spillovers that this would bring (see Dodgson 1990). In fact, while there were long-term aims to move there, it remains in Slough in Berkshire, west of London. According to Dodgson (1990), this was because an appropriate building was immediately available, and not to locate in Cambridge was to demonstrate a 'symbolic' independence from the Laboratory of Molecular Biology.

The formation of Celltech acted as a trigger for the development of the UK biotechnology industry. Since its formation, there has been significant entry into a number of sectors most notably in therapeutics and diagnostics, in biological reagents and speciality chemicals, plant biotechnology, veterinary products, and to a lesser extent in food and drink products, energy, and environmental services, as we discuss later on. The numbers of venture capital firms have also grown in the UK over the 1980s and 1990s and several such as Biotechnology Investments Limited and Apax Partners now have specialist expertise in biotechnology.

7.4 FEATURES OF THE EMERGING UK BIOTECHNOLOGY INDUSTRY

Recent industry analysis has shown that the largest DBF sectoral grouping is in the area of supply of reagents and speciality chemicals (Shohet 1994). Their products are mainly consumables used for research and development and a number of firms in this grouping are spin-offs from university departments. Often these firms provide specialist contract manufacturing of low-volume, high value-added biochemicals such as peptides, DNA sequences, monoclonal antibodies, and other molecules related to molecular and cell biology. A second important group of supply firms are the manufacturers of equipment and instrumentation (including software). Typically these companies supply fermentation equipment necessary for scaling up cell culture, as well as chromatography materials and separation machinery used in the purification of valuable proteins. Specialist software firms such as Oxford Molecular plc have developed expertise in molecular modelling and drug design software. A further 20 per cent of the UK industry are in the diagnostics sector, principally in medical diagnostics. This sector has attracted a number of entrants because of the potentially large markets and limited regulatory requirements compared to the development of therapeutic pro-

Box 3. *British Biotechnology plc*

When the Searle family decided to sell its controlling stake in the pharmaceutical firm G. D. Searle in 1985, the company's UK operations, based at High Wycombe near Oxford, were acquired by Monsanto. Within three months Monsanto ceased its R & D activities in the UK, as it already had major investments in biotechnology research in St Louis, Missouri. Using some of their redundancy payments, Brian Richards (head of pre-clinical research) and Keith McCullagh (research director) decided to set up British Biotechnology, and by six months had commitments of £2.5m. to establish a new UK biotechnology venture. They chose a site at Cowley, Oxford—close to their old work place, enabling them to recruit other ex-Searle employees without the costs of major relocation, and also near to the University of Oxford, a major international centre for research in the biological sciences. The site is near to a number of other prominent UK DBFs—notably Xenova, Celltech, Oxford Molecular, and Oxford Glycosciences. In 1992, the firm obtained a listing on NASDAQ and the UK Stock Exchange. By 1995 it employed over 300 staff. Its research concentrates on using molecular biology and synthetic chemistry to develop novel therapeutic agents against cancer, inflammatory, and virus diseases.

Box 4. *Cantab Pharmaceuticals*

When it was formed in 1989, Cantab closely followed the model more typical of many academic spin-outs in the USA. Its founder was the head of immunology at Cambridge University, Professor Alan J. Munro, an academic entrepreneur who also spent time working with the UK venture capital group Abingworth before setting up the company. Cantab is based in the city's science park which houses around 25 biotechnology related firms—the highest concentration of biotechnology firms in the UK. There are also many more there in other high-technology sectors such as computing and electronics. The firm retains its close links with the University of Cambridge in research areas such as immunology, cell biology, and the molecular biology of virus diseases. These links give Cantab exclusive rights to technology arising from joint research and, in return, the university receives royalties from sales. Several Cambridge academics—as well as a number from the USA—sit on the firm's scientific advisory board. The firm floated on NASDAQ in 1992 and on the London Stock Exchange in 1993.

ducts, where extensive costs relating to toxicity testing and clinical trials are incurred. The therapeutics sector in the UK has a number of important emerging companies specializing in a range of chronic disease areas such as inflammation, cancer, AIDS, and diseases associated with ageing. Some examples of these firms include Oxford-based British Biotechnology, which was the first to make a public offering, in 1992. Other firms following in its wake have tended to be in health care areas and important flotations include Celltech (Slough), Cantab Pharmaceuticals (Cambridge), Chiroscience (Cambridge), Oxford Molecular (Oxford), and PPL Therapeutics (Edinburgh).

The agricultural sector is also important. This sector includes seeds, clonal propagation, and animal embryo suppliers, as well as manufacturers of veterinary products such as vaccines and diagnostics. The smallest sectors are environment and food, representing less than 3 per cent of the industry. Figure 7.1 shows the UK breakdown as it was in 1993.

The average size of UK DBFs across all sectors was thirty-eight employees. This is consistent with findings for Europe, as a whole, where the majority of firms employed fewer than fifty people (Lucas et al. 1994).

Box 5. *PPL Therapeutics plc*

Like Cantab (see Box 4), PPL Therapeutics was founded on research carried out in the public sector. In this case it was technology for the genetic engineering of livestock, first developed at the Institute for Animal Physiology and Genetics (now the Roslin Institute) and funded by the Agricultural and Food Research Council (now part of the Biotechnology and Biological Sciences Research Council). The firm is based on the outskirts of Edinburgh, a region that is home to a number of agricultural and genetics research institutes, most affiliated in some way to the University of Edinburgh. The result is an important regional concentration of university departments, spin-off companies, and research institutes. Established in 1987, PPL Therapeutics has developed methods that enable high-value molecules such as human blood clotting factors to be produced in the milk of sheep and other livestock. At its founding, the firm received backing from a number sources such as the UK venture capital firms 3i, Apax, and Grosvenor Venture Managers as well as from French, Japanese, and US backers. It has developed strategic alliances with a number of European companies, e.g. Bayer in Germany and the Denmark-based Novo Nordisk. Like Celltech and British Biotechnology, it has also established US operations—PPL Therapeutics Inc., which spun out of Virginia Polytechnic and State University. Around 70 are employed in the Scottish site and around 20 in the USA.

Recent surveys and reviews of the sectoral profiles of the UK, pan-European, and US industries reveal important and consistent differences in the relative sizes of the various sectors. In the USA, between 28 per cent and 40 per cent of dedicated firms operate in the therapeutics sector (Bullock and Dibner 1995; Lee and Burrill 1995). In Europe as a whole, less than 20 per cent of firms are engaged in therapeutics. The largest number of dedicated firms in the UK operate in auxiliary supply areas such as reagents, equipment, and services. This may have important effects on the nature of clustering in the UK because the dominance of service- and supply-oriented firms may provide a weaker innovative core to the industry, in comparison to the USA, where there is a stronger nucleus of firms based around key leading-edge areas such as therapeutics (see Chapter 6 above). This difference somewhat mirrors the differences between the computer industries in the UK and USA described in Chapters 4 and 6—the UK industry

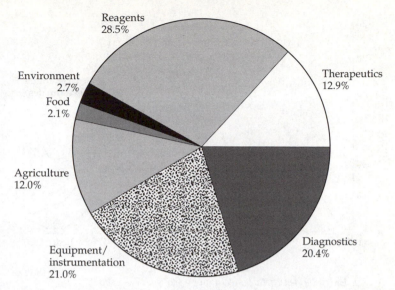

Fig. 7.1 *Sectoral breakdown of dedicated biotechnology firms in the UK (1993 figures)*

being concentrated around services and distribution whereas US clusters have a manufacturing core of hardware firms and microprocessor manufacturers.

7.5 ENTRY PATTERNS

UK data for this study were collected from a number of sources including industry databases, directories, and annual reports. Pan-European data on the biotechnology industry have not been systematically collected and some of the most useful information has come from surveys conducted by the management consultants Ernst & Young. US data sources include annual surveys conducted for Ernst & Young, and the extensive data collected by Dibner. A general difficulty with econometric studies on biotechnology is the poverty of large datasets on employment, location, and financial information. This is partly because, in both the UK and the rest of Europe, government industrial surveys do not identify dedicated biotechnology firms nor is there a separate

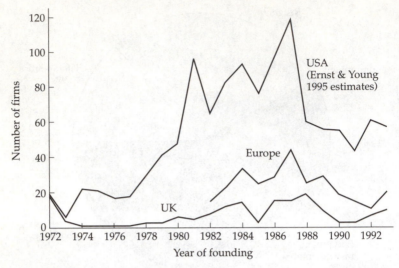

Fig. 7.2 *Entry by dedicated biotechnology firms 1972–1993*
Sources: Shohet (1994); Lee and Burrill (1995); Lucas et al. (1994).

Standard Industrial Classification (SIC) or NACE (European
Standard Industrial Code) for this 'industry'. A further difficulty
is that of comparability owing to the various definitions of
biotechnology adopted across different member states and by
different survey organizations. For all that, we can still present, in
Figure 7.2, a reasonably reliable account of entry, over time, for
the UK, Europe, and the USA.

The pattern of entry in the USA, the UK, and Europe as a whole
has been cyclical with a gradual build-up of new firms occurring
between 1982 and 1984, followed by a decline in 1985 (which
accompanied a major rise in interest rates) and a further resurgence between 1985 and 1987/8. Across Europe and the USA
there was a decline in the numbers of new firms founded in the
period 1988 to 1991 which coincided with the steep worldwide
recession, and some signs in recent years that, post-1992, the
number of new firms is picking up in Europe. According to
Dibner, just under 700 biotechnology companies were in existence
in the USA up to 1991 and 950 in 1994. Ernst & Young's surveys
have tended to take a wider definition of biotechnology: in 1995 it

was estimated that over 1,200 biotech firms had entered since the early 1970s in the USA whereas 386 firms were believed by them to be operating in Europe by 1994. Of the European firms, about 45 per cent are UK-based. In examining these trends it is important to bear in mind that only surviving firms are counted at the time the data are surveyed and that firms entering and subsequently exiting (e.g. through takeovers and liquidation) are missed. At least any bias in the sample population that this creates is in favour of the successful firms, which are our main concern here. There is also evidence that UK and US biotechnology failure rates have been comparatively low (around 5 per cent) compared to other new technology areas such as software, where the rate may be as high as 30 per cent (Garnsey et al. 1994; Barley et al. 1992).

7.6 LINKAGES BETWEEN FIRMS AND THE DEVELOPMENT OF CLUSTERS

As we showed in Chapter 6, the role of key individuals with different skills and from different organizations and the development of intricate networks have been important factors in the formation of clusters in the USA. While the topic has not been so well researched in the UK, the intensity of these collaborations does appear to be distinctly weaker, and to have remained, for the most part, bounded within areas of specialization and academic fields and less confined to local or regional areas than in the USA. Fewer alliances of UK dedicated firms with established UK multinationals can be identified than with US, Japanese, or continental European multinationals. Dodgson (1990) notes, for example, that Celltech—the first significant UK biotechnology company—was not well received by a majority of the large UK pharmaceutical companies, instead developing its early links with major firms from other countries. British pharmaceutical companies did not take up offers to buy stakes in the company or purchase shares when it was floated in the late 1980s. Its first significant contract with a UK multinational occurred in 1988, some eight years after its founding. This is one illustration of the more general observation that local ties are weaker in the UK, and clustering less marked. In one sense, this is surprising, since one would expect transaction costs to be higher in collaborations between firms which are geographically further apart. For their part, large UK firms such as Glaxo, Zeneca, and SmithKline Beecham have developed many alliances with US DBFs—in some cases acquiring them, as with GlaxoWellcome's acquisition of Affymax, and Human Genome Sciences by SmithKline Beecham.

Alliances in the UK therefore do not seem to have been as dependent on geographical proximity as those in the USA, and UK companies have been able to gain complementary assets of knowledge and resources without this close proximity. For the DBF, the advantages are the experience and resources that large firms can provide in areas such as clinical trials, regulatory approval, marketing, and distribution. For the large firms, the advantage is access to innovative techniques and frontier knowledge. Since small UK firms need to gain access to Continental, US, and Japanese markets, this may explain why there are more numerous collaborations with non-UK firms. Another factor important to US clustering is the network of alliances between one DBF and another in particular localities within for example California and Massachusetts (Prevezer and Lomi 1995). These local DBF–DBF alliances are comparatively unusual in UK biotechnology, and this may also account for the lack of intense clustering.

Acquisitions have been surprisingly rare, particularly in the UK. In the USA, there has been a small number of important takeovers: for example, the 60 per cent acquisition of Genetics Institute by American Home Products and Hoffman-La Roche's 60 per cent ownership of Genentech. Effective collaborations may explain the infrequency of acquisitions. The collaborations do the job, so to speak, and the ties to other firms make DBFs less attractive merger targets as many of their key assets are locked up in complex contractual agreements (Powell and Brantley 1992).

7.7 DATA ANALYSIS

What follows is an empirical analysis of some aspects of what has just been described. It is important to recall that the UK dedicated

biotechnology industry is much smaller than its US counterpart—
our dataset contains 186 surviving DBFs up to 1992 (151 of which
entered between 1980 and 1992) which means that a less sophisticated analysis of location behaviour and regional and sectoral
differences than that given earlier in the book for the USA is
possible.

We shall concentrate on the evidence for clusters or regional
agglomerations in the UK and on the significance of existing firms
and the science base as attractors of new biotechnology firms
entering between 1980 and 1992. Locations were drawn from the
addresses of firms at the alphabetical postcode level. Each firm
was assigned to one of twenty-four subregions (comprising one
or more counties). These subregions can be aggregated back to the
eleven standard economic regions of the UK (see CSO 1993). The
classification of regions, subregions, and counties is given in
Table 7.1. We have excluded Northern Ireland, which was designated as region 22, because of lack of data: and we have included
a distinction between Greater London and the rest of south-east
England. Figure 7.3 shows where these regions are located in the
UK in relation to each other.

Areas of concentration can be found in and around London, in
the Cambridge region, in south central England (around Oxford
and Reading) as well as in south Wales, the north-west, and in
Glasgow, Edinburgh, and Dundee regions (see Table 7.2). However the areas differ in size, in the scale of their existing manufacturing industry, and in the size of their working populations. One
way to make comparisons between these regions is to compare
the proportion of firms found in the region relative to the national
average, using the method of revealed comparative advantage
(see Archibugi and Pianta 1992: 49). Using this approach, three
types of quotient have been calculated based on (1) regional areas
(which we have called the r-quotient); (2) entry by manufacturing
firms over the time period 1980–92 (m-quotient); and (3) population employed in the region (p-quotient). The quotients for each
region appear in Table 7.3. To interpret these, the quotient can be
regarded as a unitless ratio of regional to national proportions,
where a value of 1 indicates that a region performs the same as the
national average. Values greater than one indicate a 'strength'
whereas values less than 1 indicate a regional weakness. In examining the quotients major differences between regions are

Table 7.1 *Classification of regions and subregions in the study*

Region (see CSO 1993)	Region abbreviation and subregion composition	Corresponding counties included in subregion	Subregion code
Greater London only	GL (code 1)	Central and Outer London Postcodes	1
South-east England (excl. Greater London)	SE (codes 2, 3, 4, 5)	Berkshire, Oxfordshire, Buckinghamshire, Hertfordshire, Bedfordshire	2
		Hampshire, West Sussex, Surrey	3
		Essex	4
		East Sussex, Kent	5
East Anglia	EA (code 6)	Cambridgeshire, Suffolk, Norfolk	6
East Midlands	EM (code 7)	Derbyshire, Nottinghamshire, Leicestershire, Lincolnshire, Northamptonshire	7
South-west	SW (codes 8, 9, 10)	Gloucestershire, Avon, Wiltshire	8
		Somerset, Dorset, Devon	9
		Cornwall	10

Table 7.1 *Continued*

Region (see CSO 1993)	Region abbreviation and subregion composition	Corresponding counties included in subregion	Subregion code
Wales	WLS (codes 11, 12)	Powys, Dyfed, West Glamorgan, Mid Glamorgan, South Glamorgan, Gwent, Clwyd, Gwynedd	11
			12
West Midlands	WM (codes 13, 14)	Warwickshire, Herefordshire, Worcestershire, West Midlands	13
		Shropshire, Staffordshire	14
North-west England	NW (code 15)	Cheshire, Greater Manchester, Lancashire, Merseyside	15
Yorkshire and Humberside	Y&H (codes 16, 17)	West Yorkshire, South Yorkshire, Humberside	16
		North Yorkshire	17
North England	N (codes 18, 19)	Northumberland, Tyne & Wear, Cleveland, Durham	18
		Cumbria	19
Scotland	SC (codes 20, 21, 23, 24)	Dumfries & Galloway, Strathclyde, Central	20
		Borders, Lothian and Fife	21
		Highlands	23
		Tayside, Grampian and Perth	24

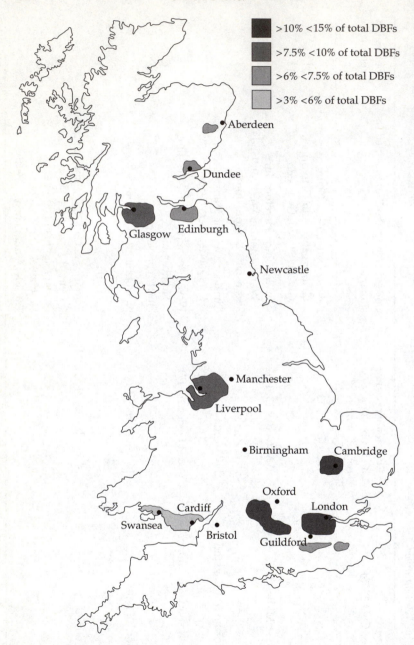

Fig. 7.3 *Location of DBFs in the UK*

Table 7.2 *Ranking of regions by number of firms per region (all sectors combined; total; number of firms is 151)*

Ranking	Regional code	% of firms	Main towns/cities in region	Equivalent regions/counties
1	1	14.5	London	Greater London
2	2	14.5	Oxford, Reading	Berkshire, Buckinghamshire, Hertfordshire, Bedfordshire
3	6	14.0	Cambridge, Norwich	Cambridgeshire, Suffolk, Norfolk
4	3	9.0	London, Guildford	Hampshire, Surrey, West Sussex
5	20	8.0	Glasgow, Falkirk	Strathclyde, Dumfries, Galloway, and Central
6	15	7.5	Manchester, Liverpool	Cheshire, Greater Manchester, Lancashire, Merseyside
7	11	6.0	Swansea, Cardiff	South Wales
=8	5	3.2	London, Crawley	East Sussex, Kent
=8	21	3.2	Edinburgh	Borders, Lothian and Fife
=8	24	3.2	Dundee, Aberdeen	Tayside, Grampian, Perth

Table 7.3 *Quotients showing revealed comparative advantage*

Region	R-quotient	M-quotient	P-quotient	Mean of r, m, p
Greater London	21.70	0.65	1.23	7.85
Rest of SE England	2.23	1.21	1.31	1.59
East Anglia	2.37	4.08	3.45	3.30[a]
East Midlands	0.38	0.41	0.36	0.39[a]
South-west	0.12	0.21	0.10	0.17[a]
West Midlands	0.67	0.41	0.42	0.50[a]
Wales	0.72	2.07	1.44	1.41
North-west	2.43	0.76	0.75	1.31
Yorkshire and Humberside	0.48	0.43	0.39	0.43[a]
North	0.45	1.31	0.52	0.76
Scotland	0.50	2.98	1.83	1.77

[a] The mean differs significantly different from 1.00 (at 5% level).

Sources: Jordan's *Database of UK Firms* (1995); Central Statistical Office, *Regional Trends* (1993); Shohet (1994).

revealed in terms of the relative strength or weakness of the DBF population.

The quotient means show that London, south-east England, East Anglia, Wales, north-west England, and Scotland have more than the average number of new biotechnology firms. Conversely, in the East and West Midlands, the south-west, and Yorkshire and Humberside regions there have been far fewer entries. These results support the figures of new entry into biotechnology shown in Table 7.2. However, some caution is needed in interpreting these quotients, since the number of firms involved is rather small, and distorting effects need to be considered. For example, the low m-quotient in Greater London is partly explained by the fact that there are proportionally more manufacturing firms with headquarters and registered offices in the London region, and hence a large denominator is used in the m-quotient calculation (though not all their manufacturing activities are necessarily located there). The low r-quotient in Scotland is caused by the relatively large area of this region.

Table 7.4 *Rankings in different sectors and regions, based on numbers of firms*

Regions: top ranking (1–5)	Health care	Supply sectors	Agri-food and environmental
1	Greater London (subregion 1)	Berks./Bucks./Herts./Beds. (subregion 2)	Cambs./Suffolk/Norfolk (subregion 6)
2	Berks./Bucks./Herts./Beds. (subregion 2)	Greater London (subregion 1)	Greater London (subregion 1)
3	Cambs./Suffolk/Norfolk (subregion 6)	Hants/W. Sussex/Surrey (subregion 3)	South Wales (subregion 11)
4	Cheshire/Greater Manchester/Lancs. (subregion 15)	Cambs./Suffolk/Norfolk (subregion 6)	Cheshire/Greater Manchester/Lancs. (subregion 15)
5	Strathclyde/Dumfries & Galloway/Central (subregion 20)	Strathclyde/Dumfries & Galloway/Central (subregion 20)	Berks./Bucks./Herts./Beds. (subregion 2)

Using our dataset which spans the period 1980–92, we have found strong evidence for regional differences in terms of entry of new firms. Can we identify differences between regions in terms of sectoral entry? To address this question, the data have been divided into three broad sectors: health (which comprises the original subcategories of therapeutics and diagnostics); supply (which comprises equipment and reagents firms), and a third category combining agriculture, food, and environment.

Analysis of variance reveals statistically significant differences (at the 5 per cent level) both between regions and between sectors in the numbers of firms. In support of these findings, we observe that a number of start-up health care firms have associations with London teaching hospitals where researchers and candidates for clinical trials are available, whereas the East Anglia region is traditionally strong in agriculture and seed production and is an area where a number of plant biotechnology firms have located. Outer London, where rents are lower but access to the capital is good, appears to attract supplier firms, including those making research reagents, instrumentation, and equipment. The triangular region connecting Cambridge with London and Oxford contains nearly 50 per cent of the UK's DBFs. This can be considered as representing a key agglomeration. The fact that this also contains a significant level of academic activity in the biological and related sciences is a point we explore later in this chapter.

7.8 ATTRACTORS

In this section we consider some of the attracting forces that draw new firms into particular localities. We examine two factors—the presence of existing employment in the biotechnology sector (in DBFs and large established firms), and the presence of a university research base. The average entry model employed in Chapter 3 relates the mean annual number of firms entering the industry to the existing level of employment in the region, employment being a direct measure of the strength of the attracting force. Table 7.5 gives the results of the regression of mean entry by DBFs on existing bioscience industry employment in the region (transformed to the natural log value).

Table 7.5 *Regression of mean entry per year in each sector and in each of eleven regions on natural log total biotechnology employment (DBFs and multinationals) in the region*

Sector	Healthcare	Supply	Agriculture, food, and environmental
In employment	0.37 (0.035)[a]	0.51 (0.047)[a]	0.12 (0.020)[a]
R^2	0.65	0.71	0.41

[a] The coefficient is significant at 5% level.

Note: Numbers in brackets are the standard errors.

The simple OLS regressions support the hypothesis that existing employment in a region (measured as both new and existing large bioscience company employment) attracts new entry in all three sectors. The sectoral differences also suggest that entrants are attracted to strengths in their own sector—with supply areas being strongest and agriculture weakest. Again, we need to be cautious about these results, for, compared with the USA, the average distance between regions is small. Being fixed in a location will hardly inhibit a firm from making alliances outside it, either within the UK or more globally. Moreover the quality of the local infrastructure, local financial incentives, and regional differences in ease of access to venture capital have not been taken into account.

There are also close links between private sector bioscience research and the university and public sector research base (Shohet and Prevezer 1996). Does it follow that, in the UK, new firms tend to congregate around an existing science base? The results of a national census of research activity (the Research Assessment Exercise) published in 1992 (UFC 1992) were analysed, which provided detailed information on research fields, institutions, and the number of full-time researchers active in each organization. The fields were divided into bioscience areas (excluding hospital-related studies such as nursing), science and engineering areas except bioscience, and non-science areas (e.g. arts, humanities, and management). Table 7.6 indicates that there is a close correlation between the total number of academic researchers in a region and the average entry per year of DBFs into

Table 7.6 *OLS regression of mean entry per year in biotechnology and in each of twenty-two regions on total academic research employment*

Variable	Coefficient	R^2
In total university research employment	0.603 (0.113)[a]	0.600

[a] The coefficient is significant at 5% level.

Note: Numbers in brackets are the standard errors.

Table 7.7 *Results of a multiple regression of mean entry per year in each of twenty-two regions in biotechnology on three components of university employment*

Variable	Coefficients	R^2
In bioscience research population	−0.046 (0.215)	0.605
In science (non-bioscience) population	0.260 (0.256)	
In non-science research population	0.456 (0.271)	

Note: Numbers in brackets are the standard errors.

the region. However, when the total academic population is broken down into bioscience, non-bioscience, and non-science groups, the multivariate regression analysis in Table 7.7 shows no specific 'attraction' effect of the bioscience or science variables alone.

Since the presence of a large university research population is likely to be found where there is a large local population, it might be that the entry numbers simply depend on the size of the total local population, rather than that they are attracted specifically to the bioscience base. One way to settle this is to normalize the data for the size of the population and the number of existing manufacturing firms. The results of a multivariate regression using normalized data are given in Table 7.8. Although none of the coefficients is significant for each independent variable, the coefficients are positive and the correlation is high (0.63), suggesting that, after normalizing for the numbers of local firms and size of the population, biotechnology entry is correlated with the presence of university research activity, though the attraction is not

Table 7.8 *Multivariate regression of ln biotechnology entrants as a proportion of the manufacturing base in each region on ln of academic research population as proportion of total regional workforce*

Variable	Coefficients	R^2
ln bioscience research population as proportion of regional employment	0.002 (0.507)	0.634
ln science (non-bioscience) population as proportion of regional employment	0.638 (0.529)	
ln non-science research population as proportion of regional employment	0.822 (0.488)	

Note: Numbers in brackets are the standard errors.

specifically associated with the bioscience element of this research activity.

This finding is in contrast to evidence in the US biotechnology industry in Chapter 6, where the science base and biotechnology firms are more often found together, at least in some sectors. Given the much smaller scale and shorter average distances between population centres, the UK findings are not entirely surprising. Roughly the same number of biotechnology firms as in the UK can be found in the San Francisco Bay area of California; as we pointed out, half of all the UK's firms are in the triangle that connects Oxford with Cambridge and London. While these three areas have strong bioscience research universities and institutes with a world-class reputation, there are other areas in the UK where relatively few biotechnology start-ups are to be found, despite highly rated bioscience university departments with strong collaborative links with industry—these include the Bristol area (in the south-west region), Birmingham (West Midlands region), and around Nottingham and Leicester (East Midlands).

Oakey et al. (1990: 68) point to the fact that, with high value per unit weight products, distribution costs are comparatively low and location away from traditional centres of production is feasible. Oakey suggests that, rather than seek the presence of a science base, founders of biotechnology firms in south-east England have tended to set up within a 30-mile radius of their previous place of work. According to Dodgson (1990) the siting of Celltech's offices in Slough was partly influenced by the proximity of potential employees from G. D. Searle's R & D laboratories in High Wycombe, close by. The founders of British Bio-technology (also ex-G. D. Searle employees) chose Oxford in which to set up the company, partly because of its closeness to their previous work location, as well as the fact that the company also has a number of close links with scientists at the University of Oxford (see Box 3). In contrast the health care firm Smith and Nephew relocated its research and development laboratories from Essex (a region with low biotechnology start-up and science base scores) to a science park site close to York University. Attraction factors were reported to include York University's highly rated research which was not exploited by other science-based companies, the city's international image, and the proximity of the firm's manufacturing base in Hull (Cookson 1993).

Universities across the UK have made major attempts to attract high-technology businesses by establishing science parks on or close to their campuses. The oldest and best known is Cambridge Science Park established in the early 1970s (see Segal and Quince 1985). Monck et al. (1988) estimated in one major study that 30 out of 36 UK science parks were associated with higher education institutions (universities and the former polytechnics). According to Allen (1995) there were 46 science parks in existence in the UK in 1995, and although there are significant differences in emphasis between parks, they generally meet three criteria as follows: (1) property-based initiatives for the establishment and growth of technology-based enterprise; (2) formal and operational links to at least one centre of technical expertise (usually universities and research institutes; (3) provision or access to some level of man-agement support and technology transfer assistance. Given the high proportion of DBFs located in science parks (particularly outside Greater London), it seems likely that this 'bundle' of factors is a more important attractor to entrants than the knowl-edge spillovers of a local science base alone. This also goes some way to explaining why we find a stronger association between DBFs and the general university research base than to the bio-science base in particular.

7.9 CONCLUDING COMMENTS

The empirical analysis has suggested that new start-ups are attracted by the existing base of employment in related sectors, but there is less evidence of the intense networks and linkages in highly localized areas which typify clusters in the USA. UK policies have focused on supply-side issues at a national rather than regional level—ensuring that academic centres of excellence in biotechnology receive adequate funding and ensuring support across a range of sectors, e.g. in food and chemicals as well as health. More recently the coupling of the science and technology base to industrial user needs has been emphasized through the Foresight process. Regional initiatives have been limited, but include the formation of development agencies for Scotland and Wales (there is no equivalent for England), which have devoted some resources to biotechnology, such as the Biotechnology Group of Scottish Enterprise established in 1992. However, to date, most regional technology activities have concentrated on attracting inward manufacturing investment. In the USA, state-level activities to resource biotechnology, e.g. in Maryland and North Carolina, have deliberately aimed to create regional strengths in this field, an approach quite different from that of the UK, and more akin to other parts of Europe such as France and Germany, which have stronger regional technology policies.

The science park concept which aimed to encourage high-technology firms to locate near to universities and to allow university spin-offs to locate close by, has had mixed success (Macdonald 1987), although the empirical analysis in this chapter suggests that many new biotechnology firms have located close to universities and into science parks. The analysis also suggests that a strong bioscience research base alone is not sufficient to influence the location of new entrants and that synergies with the science base and with other firms in the vicinity have yet to lead to clusters on the same scale of the USA.

It would be inappropriate to attempt to transplant policies that have worked in the USA into the UK without a careful consideration of the different structural conditions—not least differences in local governance structures, geographical scales and travelling times, industry structure, labour mobility, education and training systems, and attitudes towards entrepreneurship. The availability of early stage finance has clearly also been an important factor for US growth, and barriers are now being lifted in the UK. The public capital markets such as the London Stock Exchange, NASDAQ in the USA, and the recently initiated Alternative Investment Market (AIM) in the UK provide important sources of capital for firms and exit routes for investors. In 1996, around twenty-five UK biotechnology firms were listed, representing the bulk of publicly quoted biotechnology firms in Europe. However, linkages between industry, scientists, and finance providers remain weaker than in the USA and policies which improve networks that can create or strengthen these channels are therefore attractive.

8

Comparison and Interaction between Computing and Biotechnology

MARTHA PREVEZER

INTRODUCTION

This chapter is divided into two parts. The first compares the processes of clustering in the two industries—computing and biotechnology—and traces differences back to the nature of the technologies. The second part looks at the interaction between the technologies, and specifically the effect computing has had on biotechnology and the implications for clustering.

PART 1 A COMPARISON OF CLUSTERING IN COMPUTING AND BIOTECHNOLOGY

Chapters 4 and 5, 6 and 7 have analysed clustering in computing and biotechnology in both the USA and the UK. We have looked at the process through the entry of firms into clusters and at the effect on the growth of incumbent firms of being situated in clusters, and we have found different factors have affected entry and growth. We have compared these processes of entry and growth in the US and UK computing industries, and, less formally, in the US and UK biotechnology industries. We have found different structures of the industries in the two countries and hence different entry patterns and growth rates in the two countries. It is clear that some degree of concentration of the industries in specific locations characterizes both industries in both countries. In computing, the dynamics of clustering on entry and growth is similar, in important respects, in the two countries, despite the different structures of the industry and patterns of sector attraction. We traced some of these differences back to the diverse histories of the industry in the two countries and in particular the later development of the industry in the UK, in large part in response to developments in the USA.

The first part of the present chapter focuses on differences between the two industries in the degree of clustering and specialization between US states.[1] We summarize and compare the results of our entry and growth models and relate these results to the structural differences between the two industries. We go on to look at the different role of the incumbent large companies in the origins of the two industries and at how important location within a cluster was to incumbent companies in the two industries. We relate the different roles of incumbents in the two industries to the degree to which entrants might have been competence enhancing or destroying to established companies in the two industries.

We then examine the role of the science base and why it has been more important in the case of biotechnology. We move on to look at the different types of collaboration in the two industries, distinguishing the scientific-industrial collaborations in biotechnology from the inter-industry collaborations in computing. Related to this theme we examine the role of alliances in the two industries, using a study by Hagedoorn and Schakenraad which has compared the numbers, motivation, and organizational forms of alliances in information technology and biotechnology. From this we look at information on the different structure of networks between the two industries and, related to this, the role of network externalities, with much greater interconnectedness in networks in IT than in biotechnology. We contrast the type of compatibility that is a feature of the different technologies in IT with the creation of product niches and local monopolies in biotechnology and the product races that ensue to win these local monopolies.

Finally we look at the different role of users in the two industries—who the users are, how confined they are to industry or how pervasive throughout the economy, and what their role is in innovation. This in turn has been important in the degree to which the existing structure of industry has been transformed in

---

[1] This discussion draws on an earlier paper of ours, Swann and Prevezer (1996).

computing, in contrast to the stability of the existing structure and importance of sunk costs in biotechnology.

8.1 THE DEGREE OF CONCENTRATION AND CLUSTERING IN COMPUTING AND BIOTECHNOLOGY COMPARED

The degree of geographical concentration in the computing industry in 1988 and in the biotechnology industry in 1991 are compared in the pie-charts in Figure 8.1. These show that the computing industry was more densely clustered with a larger proportion of companies concentrated in fewer states. Over half of the computer companies were in three US states in 1988—California, Massachusetts, and New York—and these three states were the most prominent for all sectors of the industry. In the biotechnology industry, there was substantial clustering, as was shown in Chapter 6, but to a somewhat lesser degree than in computing, with the top three states accounting for under 40 per cent of companies. In both industries, California was the state with the greatest concentration of companies—over 35 per cent of companies in computing and over 23 per cent of companies in biotechnology. But in biotechnology a larger number of states attracted sizeable numbers of companies compared to computing, so the distribution of companies between states has been slightly more even (see Figure 8.1).

Comparing the distribution between sectors: in computing all sectors were concentrated in the same states; in biotechnology this was less true. Health care and equipment sectors were concentrated in California, Massachusetts, New Jersey, and Maryland. But in sectors developing more recently such as agriculture, chemicals, and waste, although California still had the most activity, some other states also attracted populations of companies. This suggests greater diffusion and specialization between states in biotechnology than in computing.

Looking at existing SIC classifications of industry and their innovativeness, Feldman found different specializations between different states in their innovativeness scores. These scores were based on the 1982 census and used the Small Business Administration census of innovation citations from scientific and trade journals. By this measure of innovations in different industries

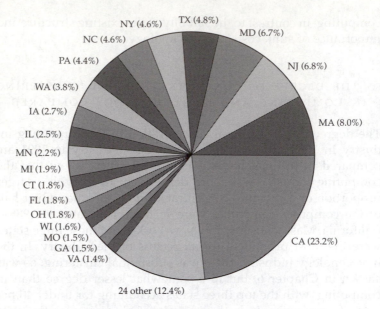

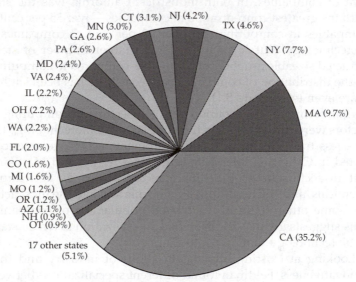

Fig. 8.1 *(a) Distribution of biotechnology companies by US state, 1991. (b) Distribution of computer companies by US state, 1988*

per 100,000 manufacturing workers, California and Massachusetts were most innovative in computers (SIC 357), in measuring
and controlling instruments (SIC 382), and in electrical components (SIC 367). New Jersey and New York had the highest scores
in innovativeness in drugs (SIC 283) and medical instruments
(SIC 384). Also relevant to our industries, Pennsylvania and New
Jersey were found to be most innovative in general industrial
machinery and equipment (SIC 356), and California and New
York in communication equipment (SIC 366) (Feldman 1994: 38).
Roughly speaking, high scores in innovativeness in computers,
components, measuring and controlling instruments, and communication equipment are relevant to the computing industry;
and drugs, medical instruments, some measuring and controlling
instruments, and some general machinery and equipment to the
biotechnology industry. It should be borne in mind that the
census of 1982 would not capture much of the then nascent
biotechnology industry. However, the strength in pharmaceuticals in New Jersey and New York has continued to be relevant to
that industry, and the importance of the 'older' industrial states
(New Jersey, New York, Pennsylvania) in equipment manufacture of various sorts also comes out alongside the strength of the
'newer' industrial states of California and Massachusetts in newer
forms of instruments and equipment.

Turning to the division in our populations of computing and
biotechnology industries, described more fully in Chapters 4 and
6, what is striking is the preponderance of smaller firms in the
software and peripherals sectors of computing—over 50 per cent
of all the firms. Average employment per firm in California and
Massachusetts in software was about 700 employees, and in peripherals firms was under 1,700. This contrasts with the components sector which was dominated by large companies with
average employment in California and Massachusetts of 17,000
per firm. Within biotechnology, there was more of a mixture of
very small and very large companies in biotechnology in most
sectors. In biotechnology 75 per cent of firms were in therapeutics,
diagnostics, and equipment sectors. The average number of employees per firm in therapeutics was over 2,000 employees, mask-
ing, on the one hand, average employment in small dedicated
biotechnology firms in therapeutics of only 130 employees, and
on the other hand 21,000 employees per firm in the large multina-

tionals assigned to this sector of the industry. It should be noted, however, that our sample for the computing industry by no means captures the whole of employment in the industry, seriously underestimating the number of firms and employment there. Our biotechnology sample captures a much higher proportion of the total population of firms.

8.2 STRUCTURAL DIFFERENCES BETWEEN THE TWO INDUSTRIES

The computing and biotechnology industries are structured in different ways and this affects the interdependencies between their different sectors. The computing industry is divided most naturally into sectors specializing in different technologies: thus there are components, hardware, software, peripherals, systems sectors, and so on. This is a crude classification and there are many differences within sectors; but broadly, each sector has a distinct set of technologies with companies specializing in that sector. These technologies combine to produce the end-product. For example, both hardware and software companies are involved in creating the final product for the consumer. These interdependencies create positive feedback between the sectors: the creation of companies in one sector leads to the need for the creation of companies in another sector. End-markets in computing are not confined to one sector of industry but have been created across the whole economy.

The biotechnology industry by contrast has had very similar technologies in use between its different sectors. It divides most naturally into sectors according to application to a particular industry. For example therapeutics and diagnostics companies make products for the pharmaceutical industry. Agricultural and chemical firms are so defined because they make applications for those industries. Food or new enzymes companies make products and applications for the food industry. Most companies are using similar technologies of recombinant DNA, hybridoma technology, fermentation, etc., especially in the first generation of the industry. There are some exceptions to this classification. Some diagnostics firms are making applications not only for the health care sectors but for the water and food industries. Research tools and equipment companies create applications for the whole range of industrial sectors and research establishments. And many environmental applications are quite novel, so that a new sector has been created outside the existing industrial structure. But the distinction broadly holds that biotechnology firms depend on existing companies in their own sector of application for their market and for the joint development of their products. Links have tended to run vertically downstream to user industries for each sector rather than between sectors, with little technological interdependence between sectors. There has been more rapid development in sectors where those vertical links with user industries have been strong. Diffusion of technologies has been slower in sectors with weaker links. Due to the lack of technological interdependence between sectors, feedback between sectors has been weaker.

8.3 SUMMARY OF RESULTS OF MODELS FOR ENTRY AND GROWTH INTO COMPUTING AND BIOTECHNOLOGY AND INTERPRETATION

The models that help us to understand what influences the entry of new firms into clusters in the two industries, and the help to the growth of incumbent firms of being part of a cluster, have been described in some detail in earlier chapters. We found that the strongest effects on entry into computing clusters were cross-sectoral attractors, with 'hard' sectors—components, hardware, and systems sectors—attracting 'soft' sectors in the USA. In the UK, strength in components and hardware also encouraged entry into several sectors. However, the presence of peripherals and services sectors also encouraged entry into other soft sectors— services, software, and systems—which were not particularly attracted by strength at a cluster in hardware and components. In biotechnology the strongest attractor to entry proved to be the strength of the science base at a cluster. There was some cross-sectoral attraction, with employment in therapeutics attracting equipment and agricultural companies and *vice versa*, and therapeutics attracting diagnostic companies. However, these cross-sectoral effects were confined to that group of sectors and positive feedback did not pervade the whole industry in the way that it did in computing. There was much less entry into the other group of sectors in biotechnology: chemicals, food, waste, and energy.

The effects of a cluster on growth of established companies appear to be very much the same in the two industries. In both, it was employment within the company's own sector and cluster which promoted the growth of the company, whereas the strength of employment in other sectors at that cluster tended to reduce company growth. In biotechnology the strength of the science base at a cluster if anything discouraged growth. However, there were some differences between the two industries. In particular growth rates in computing—11 per cent per annum overall—were almost twice as high as in biotechnology. In computing, the effect of own sector strength was particularly pronounced for the 'hard' sectors—components, hardware, and systems. In biotechnology growth rates were pretty much the same across sectors—around 6 per cent per annum.

In comparing the two industries in the USA, there are several distinctions to be drawn. The links between sectors which encourage entry into computing are significantly stronger than in biotechnology. These strong links in computing in the USA have been between the 'hard' sectors such as components, systems, and hardware, and the 'soft' sectors such as software, peripherals, and distribution. This may be attributable to the technological interdependence discussed above. In biotechnology there is no equivalent division into 'hard' and 'soft' sectors, as sectors are not divided along such technological lines. As sectors are divided according to industrial application, as discussed above, these technological interdependencies do not exist. Moreover the intersectoral links in computing are more pervasive between most sectors, whereas in biotechnology they exist only between a group of sectors mainly in health care and equipment. Development in these sectors has not affected entry into the other group of sectors such as chemicals and food.

The two industries also differed in the extent to which the negative effects of clustering were present. We attribute the negative effects to congestion and other saturation costs that arise when clusters become overcrowded. These negative effects were much stronger in computing than in biotechnology. This may be due largely to the significantly greater age of the computing industry. It is also likely to relate to the greater density of clusters in computing than biotechnology, as we saw in Figure 8.1.

We have also noted differences between the two industries in the extent to which clustering effects have been driven by demand-side, rather than by supply-side, motivations to cluster. We conjecture that the demand effects on clustering may have been stronger in biotechnology, with entry driven by the creation of new markets in the research base and in research-oriented companies such as those in the therapeutics sector; and also new markets in related end-users in the health care sector, such as hospitals using new diagnostic and instrument kits. Supply-side links, where firms cluster to absorb tacit knowledge from the science base, have also been important, but possibly to a lesser extent than in computing. There, the supply-side motivation for firms to cluster, to absorb knowledge spillovers, has been thought to be the chief cause of links between companies in different sectors and a main dynamic for clustering, as technological links and compatibility are crucial in computing. Clustering to take advantage of new end-markets has been less pronounced in computing, as those end-markets themselves have been diffused throughout the industrial, financial, and domestic economy, and not concentrated at particular locations.

8.4 DIFFERING ROLE OF INCUMBENTS IN THE TWO INDUSTRIES AND DIFFERENCES BETWEEN ENTRANTS AND INCUMBENTS IN ABSORPTION OF SPILLOVERS

There are some similarities between the two industries in the way that entrants and incumbents respond (differently) to various stimuli: entrants in both industries are attracted by opportunities created, or spillovers occurring, from other sectors in their industry and, in the case of biotechnology, by research spillovers from the science base. They are not attracted by strength in their own sectors. Incumbents on the other hand, in both industries, are stimulated more by strength within a cluster in their own sector, perhaps because they are effective at absorbing spillovers that arise in their own sector. They do not absorb spillovers arising either from other sectors or from the science base. This may be a result of the differences described in Chapter 6 between entrants and incumbents generally: entrants being smaller and more 'extrovert' companies, more flexible than the larger established incumbents, with fewer routines and less hierarchical organizational structures. Entry is often driven by opportunities created through synergies with other sectors or with the science base that do not fit within the existing value chain of the incumbent. Incumbent firms, on the other hand, being larger and more insular or 'introvert', look inside their own company for many of the auxiliary skills of financing and management that are required by smaller entrant firms outside their companies. Incumbents are efficient at seeking out opportunities within their own sectors, which tie in with the existing value chain. They are not so efficient at absorbing spillovers outside that sphere, thus leaving opportunities for new entrants.

There are, however, differences between the two industries in the roles that entrants and incumbents play. In particular, the role of incumbent companies was different in the origins of the two industries, and these differences have persisted. In computing, firms such as IBM, Fairchild, General Electric, Texas Instruments, and Lockheed established R & D facilities in California and were highly influential in spawning spin-off companies that together with the older companies formed the backbone of the early cluster. The extent of information exchange between former employees of Fairchild—the 'Fairchildren' as they were called—and the parent company is thought to have been significant in the way that the cluster forged ahead in creating and establishing new technologies. Information flowed, both due to high job mobility within the area between the incumbents and new entrants, and also due to informal technical information sharing by, for instance, engineers from different firms. The role that incumbents played in the biotechnology industry was somewhat different, more as sponsors and patrons of the new companies than as rivals or competing directly within the same market. For instance Eli Lilly sponsored the insulin conference in 1976 to stimulate research into alternative methods of producing insulin; it backed the creation of Genentech with finance and through collaboration. Kabi Vitrum played a similar role in the early days of the industry, sponsoring Genentech's research into human growth hormone. In the chemicals area Monsanto occupied a similar leading role in the early 1980s. None of these established companies needed to locate in the centre of the clusters that were forming on the east or west coasts in order to create these links with the entrants. This contrasts with the computing companies where the location of R & D facilities in the cluster was felt to be necessary to the larger established companies for them to absorb the emerging technologies, and in turn played a role in diffusing existing skills throughout the area.

This type of involvement reflects the distinct interest that these established companies had in requiring these new companies to create new techniques and technologies which would assist the established companies in their own research areas. In this way the entrants in biotechnology could be said to be competence enhancing for the incumbents to a greater degree than in computing, where entrants were more directly challenging or competence destroying. In biotechnology the relationship between entrants and incumbents was more complementary, with entrants specializing in research and having closer links with the science base, and requiring the complementary assets downstream in production, marketing, and distribution from the incumbent companies in order to commercialize products. We shall return to this relationship in discussing the differences in the types of alliances that formed within the two industries.

8.5 ROLE OF THE SCIENCE BASE

The role of the science base has been significantly more important to the biotechnology industry than to the computing industry in a number of ways, and helps to explain why clusters have formed around the science base in the one industry and not in the other. As described in Chapter 6, the roles of the science base have been varied in biotechnology and have continued to be important beyond the early days of the industry. The science base has been a continuing source of new technologies, creating incentives for all companies in biotechnology to establish firm links with the science base to keep abreast of, and monitor, latest developments in new technologies that might be of interest to them. The science base has also provided a distinct role in biotechnology in providing founders of new companies, especially in the early days of the industry, with a high proportion of new companies founded by scientists from within the science base eager to commercialize technologies originating within the science base. The role of key 'star' scientists in influencing the location of the founding of new enterprises has been well established (see Chapter 6), and the effect of the involvement of leading scientists in new firms on those firms' reputations and public valuations has also been established (Stephan 1994). Scientists have continued to be used as scientific advisers in the new firms, to maintain links with the science base. This in part reflects the nature of the new biotechnologies, which have required the specialisms of different parts of the science base—molecular or medical specialist knowledge for example—alongside those skills developed within industry.

Collaboration through this variety of linkages between the science base and industry has been less apparent in computing. There, beyond the initial direct involvement of the science base in the origins of the industry, collaboration has been more inter-industrial between different parts of the industry than between the industry and the science base. This is reflected to some extent in the ranking that Feldman found in the importance of industrial R & D, the importance of related industries, and the importance of university R & D to innovation in the computer industry (SIC 357). She found that some of the leading states within our clusters—California, Massachusetts, and New Jersey—ranked most highly in terms of numbers of innovations yielded per unit of innovative input of industrial R & D and inputs from related industries. However, the states that ranked most highly for use of university R & D were Connecticut, Minnesota, and New Jersey (Feldman 1994: 41). California ranked fifth and Massachusetts eighth in terms of innovations yielded per unit of input from university R & D. California and Massachusetts, the leading states in the formation of computer clusters, relied on information from industrial R & D and from related industries for innovation. They did not use university research in the integral way that occurred in biotechnology.

8.6 ROLE OF ALLIANCES

Inter-firm collaboration in the form of alliances between firms increased markedly in these high-technology industries, in particular during the 1980s (Hagedoorn and Schakenraad 1990). We use the study done by Hagedoorn and Schakenraad of these inter-firm agreements in the fields of information technology and biotechnology to illustrate some of the different characteristics of such inter-firm alliances between the two industries. There were differences in the size of population of alliances between the industries, with over 2,700 cases of inter-firm agreements in information technology collected in their MERIT-CATI databank compared with 1,200 agreements in biotechnology. There was substantial growth in the numbers of agreements in both industries during the 1980s, with a major boost in numbers in the second half of the decade.

Turning now to the organizational modes of these alliances, they have distinguished between six forms of agreement: joint R & D arrangements; joint ventures entailing the setting up of a separate joint company; technological exchange agreements encompassing technology sharing; cross-licensing or mutual second sourcing; one-directional technological flows through licensing; direct investment by one party into the other; and a variety of customer–supplier agreements, mediated by contracts between the two firms concerned. In both industries joint R & D arrangements were the commonest form, about 30 per cent of agreements being of this type in both IT and biotechnology. However, there were differences between the industries in preferences for other forms of agreement, with more mutual technological exchange agreements, one-directional technology flows and more joint ventures in IT than in biotechnology, and more direct investment and contractual customer–supplier relationships in biotechnology. This might be thought to reflect the greater prevalence of more equal relationships between partners in IT, with more contractual and unequal relationships between firms of different sizes in biotechnology. Hagedoorn and Schakenraad point to the importance of cooperative agreements between the small and large companies in biotechnology, with large established companies engaging in a substantial share of cooperative agreements with small high-technology companies (Hagedoorn and Schakenraad 1990: 7).

They also looked specifically at the motivation behind these alliances and several differences are apparent between the industries. Basic research, the monitoring of technological opportunities and entry, together with technological complementarities and reduced innovation lead times through these complementary competences, appeared to be more important in biotechnology, especially as they led to joint ventures and direct investment agreements. Lack of finance was also mentioned more frequently as a motive in biotechnology. In IT, on the other hand, market power and the influencing of market structure featured more prominently as a motivating force, something largely beyond the control of biotechnology companies. The horizontal matching of core activities was much more prominent as a motive for direct investment agreements in IT industries. Control over partners and tighter customer–supplier relations were also more important as a motive for direct investment in IT than in biotechnology; this may reflect greater direct competition and need to control competition in IT than biotechnology. In terms of what Hagedoorn and Schakenraad term strategic positioning within the two industries, biotechnology agreements seemed to display greater longer-term positioning, with less emphasis on economizing on costs than IT agreements, where costs were given a greater priority in strategy.

So although both collaboration and alliances have been extremely important in each industry, and a striking feature of the industrial landscape in these high-technology areas, there have been significant differences in the types of collaboration and in the forms and motivation behind these alliances in the two industries. These differences may be traced back in part to the different structures of the industries, with vertical relationships between entrants and incumbents being more important in biotechnology, and 'horizontal' relationships involving mutual technology exchange in computing. There is a corresponding geographical dimension to this, although this has not been specifically measured when comparing the two: alliances between entrants and incumbents in biotechnology span geographical distances quite easily, and are more contractual and formal types of relationship, in which technology transfer can be organized across geographical boundaries. In computing, on the other hand, one suspects that the more mutual technology exchange agreements between more equally sized partners may have required them to be closer together.

8.7 STRUCTURE OF NETWORKS

Another dimension of the relationships between firms, which also has a geographical aspect to it, is the degree to which they are bound into networks with each other. Network externalities assume a much more important role in computing than in biotechnology, with compatibility between different technologies within the industry being a key characteristic of computing and again traceable to the different structures of the two industries. In contrast, the biotechnology industry has been characterized by the creation of product niches, distinct from each other. Competition has frequently taken the form of races between teams to make specific products such as the interferons, tPA, or interleukins, by different methods, with no question of compatibility between firms. The winners of these races find themselves with a local monopoly of the product, established, and fiercely defended, through patenting.

The importance of tight technological networks in computing is reflected in the much greater intensity of relations in computing than in biotechnology, as measured by the density of networks (Hagedoorn and Schakenraad 1990, 1992). Measured on a multi-dimensional scale, the intensity of cooperative relationships in alliances is much greater in IT than in biotechnology, and shows many more multiple cooperative relationships between two firms and between distinct groups of firms. In biotechnology, alliances are represented in much sparser networks and more diffused interconnections. Hagedoorn and Schakenraad found distinct geographical groups of firms through intra-Japanese, intra-US, and intra-European alliances. However, those geographical areas are not equivalent to the much tighter clusters within the individual states of the USA.

In a later study of networks in information technologies, they used a measure of 'degree centrality', which captures the total number of relations enjoyed by each firm in any network, and found an intensity of network relations of 40 per cent in the late 1980s. This was considerably higher than the 11 per cent and 17 per cent that has been found for networks of alliances in biotechnology in California and Massachusetts (Prevezer and Lomi 1995).

Kogut et al. (1995), looking at semiconductors specifically, distinguished between the degree centrality (or network density) and the 'betweenness centrality', measuring the dominance of particular firms in the pathways of relationships between other firms, as these affect the entry of new firms. They found that network density alone did not stimulate entry, whereas the existence of a centralized network, dominated by a few leading firms, did encourage new start-ups into this sector. They interpreted this as being due, at least in part, to the importance to the entry of new firms, in particular, dominant, standard-setting firms, in the semiconductor market. This again brings out the importance of compatibility and standards in computing, which do not operate in an equivalent way in biotechnology, with implications for the importance and the structure of networks in those industries. Technological compatibility, being more important in computing, creates denser networks involving leading firms setting technical standards; such tendencies reinforce the importance of geographical proximity and strengthen the technical advantages of being located in a cluster.

8.8 ROLE OF USERS

Another difference between computing and biotechnology, referred to above in the discussion of the different structures of the two industries, is the role and pervasiveness of users in the two industries. In computing, end-users have pervaded the whole of the economy—throughout the industrial, domestic, and financial sectors and into almost every walk of life. In biotechnology, into the 1990s, users have chiefly been established companies within existing sectors of industry. Dedicated biotechnology companies alone have been unable to commercialize their technologies into products which they can sell directly to final consumers.

There have been, and are increasingly, exceptions to this in biotechnology, as the industry matures. Instruments and diagnostic kits have been sold to research establishments and to end-users such as hospitals and doctors, as well as to industrial users. In addition, the selling of products to a variety of industrial sectors is increasing, with applications of diagnostic testing, for instance, spreading out of purely health care areas into water, food, fingerprinting, and other security and identification applications. Environmental applications will also probably be sold to a greater variety of users than polluting industrial users for remediation purposes.

In computing, the role of the end-user in innovation, initiating the dynamic for the development of new computers and applications, has been correspondingly much more widespread in this industry than in biotechnology. The role of the user in stimulating innovation in scientific instruments has been found to be important (Hippel 1988). This is one key area in the biotechnology industry where users, particularly in research establishments, have been involved in stimulating the development and commercialization of new instruments to meet new research needs. It is not therefore that the role of end-users in biotechnology has been insignificant: it has been more confined to specific sectors of the industry.

This brings us to our final distinction between the two industries: the role of the market in the evolution of the two industries. The computing industry, once established, is thought to be a leading example of forceful 'organic' market-led growth. Growth has taken place through the creation of capabilities by and within networks of specialized firms whose main nexus of coordination has been the market, rather than in large organizations enjoying internal economies of scale and scope (Langlois 1992; Baptista and Swann 1996). The size, diversity, rapid development, and unknown character of the market for microcomputers has meant that no single organization could develop internally all the technological capabilities required (Langlois 1992).

Chapter 6 listed the variety and profusion of state policies and initiatives in biotechnology which have been designed to influence the location and evolution of the industry. The chapter described the success of such initiatives in causing clusters to migrate to other states within the USA, away from the original centres of the industry. In computing, on the other hand, Silicon Valley has maintained its momentum as the most innovative cluster in the industry. This has been attributed by Saxenian (1994) to the evolution of fluid, intense channels of communication through the variety of social and commercial networks in the area. This type of input has not been created through government intervention, and is probably not susceptible to influence via more formal policy-making. Of course governments can help to foster conditions which make job mobility and information exchange within an area easier, for instance through the creation of research parks. But making these facilities work in the unpredictable and unplanned ways which turn out to be most profitable is usually beyond the capabilities of policy-makers, who mainly work from outside the industry itself. We suggest that there may be a difference between the computing and biotechnology industries in the degree to which they are able to be influenced in their location decisions by policy inducements.

What we have seen in this comparison between the computing and biotechnology industries are differences that spring from the structural distinctions between the industries in their technological specialization. Structure has affected the different relationships between entrants and incumbents, different types of collaboration, the way alliances have been motivated and their organizational forms, the structure of networks in the two industries, the pervasiveness and influence of users in shaping market demands in the two industries, and the susceptibility to policy measures in shifting the location of the industries and in the migration and diffusion of clusters from their original sites.

In the second part of this chapter, we consider the various ways in which the two industries have interacted, and in particular the influence that the computing industry has had on the technological development of the biotechnology industry. We trace the locational implications of these influences and interactions, the degree to which the biotechnology industry has been drawn to centres of computing excellence in the formation of new leading-edge technologies requiring the convergence of these two technologies; and the degree to which computing skills have become so codified, transportable, and diffused throughout the economy as not to influence the success or location of biotechnology companies.

PART 2 THE INTERACTION OF COMPUTING AND BIOTECHNOLOGY

Has the emergence of a new technological sector been contingent on the presence of an earlier complementary technological sector?

We shall see whether the emergence of biotechnology has been directly related to the presence of computing clusters. Biotechnology depends upon the ability to analyse, process, and create models from vast quantities of information and to link information of different types. The role of computers in biotechnology includes data collection, assembly, retrieval; nucleic acid and protein sequencing; the generation of maps of protein structure from nucleotide sequences; the simulation of molecular processes and molecular modelling; the marriage of computers with bioprocessing equipment making more sensitive biosensors and transforming experiments; rational drug design involving new search procedures using the knowledge of protein structures derived from these techniques; and more recently irrational drug design using genetic algorithms to model the processes of natural evolution. We also look at recent developments in more general computer tools such as use of the Internet and e-mail and how that is affecting communication between firms, and between firms and users.

These different types of use of computing have varied implications for clustering. Their role in data collection, assembly, and retrieval, whilst fundamental, is also widespread and fairly routine. However, the location of the main databanks and library resources, as public goods, has been an important part of the specialized infrastructure of an area, with clustering implications for companies in those areas. Sequence analysis by itself has also become relatively widespread with the development of standard equipment which can be customized to companies' or users' requirements. Molecular modelling and the determination of protein structures using computers has, however, been a more specialized task, with new start-ups in the early 1990s playing a more prominent role. Yet even this has become more widespread in the mid-1990s, with, for instance, a protein modelling service available by e-mail. Rational drug design is the marrying of some of these techniques to transform the way traditional screening and experiments have been done; the role of specialized companies liaising with older drug companies is important. Applying computing technology to biosensors, and to design experiments capturing experience and qualitative judgements, is also specialized, but with a different set of companies developing these technologies; some of these are subsidiaries of existing large biotechnology equipment or computing companies.

Broadly one would expect to see differences in the diffusion of these different types of computing technology and biotechnology reflecting different stages in the life cycles of the technologies. There are also implications within the technologies themselves for how specialized and localized they are likely to be: some of the developments require closer collaboration to build software for particular uses. This would seem to require greater proximity between the different types of company. This tendency is offset, to some extent, by the spread of information about such developments; and the greater ease of collaboration using such tools as the Internet; and several of the key companies are not located within traditional clusters but are based in states such as Montana and Utah, as well as California and Massachusetts.

8.9 DATA COLLECTION, ASSEMBLY, STORAGE, AND RETRIEVAL

There has been an explosion of information in molecular biology of sequencing data of nucleic acids, peptides, and proteins, with information growing exponentially. Millions of base pairs of DNA sequences are now known and must be analysed; there are hundreds of restriction enzymes and cloning vectors to be tracked. Computation systems are the necessary tools to manipulate these different types of knowledge.

There has grown up during the 1980s a much greater and more systematic use of databases, with recognition of the need for standardization and networking between them. These databases are in the public domain. There are, in the mid-1990s, around half a million nucleic acid sequences in GenBank compiled by the National Institutes of Health (NIH) at their National Center for Biotechnology Information (NCBI) in Maryland. There are also the NIH's database BIONET, which uses GenBank and two other databases, the Molecular Biology Computer Research Resource (MBCRR), and the National Biomedical Research Foundation's nucleic acid and protein sequence databases, called the Protein Identification Resource, in Maryland. The MBCRR has developed computer and statistical methods to uncover patterns in DNA, RNA, and protein sequences. The Brookhaven Databank, New York, holds 2,500 sets of coordinates of three-dimensional protein structures. By 1996, the Institute for Genomic Research (Md.) had sequenced 174,000 expressed sequence tags and identified over 8,000 new human genes. The concentration of these public databases in Maryland has been one element in the attraction of companies to that state. These databases are becoming more sophisticated and interactive with systems linking genetic maps of organism to their clones and to DNA sequences; the NCBI has developed a database Entrez which jumps among the domains of programmes of DNA and protein sequences (*Genetic Engineering News*, July 1987; *Bio/Technology*, Mar. 1995).

European resources are concentrated at the EMBL data library in Heidelberg, the European Bioinformatics Institute (EBI) and at the European Nucleotide Sequence Centre (ENSC). There is also a prominent protein sequence database with 40,000 protein sequences, SwissProt compiled by Amos Bairoch based in Geneva, with close ties to the EMBL. It is argued that Europe needs more of such types of data-handling capacity as it lags behind the USA in its public database capacity. Some of the leading companies, however, that specialize in combining data on molecular, protein, and DNA structures, are European, such as Oxford Molecular in the UK and Biostructure in France, which have recently merged.

8.10 SEQUENCE ANALYSIS AND MAP GENERATION

Some of the main tasks of sequence analysis are set out below:

- determine nucleotide frequencies;
- locate restriction enzyme cleavage sites;
- find pair-rich regions and symmetries in nucleics;
- translate amino acid sequences;
- reverse translate to find nucleic acid sequences;
- find secondary structures of RNA molecules and proteins;
- generate genetic maps from nucleotide sequences;
- identify hydrophobic (-philic) protein regions;
- compare protein sequences.

In the early 1980s the leading centre for developing sequence analysis was the genetic engineering programme MOLGEN based at Stanford, bringing together computer science and molecular biology, cataloguing 500,000 sequences to compare with unknown ones. The programme also began applying artificial intelligence languages from MIT's AI laboratory to assist scientists in choosing a sequence of tasks to satisfy experimental goals, making use of the generic nature of basic strategies in cloning experiments and making use of these skeletal plans and knowledge of vectors, hosts, and insertion methods to pick optimal experimental methods (*Bio/Technology*, Sept. 1983).

Since then, from the mid-1980s, there have developed more standardized systems for analysing the databases of GenBank and the Protein Identification Resource, for instance. Companies such as International Biotechnologies and Beckman Instruments have condensed such information from GenBank into disk format, making it more accessible. Leading companies involved in this diffusion have been based in many different states: IntelliGenetics, Applied Biosystems, and MicroGenie in California, BIT in Oregon, CompuGene in Montana, Genetics Computer Group and DNAstar in Wisconsin, and IBI in Connecticut. IntelliGenetics has been in the forefront of developing hardware and software to sequence data from large databases and libraries and to analyse sequences.

By the early 1990s, there existed sequence analysis packages such as MacVector, GeneWorks, or MacMolly designed for the Macintosh with accessible graphics, performing sequence and restriction analysis and creating genetic maps and making predictions about protein structures. Software has been combined with automatic instruments, with companies specializing in providing software for editing, comparing, sorting, and managing data, working with automatic synthesizers for sequencing and amplification developed by Beckman Instruments, Applied Biosystems, or Pharmacia LKB. Genetics Computer Group GCG (Wis.) have created a package for comparing sequences, assembling fragments, and searching databases; IntelliGenetics (Calif.) have developed a range of software programmes which they would customize for their scientists and users for instance collating DNA sequences from patent applications, or their SpeedReader programme which would read and analyse sequences (*Genetic Engineering News*, July–Aug. 1991; *Bio/Technology*, July 1992).

Both hardware and software companies in this field have become geographically spread out, with developments occurring in Hitachi Software Engineering America (Calif.), Riverside Scientific Software (Wash.), Biosoft in Cambridge and Oxford Molecular in the UK, Biostructure in Strasbourg in France, or SoftGene in Berlin, Germany. Companies have also specialized in screening different types of libraries: Iterex (Calif.) and Selectide (Ariz.) looking at peptides, Cetus (Calif.) focusing on phages, Stratacyte (Calif.) specializing in antibodies, Cephalon (Pa.) screening neurological activity, Ligand Pharmaceuticals (Calif.) looking at receptors, Neurogenetics (NJ) focusing on neuroreceptors, or Panlabs (Wash.) and NovaScreen (Md.) looking at a range of receptor binding and enzyme inhibition assays (*Genetic Engineering News*, Jan. 1992).

8.11 PROTEIN STRUCTURE, MOLECULAR MODELLING AND SIMULATION OF MOLECULAR PROCESSES

Molecular modelling to determine the structure of proteins and to understand molecular processes has become one of the main routes of development of the technologies from the mid-1980s combining both computing and biotechnology. Prior to computers, the three-dimensional structure of proteins was copied using ball and stick figures. It is difficult to predict the tertiary structure of a protein from its amino acid sequence alone, unless the sequence is homologous to some other protein whose X-ray crystallographic structure is already known, and even this is not enough. The active form of the protein is the folded version of the amino acid. Folding patterns are critical and details of patterns scanty. No two proteins fold in the same way. Interactive computer graphics have become an important tool for designing new proteins and solving the three-dimensional structure of proteins. In 1986 the crystal structure of only 200 proteins was determined. Prior to computers it took between five and ten years to move from the test tube of a purified protein to having the atomic coordinates of that protein (*Bio/Technology*, Apr. 1986).

With computers, the shape of molecules can be manipulated on the screen, drawing road maps of chemical receptors and using these to link to how drugs will be received, showing which structure in a drug to change to achieve the specificity needed to make it effective. There are clear links therefore between advances in molecular modelling and applications in what has come to be called rational drug design. Research on protein structures concentrated in the mid-1980s on new therapeutics, with computer simulations being used to understand intermolecular interactions of complex molecules like proteins and nucleic acids. The Brookhaven National Laboratory's Protein Data Bank (PDB) coordinate system has become an industrial standard so that companies could obtain a tape of coordinates of a molecule that had been solved and was on file at the PDB. Once these molecular coordinates had been obtained, programmes could convert them to their three-dimensional structure.

Early collaborations in this field occurred between UCSF's Peter Kollman and Genentech for instance, creating new protein moieties and establishing a database of structures of proteins using computer simulations. These techniques supplement and to some extent will replace X-ray crystallography (*Genetic Engineering News*, Sept. 1987). Other collaborations have included that between Tripos Associates (Mo.) and the Molecular Science Group in Utah working on graphics interfaces, and that between Tripos and Tom Blundell in London to develop software packages to model proteins by homology, comparing structural motifs. The computing automated the matching process and fitted the coordinates of proteins to the standard coordinate system at the PDB.

Calculations involved in formulating configurations require massive computing power. These developments have therefore awaited advances in computer power and speed with the spread and cheapening of supercomputers in the late 1980s supplied by such companies as Gay Research Inc. (Minn.), Convex Computer Corp (Tex.), Silicon Graphics Inc. (Calif.), IBM from 1990, or Hewlett Packard from 1991. Three companies dominated the software in this area: Polygen/Molecular Simulations Inc. (Mass.), Tripos Associates (Mo.), and Biosym Technologies (Calif.). Since then, by 1992 the software technologies had diffused both geographically and in accessibility. A company in Ontario,

HyperCube, developed a new system, HyperChem, out of a collaboration with Autodesk (Calif.), making molecular modelling accessible to personal computers with a package that would run on any IBM compatible 386 or 486. The package could construct proteins and nucleic acids with fully integrated molecular mechanisms; it was designed, marketed, and priced to make it available to universities. Similarly there have developed drawing programmes for presentations and research such as ChemDraw 3D or ChemText done by Molecular Simulations Inc. (Calif.); Tripos (Mo.), and Biosym (Calif.); Autodesk and BioCad Corp., both based in California, have developed new and cheaper molecular graphics programmes. Software procedures have thus become more compatible, flexible, and able to incorporate new functions and to interact with users to a greater extent (*Bio/Technology*, Jan. 1989).

Protein modification has become an important commercial application of modelling software. This offers the potential to alter a molecule's characteristics: its specificity, affinity, or activity and stability. Again the software market has awaited advances in supercomputing necessary to examine the bonded and unbonded atomic states, to calculate attractions and repulsions of atoms, and to distinguish between atomic states.

Interaction between software developers and users has been another critical element in the process of diffusion. For instance Novo Industri in Denmark bought its basic modelling system from Polygen and adapted it to its needs. This was felt to be accessible to experts, but not to chemists. Novo subsequently wrote a basic package to perform some of these functions and has made it commercially available to outsiders. Biosym Technologies, one of the leading suppliers of molecular modelling software packages, stresses the importance of interaction with the users, to apply their products to users' needs. They use their contract research networks to feed back information to the companies they supply. Agouron Pharmaceuticals (Calif.), a leading company in rational drug design, has also used Polygen packages interactively, requesting Polygen to upgrade parameters, to contour information, and to modify algorithms, adapting the packages to their needs. Users are now including major pharmaceutical companies as hardware platforms and workstations are becoming cheaper. The new systems that Biosym develops are designed to deal with data processing and integrate many of the previously specialized procedures (*Bio/Technology*, Jan. 1989).

More recent developments in the mid-1990s have shown how diffused these previously specialized technologies can become. It is now possible to have protein modelling done, translating amino acid sequences to protein structures, by e-mail. A service named Swiss-Model uses an automated, knowledge-based, protein modelling tool named ProMod, implemented under the World Wide Web. There are drawbacks to its methods: knowledge-based systems extrapolate a model from the known structures of related family members and sometimes results are wrong or the resolution of the model is low. However, this free one-hour service demonstrates the speed with which such technologies can become standardized, can cheapen, and can be diffused, with access available to any scientific user with an appropriate e-mail facility (*Bio/Technology*, July 1995).

8.12 RATIONAL DRUG DESIGN

The rational designing of drugs has been a clear development out of advances in molecular modelling and simulation of molecular interactions. With rising research costs, rational criteria have been needed to prioritize compounds for testing. Computer modelling programmes, predicting the structure of proteins and the interaction of drugs with proteins, have become a useful tool in organizing drug research. Advances in knowledge of sequences have also been important. Research methods have been reversed; instead of observing the disease and responding through finding the right sequences, research is starting with the knowledge of sequence and protein structure and can anticipate or predict the nature of the disease and design particular drugs to deal with it.

Rational drug design began with Ehrlich's turn-of-the-century definition of a receptor as a molecular entity to which a drug binds. Receptors were mostly proteins binding their ligands through interactions between different shapes. Understanding the three-dimensional shape and designing drugs to accommodate that shape has required advances in three major areas of technology: X-ray crystallography, NMR imaging, and developments in computers. Data are generated from protein crystallography or NMR or are extrapolated from homologous proteins; these are integrated with sequence data, giving computational chemists their raw material. They construct mechanical models of the three-dimensional structure of the drug. NMR magnetic fields have advanced in strength; X-ray developments with time-resolved studies have meant that it is possible to visualize intermediates of chemical reactions on a nano- and picosecond time scale. This allows for the development of drugs to bind short-lived intermediates and not just starting- or end-products. In 1992 167 new X-ray crystal structures and 59 new NMR structures were published in the biomedical literature (*Bio/Technology*, Dec. 1994).

To model the drug's dynamics requires: computer programmes to take account of its quantitative structure to capture its activity relations; quantum chemical programmes to calculate binding energies and visualize electron effects; conformational modelling to understand the dynamic drug receptor surfaces; and database systems to retrieve structures and scan for toxicity and other qualities. It requires the interaction of several disciplines: biological assayists, protein biochemists, synthetic chemists, pharmacologists, and computational chemists. Computer software and hardware developments, with software to search chemical databases for candidate drugs, algorithms to assemble drugs within the target molecule's binding site, and programmes to predict the 3D structures of proteins, have been prerequisites for these advances in drug design (*Bio/Technology*, Feb. 1990).

There has been a batch of start-up companies mainly in the early 1990s exploiting rational drug design. They interact with the older established pharmaceutical companies which are also concerned to absorb these new techniques. New companies have included Agouron Pharmaceuticals based in California determining structures using computers, Arris Pharmaceuticals (Calif.) using artificial intelligence programmes for drug design, Immuno Pharmaceutics IPI (Calif.) combining proprietary software with rational methods, BioCryst in Birmingham, Alabama, improving the effectiveness of conventional chemotherapeutics, and Vertex Pharmaceuticals in Cambridge (Mass.) designing suppressants to treat autoimmune disorders (*Genetic Engineering News*, Jan. 1992).

Within the large companies and older biotechnology companies, interdisciplinary teams have been set up developing systems and applications of computational chemistry, for instance in Merck, Abbott, Genentech, Bristol Myers Squibb, and SmithKline Beecham. Abbott has been designing a therapeutic agent for Parkinson's disease, Merck working on prostate drugs, and SKB and Genentech on rationally designed chemotherapeutics for AIDS. These methods are altering research procedures, shortening research times, rather than affecting trial times, and will not entirely replace traditional methods but are being used to supplement them (*Scientific American*, Jan. 1990).

Further developments in these methods continue, with advances coming from the science base. For example X-ray crystallography and NMR spectroscopy give snapshots and cannot represent *in vivo* changes in shape when receptors bind their ligand. Efforts are being made to capture the change that occurs in molecular shape in moving from its unbound to bound state. A team at Harvard is using a structural database-searching programme to identify the rigid core structure. Further challenges include designing drugs where the target structure is unknown; efforts are being made in this direction at UCSF in designing antimalarial drugs, using the structure of related known proteases. Specialized Dock 3.0 software to search for ligands from the Fine Chemicals Directory with molecular display software MIDASPLUS is being used to find compounds with the right inhibitory effect. Advances in atomic force microscopy and electron microscopy are increasing the tools available; such tools are computationally intensive and would not be possible to use without parallel computers capable of turning out a teraflop (one trillion calculations per second) (*Bio/Technology*, Dec. 1994).

8.13 'IRRATIONAL' DRUG DESIGN

There is also a new field emerging of 'irrational drug design' using genetic algorithms to mimic the natural selective process as a method for drug development (*Bio/Technology*, 1995). There is disillusion with the expense and labour intensity of rational drug design methods, which are not producing quick results, leading to further technological developments. New products are going to evolve rather than be designed. These new methods call into question the rational drug design methods of graphic representations of how the target molecule and mutations of its ligand interact, designing molecules with the best hypothetical fit. Recent developments have shown that molecules completely unrelated to the natural ligand may have greater affinity for the target and suggest that mutation is not the sole factor contributing to natural selection. Computer-generated 'artificial life' (a-life) models are being constructed, consisting of populations of algorithms that behave like individual organisms, with each algorithm responding uniquely to its local situation in a changing environment. The interactions of the algorithms create a computer-generated ecology in which algorithms compete to be successful. These virtual laboratories are being used to test hypotheses and gain insights into natural processes. These advances will in time also filter out into the commercial world, affect the way that companies do drug research, and alter the kinds of products that are available in the market place.

The cumulative nature of this type of technical advance is clear. Advances in this field of drug design could not be made without parallel advances in a series of other technologies, computing being one of them. The locational implications of these advances are less obvious. The science base continues to be important in developing basic leading-edge research, and traditional centres of excellence appear to be retaining their reputations for being in the forefront of such research. There does appear to be some initial clustering in traditional centres in California and Massachusetts with some prominent new start-ups choosing to locate there. It is not clear whether proximity to software specialists in this area has been a reason for being based there. Certainly there is evidence of interaction between these start-ups and the development of new software for these very specific purposes, and such interactions may be easier to accomplish within clusters. There are also examples, however, of more diverse locations for start-ups. It is also the case that the established companies based outside the main clusters of biotechnology have been active in absorbing these technologies to transform their drug research methods.

8.14 BIOPROCESSING, THE DESIGN OF EXPERIMENTS,
AND NEW EQUIPMENT

The field of changes in bioprocessing and experiment design has required developments in equipment which have incorporated advances in computing technology. Early collaborations, for instance between Genentech and Hewlett Packard in the early 1980s, entailed a joint venture, combining Hewlett Packard engineers and a Genentech scientist, to develop instruments and related systems (*Biotechnology News*, Aug. 1983). Since the mid-1980s there have been many developments combining chemical components and integrated circuits within instrumented fermenters and biosensors in order to acquire and analyse data and make feedback and control more sensitive and sophisticated. By the late 1980s artificial intelligence programmes were being incorporated into software to translate intuitive understanding of experiments into bioprocessing procedures. James Bailey at CalTech built a software system called MPS for manipulating biosynthetic pathways, developing computer-aided design in experiments. Companies such as IntelliGenetics (Calif.) have commercialized this knowledge, creating software programmes such as BioPath for engineering metabolic pathways, StrateGene incorporating artificial intelligence for understanding bioprocessing procedures, or BioSep to simulate different separation routes, using an engineering input to design the programme (*Genetic Engineering News*, June, July 1988).

The incorporation of personal computers into fermenters and bioreactors has meant that the user can choose different cell culture parameters to grow organisms, with control loops for all the major phases of the biochemical process. These have replaced the strip chart recorders and manual data logging. There have been collaborations between computing companies such as IBM and equipment companies such as New Brunswick Scientific (NJ) to develop software to give supervisory controls over the environmental conditions which need to change over the course of a process. Programmes such as BioFlo I, II, and III are developments out of this, with microprocessor control for pH, oxygen levels, agitation, or temperature, with greater sophistication in control loops and precision as each new programme evolves. IntelliGenetics' BION programme contains language specific to biologists and is a knowledge-based system, asking how a conclusion was reached and receiving an explanation. IntelliGenetics have developed a series of knowledge engineering environment (KEE) systems which play out strategies. Other equipment companies in the early 1990s in this area with an array of fermentation control PC-compatible software packages have included ICN Biomedicals (Calif.), Application Dependable Instruments (Calif.), and Sulzer Biotech Systems (NY) (*Bio/Technology*, Sept. 1983; *Genetic Engineering News*, Sept. 1988).

Hardware has become cheaper since the early 1980s, when there was time sharing of the expensive Digital Equipment Corp. systems. During the 1980s Xerox developed scientific workstations that support these knowledge-based systems. Some of the other traditional biotechnology equipment and computing companies have entered this field, developing microcomputer tools for biotechnologies. These include Beckman Instrument's Spinco Division (Calif.), International Biotechnologies Inc. (Conn.), DNAstar (Wis.), Westco (Conn.), and CompuGene (Mo.), and the headquarters of IntelliGenetics, IntelliCorp (Calif.). Beckman Instruments has developed its Biomek 2,000 Laboratory, an automated workstation with assays, sample preparation procedures, and 3D reconstructions, as well as image analysis, morphology, image processing, and image measurement. As with other fields of development in computing and biotechnology, bioprocessing equipment developments have been assisted by the advances in parallel computing, especially in image processing of electron micrographs. For example, in 1992, in calculating the solvent-accessible surface area of a protein, parallel computers were 30 times faster than an IBM mainframe, and 75 times faster than a Convex super-minicomputer (*Bio/Technology*, Sept. 1984, June 1992).

8.15 CONCLUSIONS

Some sort of pattern in the convergence between computing and biotechnology is discernible. In each distinct area of specialization where computing and biotechnology meet—data manipulation, sequencing analysis, molecular modelling, rational drug design, process and experiment control, and design—a movement can be detected from initial specialization often located close to the core development of the technologies, with a handful of companies locating near those developments, to a widespread diffusion of the technologies through new companies being based in many diverse locations as well as diffusion into older established companies with their locations outside the original biotechnology clusters.

This diffusion has been assisted by companies making the technologies themselves more accessible to non-specialists and by the wide spread of such information through the internet and e-mail services, which makes knowledge of these advances more common, and goes some way towards assisting setting up collaborations and links with users. Such processes of diffusion have been affected by the stage in the life cycle of the particular computing technologies, with, for instance, data manipulation techniques being relatively advanced in their development and therefore in common usage when the convergence with biotechnology occurred. Other computing technologies relevant to biotechnology such as molecular modelling, have been developed to a greater extent in conjunction with biologists, although their spread into more generalized user-friendly packages seems to have been fairly rapid in each segment of the market.

One clear characteristic of the convergence of these technologies in each distinct segment has been the co-evolution of techniques, with advances in modelling or drug design dependent on prior or simultaneous developments in related tools and techniques such as developments in X-ray crystallography or NMR tools. This intertwining of the evolutionary paths of the different technologies has made it increasingly difficult to distinguish between computing and biotechnology skills, as the blending of specialist skills in the variety of disciplines that are contained under both broad headings becomes more essential and more commonplace.

9

Clusters and Competitiveness: A Policy Perspective

PAUL TEMPLE

INTRODUCTION

Over long periods of time, economic growth and prosperity have depended upon a progressive development of international specialization. Much of this volume is devoted to showing empirically that the industry cluster is an important means of understanding that process in both computing and biotechnology. This chapter addresses some of the policy issues that emerge from this analysis, setting them in the broader context of knowledge-based specialization. The chapter is organized as follows.

Section 9.1 describes the challenges currently facing economic policy in the advanced economies, especially those posed by unemployment and rising inequality. It argues that, if the dangers of protectionism are to be avoided, then successful policy will require, among other things, the development of knowledge as a strategic resource. Section 9.2 examines some of the policy implications that emerge from viewing knowledge as a resource, concluding that the concept of the industry cluster is sufficiently flexible to embrace the complex processes that describe technological change. Section 9.3 looks at the issue of cluster performance. It shows that, of the various reasons for cluster formation, knowledge-based clusters form a special case for public and private sector partnership since the key determinants of performance turn out to be things which bear a close resemblance to what economists call *public goods*. These take the form of shared visions, trust, and standards. In turn these public goods help and encourage resources to flow along innovative paths while stimulating the specialization which encourages innovative entrepreneurship. However, unlike the public good of the textbook the public goods described here are not easily produced—public–private sector partnership is frequently an essential ingredient. Section 9.4 discusses the possible purposes of intervention that encourages clustering: reaching critical mass; promoting collaboration; coordinating investments. Section 9.5 examines the UK policy context and policy options: industry policy; science policy; Foresight; regional policy. At present these areas of policy are not integrated. The encouragement of cluster formation is a way of combining them. Section 9.6 contains some proposals for future policy.

9.1 THE POLICY CHALLENGE

The 1990s are witnessing a steady, but persistent, shift in the focus of economic policy among the advanced economies of the OECD. In macro policy the basic guidelines set for the 1980s—involving the elimination of inflationary responses to supply-side shocks—has given way to a widespread concern for the levels of unemployment and inequality that have emerged. Central to the concern is the realization that a more stable macro-economic environment has not encouraged a rate of growth of investment sufficient to reduce the current high levels of unemployment in the OECD—7.7 per cent of the workforce (OECD 1996).

Alongside the growth of unemployment is a general increase in inequality—a reversal of long-standing trends—that is threatening to recreate social divisions not yet seen in the post-Second World War period. In part, of course, increasing inequality is itself a result of the growth in unemployment. But not wholly so; unlike many of the European economies the USA has not witnessed a large increase in unemployment. On most measures, however, levels of inequality are higher in the USA than elsewhere.

The obvious danger in this scenario is the development of protectionism—the pursuit of mercantilist policies in which each economy seeks to stabilize employment by deterring competitive imports. In the extreme case, this becomes a dangerous negative sum game where each country attempts (ultimately unsuccessfully) to export unemployment while at the same time compromising that further international specialization which is the foundation of technological change and economic growth. The challenge for the OECD economies will be their ability to tackle the problems of unemployment and inequality through policies designed to encourage a pattern of growth and investment which is consistent with a progressive development of the international division of labour. In short, the leading objective of policy needs to be seen in terms of the promotion of international competitiveness.

A competitive economy can be thought of as being one whose tradable sector is able to grow in accordance both with international specialization and with the maintenance of high levels of employment. Now the resource which above all distinguishes the OECD economies from other less developed economies and upon which competitive advantage can be based is, loosely, knowledge—both the skills and educational attainments of the workforce and the sophistication of the technological infrastructure. The importance of knowledge as a resource has been repeatedly recognized by a wide variety of voices. Recently for example, the European Council's White Paper on industrial policy saw 'global competitiveness as a key factor in growth and employment' and that the objective for policy was 'the bolstering of the EU's presence in the markets of the future, particularly in telecommunications, information, biotechnology, environmental protection, new materials, and energy' (quoted in CEC 1994).

The measure of success of policy aimed at boosting competitiveness through developing knowledge as a resource should be seen in the growth of the tradable sectors of the advanced economies. In its turn, this would permit the expansion of other areas of the economy—not necessarily directly tradable—which are associated with general increases in the standard of living. These areas include housing, health, and education—areas which also require the intensive use of skilled labour. If this can be achieved, then the advanced economies may be able to escape the trade-off between increasing inequality and unemployment which appears to be currently explaining the differential experiences of the USA and the EU, according to the degree to which their labour forces are deregulated.

How far are the facts of international specialization in the advanced economies consistent with the hypothesis of increasing knowledge intensity of production? An attempt can be made to measure the knowledge intensity of production. The formal expenditure of the R & D departments (of mainly large firms) is recorded on a reasonably comparable international basis, although it hardly captures more than a fraction of the role that knowledge plays. R & D expenditure is nevertheless closely related to other measures of technological sophistication like industrial standards and innovation counts (Swann et al. 1996). Figure 9.1 shows how rapidly the ratio of R & D expenditures to value-added in manufacturing industry has grown for the largest six economies in the OECD: in the USA it represents more than 8 per cent of manufacturing GDP, compared to a little more than 6 per cent in 1973. The spectacular rate of increase in the knowledge intensity of Japanese production is well in evidence with R & D intensity more than doubling over the same period. The UK also registers an increase, but at a rather slower rate, and indeed, in a ranking, the UK slips from second place to fifth.

Although the evidence presented in Figure 9.1 suggests that growing knowledge intensity is a universal experience for these six major economies, and this is consistent with our hypothesis about the nature of international specialization, it is important to realize that the path of adjustment differs substantially between

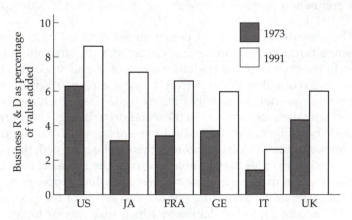

Fig. 9.1 *The growth of research intensity in manufacturing*
Source: OECD.

the economies: how far is growing research intensity due to a *levels* effect—i.e. the faster growth of research-intensive sectors (the so-called 'high-tech' industries) and how far is it due to a *rate* effect—the general growth of research intensity within sectors. Research by Peck and Temple (1996) has shown that for all the G6 economies both these effects are positive, but that their relative importance is very different. In economies experiencing the fastest rate of growth of manufacturing output, Italy and Japan, the bulk of the increase is due to a rate effect, while in the UK the bulk of the increase has been due to a shift of resources into sectors which are more research intensive. The sectors of particular importance in this regard are aerospace, data-processing equipment, and pharmaceuticals. It is worth remarking that these are all areas where multinational activity has been important, and in the case of aerospace and pharmaceuticals, these are also areas where government purchases are important.

The fact that the rate effect appears to be so important in explaining success suggests that policies aimed at the knowledge resource should not be conceived solely in terms of high-technology industries: knowledge-based clustering may be an increasingly important phenomenon even in mature industries. It is better perhaps to think in terms of the comparative advantage of nations moving into earlier stages of the product cycle, not just in research and innovation but also in the rapid diffusion of new technology and organizational best practice, than to think in terms of the build-up of so-called 'sunrise' industries. This is particularly important for the UK, which has been, on the basis of the evidence in Peck and Temple (1996), least able of the major six economies to increase the research intensity of its industries.

An excellent example of how, in a mature industry, development paths can differ is provided in a comparative study of two cutlery industry agglomerations based around Sheffield in England and Tsubame in Japan (see Hayter and Patchell 1993). They argue that the 'Japanese experience suggests that ... industrial evolution is a learning process in which accumulated expertise developed in an industry can be used to shape future industrial adjustment'. In Sheffield by contrast, the accumulated expertise was collectively allowed to go to waste as the majority of firms followed policies of cost minimization based on known technologies. This suggests that a vital question for policy is why there should be systematic differences in the performance of industry clusters. This is addressed in section 9.3 below. First, however, it is important to consider, in a more general fashion, the role of policy in developing the knowledge resource.

9.2 KNOWLEDGE AS A RESOURCE: IMPLICATIONS FOR POLICY

If knowledge as a resource is indeed the key to understanding the future performance of economies such as that of the UK, then what does this imply for the policy-maker? First, it needs to be explicitly recognized that the translation of the competitive potential of society's knowledge-based resources into competitive performance depends upon highly complex social processes; perhaps five distinct processes are important determinants of technological change and long-run competitive performance. Moreover, aspects of them could be, and to a varying degree have been, regarded as *objectives* for aspects of government policy. We may distinguish between:

- the *generation* of new knowledge;
- the *translation* of new or existing knowledge into innovative products and processes, i.e. innovation/entrepreneurial function;
- the *diffusion* of innovations;
- the *exchange* of knowledge-intensive goods and services;
- the *absorption* of knowledge and learning and its coordination within the technological infrastructure (the public good function).

In the first three the reader will recognize the classic tripartite division of technological change into processes of invention, innovation, and diffusion. The first is widely regarded as an objective of science policy while the first three together constitute science and technology policy. If the role of industry policy is indeed becoming refocused on the development of competitiveness, then we can see, given our earlier discussion, that technology policy and industry policy are effectively converging. However, it can be argued that the fourth and the fifth processes are also fundamental in understanding the mechanisms by which the knowledge resource is translated into competitive performance, and although less well recognized and documented, effective mechanisms in these areas are important in explaining the story of successful clusters. This is because they can have a considerable impact in reducing transactions costs when innovative firms use the market to solve problems. One especially important example of the exchange of knowledge-intensive services is the hiring of skilled personnel. As far as the absorption of knowledge into the technological infrastructure is concerned, it is now widely recognized that standard-setting activities of all kinds are an increasingly important means of generating localized public goods.

Second, all of these processes are subject to market failure and hence it needs to be recognized that the more knowledge intensive production becomes, the more relative economic performance will come to depend upon institutional mechanisms for correcting, or at least mitigating, market failure. The study of competitive performance therefore needs to consider *institutional* failure as much as it does market failure or government failure.

Third, we may note the changing emphasis in policy formulation in many of the OECD economies, away from the process of new knowledge creation and from the related market deficiencies (e.g. Limpens et al. 1992), which hinge primarily on the difficulties that individual firms may have in appropriating the benefits of their investments in knowledge creation. These difficulties apply particularly to so-called 'basic' scientific research, where the ultimate economic application is both uncertain and far distant. Emphasis on this set of market failures produces policies emphasizing stronger reinforcement of property rights (via the patent system) and an emphasis on 'science push', where public sector efforts to increase the knowledge stock are concentrated on basic science. Were it not for the new knowledge that emerges as a result of public sector missions in other areas such as defence or education, the USA would provide the example which came closest to a model predicated upon the exclusive importance of new knowledge creation. However, in the USA and elsewhere, the policy significance of technological diffusion processes has been increasingly recognized. Indeed the famous study of comparative technology policy conducted by Ergas (1987) distinguishes the technology policies of countries such as Germany and Sweden in terms of their tendency to focus on diffusion as the *major* objective for technology policy.

The recent emphasis in technology policy on diffusion processes is a consequence of four factors.

- The vastly greater significance which attaches to diffusion (as opposed to innovation) for the generation of economic wealth.
- The increasing importance of market failures in diffusion processes where network externalities are present (as is the case in many communications and information processing technologies), so that the benefits of adoption depends upon the size of the population of users. These situations are of particular interest to policy-makers, because quite small and temporary subsidies to adoption can have quite large impacts on the *speed* of adoption. This can give public authorities great power even if they cannot necessarily foresee the final outcome of their actions.
- The growing acknowledgement of the importance of the costs of technology transfer, a factor which until recently economists had tended to ignore.
- The role played by technological expectations on the adoption decision (of crucial importance in our discussion of policy related to clusters). It should be remembered that the appropriate policy objective is not necessarily a faster rate of diffusion. Network externalities and consequent bandwagon effects may result in the adoption of an inferior technology. It is not difficult to envisage situations in which the appropriate policy is to continue technological competition (David 1987).

Fourth, if competitive performance depends increasingly on institutional means of correcting market failures endemic in the creation and use of knowledge, then new ways must be found to limit the damage due to differing perceptions of what does and does not constitute 'fair' competition; and what measures can legitimately be taken to assist the development of so-called 'strategic' industries. In the USA, for example, much has been made of the fact that basic R & D is more likely to be located within the university system, making it much more accessible to expropriation overseas than is basic R & D in Japan, which is more likely to be located inside a private firm. Similarly, the acquisition of British or American technology through takeover by a foreign firm is much easier than in countries, such as Japan and Germany, where takeover is more difficult. Without the development of acceptable international codes of practice, national strategic considerations may limit the spread of knowledge in ways which are inefficient from the point of view of global welfare (Ostry 1991).

Fifth, it needs to be remembered that all governments are major players in the development of knowledge resources. This stems in part from their goals in other directions, notably in health, education, and defence. In the UK, for example, the government is a major purchaser *inter alia* of drugs and defence equipment. Where spillovers exist in these activities, government should take them into account when formulating policy.

Finally, the set of policy objectives should not be regarded as independent of each other. A policy directed at encouraging the rate of new knowledge creation cannot be expected to be neutral in its impact on, say, diffusion. A strengthening of the patent system, for example, may encourage the holder to charge higher prices in the early stages of the patent's life, which may of course retard the diffusion of the innovation protected; on the other hand it clearly encourages the disclosure of knowledge. In short, the social processes which beget technological change are highly interconnected and are likely to vary considerably from industry to industry and from technology to technology. In essence, policy needs to be sufficiently flexible to take account of highly specific and highly localized factors. It also needs to think in ways which integrate the processes outlined above.

This last point raises the question: what are the appropriate concepts for dealing with these social processes as part of an integrated whole, i.e. systemically? One of the advantages of thinking in terms of the industrial cluster is that it is sufficiently flexible to embrace all of these aspects vital to the process of technological change. It is therefore an important means of conceptualizing an industry policy aimed at stimulating technological change through the development of knowledge as a resource.

9.3 POLICY AND CLUSTER PERFORMANCE

What exactly *is* a cluster? In the UK, as elsewhere in the industrialized world, geographically localized specialization represents a norm, but policy is seldom developed in these terms; indeed in the popular conception, a cluster is thought to be rather exceptional and by no means always desirable. We would hesitate to describe the cutlery industry in Sheffield (clearly an 'agglomeration') in the same terms as Silicon Valley (often described as a 'phenomenon'), but why? In this section an answer is sought by considering a central policy issue—why does the performance of some clusters differ so markedly from others?

The literature relating to clusters is full of references to the variability of cluster performance. Here we examine three sets of factors suggested by an overview of both the economic and the sociological literature, and which get close to distinguishing a clustering phenomenon from a simple agglomeration. The first, suggested by the empirical analysis of Chapter 4 of this volume, looks at the cluster from the *life cycle* perspective. The second considers the role of the *innovative entrepreneur* in more detail and the factors which are conducive to entrepreneurship. The third explores a factor suggested (in particular) by the sociological literature and relates to the *governance* of the cluster.

Critical mass and diversification

The empirical work in this volume suggests that one important way of looking at variability in performance is the cluster life cycle. A corollary of thinking in this way is that there may be a policy life cycle associated with it: policies appropriate to one stage of the cluster life cycle may not be appropriate to another.

The life cycle approach outlined in Chapter 4 alerts us to one characteristic of clusters of obvious importance to the policymaker: *critical mass*. Only in clusters of a certain size will the positive feedback effects described elsewhere in this book begin to operate. This begs the question of what it is that critical mass entails. In the model, cluster size is measured by employment. However, is employment really the key dimension, or is it serving as a proxy for something else? In the context of functioning networks in Sweden, for example, Carlsson and Jacobssen (1994) refer to the 'intensity of the relationships' between the various economic agents, as well as to their technical content and direction. As will be made clear below, critical mass is best thought of as a matter not only of size, but also of technological direction, a concentration of the kinds of information exchanged.

The actions of government can in practice create sufficient concentrations of resources to produce critical mass in some sectors. As is now well known, it was defence procurement that played the lead role in the rise of the aerospace-electronics complex in southern California in the 1940s and more especially the 1950s. It is important to stress, however, that there is no evidence that this was in any sense a deliberate act of policy. Indeed in so far as location was a strategic factor in the defence industries, it is decentralization that is frequently encountered. For example, during the war, the USA War Production Department made conscious efforts to decentralize capacity, especially towards the interior, away from the east coast and the Pacific (Markusen 1987). There is evidence that any deliberate policy to centralize would have met quite fierce resistance in the rest of the USA. In 1960, two New York senators sought to redress the favoured position of southern California in DoD contracts, although an ensuing bill was annulled by the Armed Services Committee. Effectively it was too late. According to M. Scott (1994), this reflected in part the fact that 'Southern California (like parts of the Bay Area) had become a massive locus of production and labour market activity, engendering such potent agglomeration economies that it was now virtually impossible to reorganise the spatial bases of defence contracting except at unacceptably high cost'.

This case illustrates another feature of the empirical work in Chapter 4—that life cycles will differ according to the degree (and nature) of *diversification*. Essentially, two technologies began to converge in the 1950s—aircraft production and electronics—and the southern Californian complex was well positioned to exploit it. Indeed it is worth remarking that at the end of the Second World War the aircraft industry went into substantial decline. The convergence of the two technologies was, of course, one of the main stories behind the development of the ballistic missile industry in the 1950s and 1960s, the growth path of which reflected the spending trends of DoD and NASA. One of the interesting

features of the story was the different policies of the air force and
the army which, in a sense, were in competition with each other
over missile and rocket development. The army preferred development (based on Huntsville, Alabama) in its own plants while
the air force relied on a host of private contractors, many located
in southern California, but whose efforts were directed by key
coordinating agencies (M. Scott 1994). In this way the Air Force
managed to promote a form of *coordinated competition* which was
missing from the more directed Army programme, but apparently much more successful.

The role that government and the military played in the southern Californian high-technology complex does therefore illustrate
three important points. The first is the difficulty that, in a democracy, any government would find in concentrating (and hence
diverting) resources to achieve critical mass, whether through
procurement policy or other means by which economic activity
could be located. The second is that a procurement policy where
government purchases form a significant part of the market can
play an important role in a positive feedback from success to
additional investment to more success. Favouring the most competitive bids, acting as a technologically sophisticated purchaser,
and (in some circumstances) providing 'credible commitments' to
certain trajectories for design, can encourage and stimulate physical and human capital formation in those areas. The third is that,
despite the prominence given to the notion of the market as the
coordinating mechanism *par excellence*, government provided a
considerable degree of coordination to the technological development effort in the southern California context. Such coordination
can of course take a number of forms and this is an important part
of the discussion of another aspect of cluster performance which
has been prominent—the role of the entrepreneur. To this we now
turn.

Entrepreneurship and specialization

Whether at the local or the national level, the essence of strong
competitive performance lies in both the creation of technological
opportunity and the response to opportunity to innovate. The
fundamental process—essentially a coupling mechanism—which
links technological opportunity to innovative performance is

entrepreneurship. Mainstream economics has never managed to integrate the undoubted importance of the entrepreneur into standard theory.

In practice the function of entrepreneurship does not inhere in the activity of individuals, or groups of individuals, but in specific capacities. Leibenstein's (1968) catalogue is helpful; his list embraces the following six functions:

1. the search, discovery, and evaluation of opportunities;
2. the marshalling of the financial resources necessary for enterprise;
3. the taking of responsibility for management and what he terms the 'motivational system' within the firm;
4. the bearing of risk;
5. the provision of leadership;
6. the translation of new information into new markets.

Leibenstein makes the point that each of these is a conceptually separate input which could in theory be provided by a specialized market and indeed sometimes is. For example, the highly developed venture capital markets of the USA mean that the entrepreneurial function may be more narrowly focused than in economies where financial markets are less well developed. On this view, the role of the entrepreneur is essentially 'gap-filling' and 'input completing'. Of principal interest for the policy-maker in advanced economies is the question of the supply of entrepreneurship and the question of what might induce a greater degree of *innovative* entrepreneurial activity, i.e. the sixth in Leibenstein's list.

Empirical research supports the conclusion that this form of entrepreneurship is fundamental to the process by which a cluster is enabled to specialize in earlier stages of the product cycle. Work by Gort and Klepper (1982) shows that early stages in the product cycle are closely associated with new firm entry. This in turn suggests a natural division of labour between large firms and small, in which the large have a comparative advantage in 'incremental innovation', based upon their accumulated experience and technology.

Gains in economic efficiency can be made if specialization occurs horizontally along the lines of entrepreneurial function. Indeed this is fundamental to the clustering process. Complete specialization would allow the innovative entrepreneur to do what he or she does best. In such a world, risk bearing (for example) would be the function of a speculator or a venture capitalist, rather than an entrepreneur; motivation would be a managerial matter, while the search for, and evaluation of, opportunities would be the job of a specialized researcher, and so on. The geography of innovation has been shown to be strongly influenced by the location of business services (Feldman 1994). In practice, the innovative entrepreneur usually needs to integrate some or all of these activities. Since these are not areas of comparative advantage the need to integrate more of these activities involves rising marginal opportunity costs. The supply of pure innovative entrepreneurship is therefore increased whenever specialized business services are developed and contracted out. Moreover, when innovation is especially radical in nature the entrepreneur may need to integrate not only those activities described by Leibenstein but also vertically—i.e. upstream into component production or downstream into marketing and distribution.

A stimulus to entrepreneurship is therefore provided by *specialization*. Not only does the existence of specialized business services lower the costs of entrepreneurship, but, as was originally demonstrated by Adam Smith, the dedication of workers to a limited range of tasks heightens their awareness of technical opportunities. By analogy, specialization among firms might be expected to focus problem-solving activities; geographical clustering, by lowering the costs associated with exchanges of information, might also be expected to stimulate this activity. At the same time a highly trained workforce coupled with a high degree of labour mobility can substantially lower search costs for specific problem-solving exercises. Route 128 performed less well than Silicon Valley because new firm start-ups on Route 128 typically lacked 'the social networks or institutional forums to experiment and learn about new markets, technologies and organisational forms' (Saxenian 1994).

It is having to integrate and perform several specialized activities which might be performed by others that limits entrepreneurial performance. The problem is essentially one of getting resources to flow according to some more or less novel vision. Relying on markets to respond accordingly may be difficult for reasons of information impactedness and appropriability. It may also involve a power problem: if innovation requires dedicated (complementary) asset accumulation on the part of another agent then opportunism on that agent's part may be possible, i.e. there is a potential 'hold-up' problem. Although this kind of problem is frequently stressed in the literature (e.g. Teece 1986*b*) the problem of convincing that agent of the innovative potential of an idea may be just as important (e.g. Silver 1984; Langlois and Robertson 1995).

Sufficient horizontal and vertical integration allows for the *de facto* coordination of the resources required for innovation. Silver (1984) shows that there are many examples in older technologies to illustrate the hypothesis that the extent of vertical integration in industry depends upon its degree of innovativeness. Examples from automobile production are well known, but Silver also demonstrates a similar relationship in industries as diverse as textiles, oil, insurance, and meat packing. The essential point is that the more radical is the innovation the more likely it is that some vertical integration aimed at coordinating assets which are complementary to innovation will be forced on innovators, diluting the focus of their activities. Markets cannot provide their traditional coordinating function because in highly innovative contexts they do not exist. However, the requirement that a single administration provide the coordinating function is removed when several agents share the same vision of the future. Where a whole community of agents shares the same perception, the inducement to specialization may be considerable. In such circumstances a *quasi-*coordination is achieved, allowing a degree of specialization which would not otherwise be possible.

The relationship between quasi-coordination and the industry cluster is clear. The firms and agencies sharing similar views about the future define a particular *technological community*. The extent of this community embraces all those with a clear interest in how the technology develops. The relevant community therefore extends beyond any set of market-based relationships, but needs to embrace so-called spillovers and in particular must span technologies which are converging. Although there is no reason in principle why such a community should not be global, it is much more likely to be observed where informal linkages between actors reinforce market-based relationships, as well as where technology transfer is tacit.

Mechanisms which might help to promote quasi-coordination include information pooling and the consequential formation of shared perceptions regarding technological opportunities and their associated risks. The shared perception is effectively a public good, in the respect that the use of the view of the future by one agent does not preclude use by another. It is, however, an impure public good (or 'club good'), because use can only be made of it if at least some economic resources are committed to interpreting and refining it for the particular circumstance in hand. This good is promoted by the density of information exchange, one of the defining characteristics of an innovative industrial cluster.

A convergence of views regarding future technological possibilities is essential if external economies are to be created within an industrial cluster. To take a simple example: suppose the views of a defined technological community are actively articulated. The probability that a financial institution will commit resources to investigating and evaluating a particular technology will be enhanced; moreover, the convergence of views will in itself enhance the probability of particular investment projects being favourably evaluated. While the development of the division of labour along lines consistent with an articulated technological vision within the financial sector is clearly of crucial importance, it is only one example of the more general class of externalities which Scitovsky in 1963 termed 'pecuniary external economies', expressing the cumulative economic processes that occur when certain investments made by one firm enhance the profitable opportunities of other firms. Clearly, the government can add considerably to these processes by linking, say, investment in infrastructure to private investment. An upgrading of facilities tied to particular investments then reacts profitably on other firms in the locality.

At least as important as the action of the government is the fillip that common views can give to private mechanisms for cooperative ventures. The role that these play in the so-called 'Third Italy' has been widely cited in areas such as research, marketing, training, and financing. Through cooperative institutions it become possible for collections of small firms to replicate the economies that are usually thought to belong exclusively to large firms. For example, the Emilia-Romagna region of Italy has created 'overhead service' centres for a number of industries, including fashion clothing, agricultural machinery, shoes, and construction. Other agencies specifically cross industry boundaries to match buyers and sellers within the region. They therefore represent a possible mechanism for bringing further coordination to the supply chain. Clearly, R & D co-operative ventures fall under this same heading. If it is known that several firms share similar views of the future, the inducement to cooperation will be correspondingly greater. The formation of these organizations is clearly predicated on a shared view of the respective limits of competition and cooperation.

Until recently, a very different culture in the USA has tended to view such organizations as anti-competitive and hence detrimental to social welfare. In spite of the USA Cooperative Research Act of 1984, many Americans regard cooperation with suspicion, even in the field of research. They consider that R & D does not always yield the expected economies of scale and that firms may begin to exchange more information about activities closer to the market (for a discussion, see Mowery 1995).

Scepticism is in order when it comes to direct policy initiatives in areas such as cooperative research. Whereas cooperative research ventures are widely (although far from unanimously) believed to have been successful in post-war Japan, a similar experiment in Britain after the First World War, whose origins can be traced to direct comparison with research organizations in the USA and Germany, was (probably unanimously) deemed to have failed. By 1929, the Balfour Committee was reporting that despite the quality of the output of the research organizations, the information 'simply runs to waste for a lack of a properly equipped receiving mechanism within the works' (quoted in Mowery and Rosenberg 1989). The key to the failure was whether such organizations function as a *substitute* for in-house R & D, or act as a *stimulus* to it. Regarding the success of the Japanese industry research associations, which were largely based on the British model, Mowery (1995) points to the fact that government funds committed to cooperative R & D ventures must frequently be matched by commensurate industry funds, with industry generally developing the agenda, often directed at *diffusing* advanced technologies rather than *advancing* them. It is worth noting also that the learning function of R & D, as opposed to its knowledge-generation function, has been well ingrained into Japanese corporate culture, and that the successful importation of technology which was such a feature of Japan's rapid catch-up in the post-war period was predicated upon considerable in-house R & D capability. Clearly no such corporate culture existed in Britain. The familiar rule that this illustrates is that transplants of apparently similar institutions from one economic and social setting cannot be presumed to succeed in another.

To what extent should a government try to bring about a national convergence of view about the threats, opportunities and challenges facing a particular technological community? Such a consensus has been important in the industrial development of Japan, and also, to an extent, in Germany and the Scandinavian economies.

No economy has managed to shift resources so quickly into knowledge-based production as Japan. Freeman (1987) emphasizes the importance in Japan of the activities of the Science and Technology Agency which, from 1969, pioneered the use of Delphi techniques to produce a common view of long-term technological possibilities. These techniques have now been emulated in the UK, with the Foresight exercise, of which more below. As for Japan, Freeman comments, 'there is no other society where financial institutions, banks and even the Ministry of Finance devote such attention to the future direction of technical and social change'. The foundation of the forecasts is a long-term assessment of future economic and social needs and how technology can be used to meet those needs. A well-publicized basic ground-plan then serves as a basis for (and potentially a stimulus to) the planning of R & D in private companies. Its effectiveness may well depend upon the extent to which government is prepared to make *commitments* to such a vision, in terms of the sponsorship of cooperative research projects. The process may be particularly important in promoting technology 'fusion' (Kodama 1992), where the driver for innovation comes from the cross-industry *combination* of hitherto separate technologies, and where the company linkages are less transparent. Kodama cites, as evidence for the growing importance of fusion, the growth of 'non-core' R & D activities in many firms' research portfolios (i.e.

technological diversification) and the increasing number of industries per project found in Japanese research associations. It may be that the Japanese Keiretsu structure and the activities of MITI provide an ideal framework for the pursuit of technology fusion, but Kodama believes that much more important is the fact that corporate strategy is guided by three principles: 'demand articulation, intelligence gathering, and collaborative R & D.'

Germany and Sweden are also renowned for their ability to develop and sustain cooperative research programmes. In general these require formal institutional structures which in the words of Ergas (1984) 'provide a framework for dialogue and agreement'. He goes on to point out the important local dimension that such processes require if the 'external economies of manpower training, user-supplier interaction, and the development of specialised sources of supply' are to operate. Germany is particularly rich in institutions which promote dialogue both horizontally between firms and between industry and educational and research communities. One of the great strengths of the German economy is its generation of formal institutional standards. These have a similar result in some respects to the norms which delimit the nature of competition in Italy—they act in their own right as a coordinating mechanism—channelling technical change in particular directions and restricting competition in others. It needs emphasizing that many of these mechanisms in Germany have their origins in a strategic capacity that exists at a geographically localized level (i.e. in the *Länder*). If there is a recognized weakness in the German system, it is in establishing linkages *across* industries.

The governance of clusters

As we have seen, the use of markets to exchange knowledge-intensive goods and services accentuates the possibility of 'hold-up' and other forms of opportunistic behaviour. Many economists believe that, in general, the potential for hold-up will favour the internalization of exchanges under the aegis of a single firm. However, it is an important part of the burgeoning literature on clusters that supra-corporate forms of organization can also reduce the potential problem of opportunism. The performance of

clusters cannot simply be summed up in terms of localized economies of agglomeration, but needs to refer to relationships of 'trust'
(or one of its variants such as 'partnership' or 'fidelity'). In this
sense social norms or simply local 'ways of doing business' substitute for formal governance within a corporate hierarchy (see
Harrison 1992).

Where does the trust actually come from? According to Sabel
(1989), among many other writers, trust is based partly on business experience, partly on a shared culture, and partly upon
shared experience outside the workplace—in clubs, churches,
business associations, etc. Above all else these social processes
lead to clearly defined demarcation rules on where the boundary
should be drawn between areas of competition and areas for
cooperation. Thus in the textile districts of the Third Italy
for example, it is widely believed that the basis of competitive
advantage between firms is in terms of one area of competence—
design and innovation—and that there is no basis for competing
on price or on any of the myriad factors that might give one
firm a temporary advantage over another. From a wider perspective Italy shows that this form of competition can be highly
successful in creating an internationally competitive industry in
the more traditional areas such as clothing, footwear, and furni-
ture. Interestingly Porter (1990), in discussing this feature of
Italian success, refers to the strong family ties which favour
innovative firm practices by lowering exit costs. Such lowered
costs help to explain national advantage in innovative performance (Ergas 1984).

In some clusters, and in contrast to the Third Italy, governance
is effectively guaranteed by the presence of one or more large
firms surrounded by many smaller firms. This is sometimes referred to as a 'core-ring' network (Storper and Harrison 1991). In
these cases it is evident that differences in *corporate strategy* can
have considerable impacts upon cluster performance. At issue is
the degree to which the lead firm is prepared to share technology
and turn it into a (at least local) public good. Saxenian (1994), in
her important study on the comparative performance of Silicon
Valley and the Route 128 clusters, draws attention to the differences in corporate strategies between the two regions. On the one
hand, the west coast producer Hewlett Packard is, she claims,
creating 'a new model of the decentralized large firm' in 'which

the firm's divisions gained autonomy and began collaborating with other specialist producers'. On the other hand DEC's attempts to enter the workstation market were hampered by the conviction that internal architecture design (i.e. vertical integration) was the best long-term strategy, despite the difficulties encountered.

Where governance is exercised by a large firm, what matters is the nature of the *vertical* technology and information flows between the lead firm and its suppliers, but also the *horizontal* information flows between suppliers. Japan affords some interesting examples of the relationship between a lead firm and its suppliers. Many of these relate to the automobile industry where large oligopolistic assemblers procure components from a large number of mainly small suppliers. Although there is clearly asymmetry in market power, and intense competition among the smaller suppliers, there are also powerful incentives in the relationships established for the small companies to innovate and upgrade their technical capacity on the basis of technical information from the supplier, while periodic contract review permits risk sharing. One important form of upgrading is for a supplier to move from a 'drawing supplied' (by the assembler) basis, to a 'drawing accepted' basis. Once reaching this more elevated rank, which requires demonstration of sufficient technical capacity, there is then a powerful incentive for the supplier and the 'drawing accepted' supplier to cooperate on component R & D in longer-term model development (Odagiri 1992). Supplier associations, or *kyoryokukai*, also have a role in promoting both vertical and horizontal information flows and technology transfer. Nissan for example makes its long-term plans available to all suppliers in the association in order to coordinate investment by suppliers. A study by Sako (1995) showed that while these and other vertical flows of information from the customer were valued most highly by members, many reported that learning from other suppliers was actually more important, so that the association functions as a forum for informal knowledge trading, of the sort described by Hippel (1987). Although it might be thought that the more technically sophisticated suppliers would have little to gain from membership, Sako did not find that this was the case; even among this group, there were sufficient opportunities for knowledge trading for membership to be worthwhile.

Far from taking a neutral view about such associations, or even actively discouraging them as potentially anti-competitive, economic policy in Japan has encouraged the formation of cooperatives among smaller firms. Unlike the motor industry, they are not usually focused around a single customer. Regionally based, and once officially registered and approved, they become eligible for subsidies for joint R & D, employee training, and so forth. Around 47,000 cooperatives were registered in Japan in 1991 (Sako 1995).

These examples suggests that different corporate strategies can have an important role in determining the nature of flows of technical information in situations where corporate governance is effected in a *de facto* manner by the large corporation. Ordinarily, this determinant of cluster performance might not be seen as a possible concern for policy. However, we argue below that corporate strategy is heavily dependent upon the institutional context, and that if there are grounds for believing that institutions are failing, restructuring of institutions may lead to beneficial changes in corporate behaviour.

9.4 CLUSTER PERFORMANCE: SOME POLICY CONCLUSIONS

In the previous this section we posed the question: what is it that distinguishes a readily identifiable knowledge-based cluster—in which innovative entrepreneurship can be seen to thrive—from a simple agglomeration of firms in similar lines of business? In a geographically localized agglomeration, a potential competitive advantage is offered by low communication costs and hence the ability to transfer technology where technology is embedded in the skills of the workforce. But if this advantage is to be realized there must be a technological community present, whose behaviour is guided by commonly accepted standards of behaviour which favour the creation of local public goods. These standards include:

- a marked tendency toward cooperative behaviour and information exchange on the basis of a shared perception of the nature of and limits to competition;

- a coordinating mechanism which substitutes for missing forward markets in areas of rapid technological development.

The idea of a technological community needs to be interpreted widely and typically embraces not just firms in the same industry but also across industries, where so-called spillovers exist, and between educational and other institutions, and industry. A key feature of clusters is therefore a rich mix of institutions which bridge different spheres of endeavour and promote the interaction of personnel. Taken together, they result in a rapid rate of investment in the public good aspects of technology, i.e. the technological infrastructure. The importance of cooperative mechanisms is most clear in the case of R & D, the purposive generation of knowledge resources, but also ranges into areas such as marketing, general intelligence gathering, and training. The coordinating mechanism is a key feature of the cluster, since it permits innovative activity without the requirement for extensive internalization of the investment in the assets which are required for successful innovation. Hence the stimulation to entrepreneurship and specialization in business services.

All this suggests that there are three possible areas for policy intervention: (1) in the attainment of critical mass, (2) in the promotion of cooperative activities across firms and other institutions, and (3) in the coordination of investment decisions. In each of these areas a case for intervention can be made on the basis of at least one element of a 'public good', namely its non-rivalry. But the provision of these goods, however desirable, can never be guaranteed.

Attaining critical mass

Although critical mass is in some respects a rather pure public good, there are obvious difficulties attached to its creation through policy intervention. First it must be recognized that any effort to achieve critical mass must of necessity be based on an assessment of competitive *potential*. Of all the possible targets for policy it comes closest to the idea that government is able to 'pick winners'. There is also the difficulty of what precisely is the objective for policy. Most of the literature stresses that what is important is the density of information flows, not simply vertically between customer and supplier, but also horizontally between firms in the same industry and (especially important in the context of technological convergence) across industries. It is far from clear that the same volume of inward investment from the point of view of cluster size has similar impacts upon these information flows. Finally, the political problem of deliberately concentrating resources in one region at the expense of another may present insurmountable difficulties. For all that, it does appear to be a legitimate objective for policy to attempt to influence the impact of inward investment upon the nature of those flows; such an objective may be an important adjunct to policies aimed at attracting inward investment by large transnational firms whose investments may be sufficiently large to generate critical mass.

Promoting collaborative behaviour

Policies designed to stimulate cooperative research behaviours are today commonplace. In Europe for example, both the Esprit and Eureka programmes have precisely this objective, while it was a vital element in the UK's earlier Alvey programme in the mid-1980s. Of course all the usual arguments in favour of (and against) cooperative R & D can be used for these programmes, including the avoidance of duplication and the spreading of risk. Such arguments apply with particular force where the technologies being developed are enabling or generic in nature (Nelson 1984). The interesting point of departure for these programmes is that they are based on a belief that one of the factors preventing a more competitive European industry is the rather high technological communication costs across national borders, and that these costs could be rapidly reduced by encouraging cross-national linkages. Applications for funds to support research need to be made therefore by consortia which span national borders. Since publicly supported collaborative R & D projects tend to be directed at upstream, riskier, 'pre-competitive' research there is a problem in evaluating these programmes, which almost by definition have longer-term and less tangible pay-offs. However, a number of studies have indicated that the development of personal contacts has been one of the most positive outcomes of the Eureka project (e.g. Watkins 1991). If a rapid reduction in communication costs is seen as part of the justification for pan-European R & D efforts, then a stimulus to cooperative efforts and a potentially rapid reduction in transaction costs can be seen as a justification for supporting *geographically localized* consortia. Again, if specific communication costs (e.g. between universities and business) are perceived to be a problem, then this could be a condition for qualifying bids.

Public support for R & D in collaborative schemes such as Eureka and Esprit lays itself open to a potential free rider problem, in that firms will substitute the publicly financed effort for their own efforts. In principle additionality may be reduced whenever the design and objectives of projects are to stimulate in-house R & D. Most in-house R & D appears to be carried out in fields very close to firms' core competencies, reflecting their cumulative and idiosyncratic experience. That few firms (except the very largest) feel able to indulge in basic R & D is well known, but that few are able effectively to explore and track alternative technologies is perhaps less well known, but probably just as likely to generate additionality. Basic, generic, and tracking R & D are also more suitable for collaborative projects than closer-to-market development work, where problems over intellectual property rights generally loom larger.

A focus for collaborative schemes may therefore centre upon tracking mechanisms as well as upon more basic research. Although this may be thought more in the nature of defensive R & D (Quintas and Guy (1995) term it 'insurance' R & D) it is not clear that over longer time horizons such R & D will not react back on firms' own core efforts and enable them to shift, with greater probability of success, their own technological focus. The study by Quintas and Guy (1995) indicated that the Alvey programme was particularly important in stimulating business linkages with the academic world, and hence providing access to academic knowledge. The case of R & D is of course only one example (albeit an important one) of a wider range of activities, including training, where incentives to cooperative behaviour have public good outcomes. Economists have of course debated whether the stimulation of cooperative behaviour may inevitably result in collusive, anti-competitive behaviour. Even where cooperation is in so-called pre-competitive areas, the lines of communication opened up may make collusive behaviour elsewhere more probable. We may only note here that this is rather less likely in the case of *local* collaborative efforts, where these are set up to meet the challenges of international markets. The argument is less clear in the pan-European programmes constituting Esprit and Eureka.

If, given suitable objectives, incentive mechanisms for local cooperative behaviour are considered desirable, then the question of finance needs to be considered. Since it is commonly supposed that technologies are embedded in social and organizational processes, then the benefits from the outcomes of such behaviour may well also be local. For this reason the use of general (national) taxation to finance local benefits may be inappropriate. On the other hand, it is far from clear that all or even the majority of the benefits are appropriated locally—a highly competitive industry for example may find many of the benefits flowing to customers in overseas markets. However, assuming for the moment that, at least to a first approximation, benefits can be appropriated locally, there are two good reasons for using local sources to finance public goods. One is the political principle of subsidiarity, which in this context can be taken to mean that decisions concerning spillovers should be taken at the most decentralized level containing the spillover. The second is the famous argument put forward by Tiebout (1956) to the effect that economically efficient provision of public goods is possible where there is sufficient differentiation of outputs between localities, and sufficient mobility among consumers, for the latter to locate according to their valuation of the different bundles of output. For example, firms who value low-cost access to a university with a particular excellence will be prepared to pay a higher rate of business tax to gain access to that resource. Taken together these issues have great significance for the geographical domain over which economic policy should be conducted.

Coordinating investments

The final area for considering policy intervention, and highlighted by the study of cluster performance, is required by the fact that the usual mechanism for coordination of resources—that of the market—is simply missing in many innovative contexts. Policy responses can and have been various. In Europe fashionable approaches to increasing the coordination of investment have included the rationalization of industry and the promotion of national champions. A rather more decentralized and currently popular approach to improved coordination focuses, however, upon a convergence of views across relevant economic agents about the development of technology which can in principle be promoted by adopting the Foresight process, discussed in the following section.

9.5 THE UK POLICY CONTEXT

We have argued that the basis of competitiveness for the advanced economies will be the ability of the economies concerned to generate investments which make relatively intensive use of knowledge. The fact that the mechanisms which are conducive to this process are highly dependent upon individual institutional contexts is a potent reason for supposing that local, possibly national, characteristics may be vital in determining which regions and which nations benefit from technological change and the freer international movement of goods, services, and capital, which are the main elements in the so-called 'globalization' of the world economy. Variations in local characteristics may therefore have a powerful influence on persistent differences in growth rates. Thus, curiously, the development of knowledge-based specialization provides a counterbalance to the forces of globalization, which have generally received much more attention. Something very similar may be said about the impact of the Single European Market, where the process of economic integration may tend to generate knowledge-based clustering as national industries begin to unbundle (*The Economist* 1996).

Effective institutions may eliminate some of the market failures in each of the five processes vital to knowledge-based investment outlined in section 9.2: to wit, the generation, translation, diffusion, exchange, and absorption of knowledge. It follows that appropriate policies must be based on an assessment of the existing institutional structure, its strengths and weaknesses. In some sectors of economies, the private sector has managed to create, largely unaided, effective institutions which reduce the impact of market failure. Elsewhere, the interventionist policies of

284   *Paul Temple*

government agencies have played an apparently vital role in promoting technological change. Again, there can be no question of
expecting policies which apparently work in one context to work
in another. Successful policy must be based on an audit of the
institutional background to the key processes of technological
change identified above. The mechanisms operating in the UK
have, to a degree, their own idiosyncratic character which
influences performance, and these must be addressed by policy.
Of particular concern in the UK is the relationship between
its institutions and the ability of the economy to generate technological resource.

What is this relationship? As far as the measurement of the
accumulation of competitive potential, or resource, is concerned,
the evidence is actually rather bleak, as Figure 9.2 makes clear.
Using measures of cumulated stocks of patents, R & D, and physical investment, each of which may be regarded as belonging to
conceptually distinct aspects of technological activity, it appears
that the UK share of the total for each indicator for the G6 actually
fell faster in the period between 1980 and 1992 than between 1970
and 1980.

Although the need for knowledge-based investment may have
been reduced by the high share of multinational inward invest-

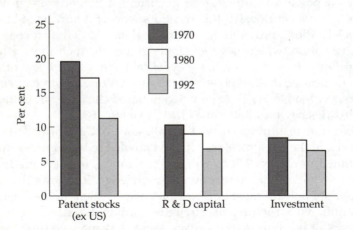

Fig. 9.2 *UK shares of G6 technological activity*
Source: OECD/Peck and Temple 1996.

ment taken by the UK during the 1980s, enhancing the ability of the economy to benefit from international spillovers, nevertheless a failure to generate knowledge-based investments has been a *proximate* cause of a lack of competitiveness in UK manufacturing (Peck and Temple 1996). This does not of course imply that policy should necessarily concentrate on incentives for investment, but needs to consider the deeper-seated *institutional* reasons for the UK's poor investment record—whether in physical equipment, workforce skills, or research and development. Here the debate has focused on a distinction between two contrasting institutional forms of capitalism—the 'Anglo-Saxon' model and a 'Japanese-German' model. The growing emphasis on corporate governance in the performance debate marks a shift away from the attention that policy gave in the 1980s to the UK labour market and its idiosyncratic institutions.

The essential difference between these models is the system of corporate governance they propose (Morris 1994). The relevant point of departure is the extent to which the Japanese-German model favours longer-term knowledge-based investment because of the low or zero risk of hostile takeover. The threat of hostile takeover in the UK may be having a considerable systematically negative impact upon R & D and other types of longer-term investment. Among the various reasons that have been advanced for this proposition is the so-called 'signal jamming' mechanism (Stein 1989) in which investors are unable to distinguish between cuts in dividends which are needed to undertake current investment opportunities and those which are the result of poor management.

It should by no means be supposed that the Anglo-Saxon model is deficient in all respects related to knowledge-based investment. Indeed it seems clear that the highly diffuse ownership patterns characterizing the Anglo-Saxon model have the potential to favour riskier technology-based developments through their diversification possibilities. Thus the USA and the UK have the most highly developed venture capital markets. It seems clear that venture capital institutions have had the most powerful impact in the USA (e.g. in Silicon Valley), not only in terms of funding riskier investments, but also in supplying a vital coordinating mechanism (Langlois and Robertson 1995). In the UK, however, the evidence is less clear cut, and recent studies have been critical of the industry's contribution to new technology ventures. According to Murray and Lott (1995) the market has favoured management buyouts and buy-ins. Once these are excluded, technology has been far less significant in the UK than in the USA.

For institutional reasons, then, quoted companies in the UK may follow different investment strategies from those in say Germany or Japan or indeed most European economies. Institutions in the UK are less likely to favour those requiring substantial amounts of trust, as for example in cooperative R & D projects. The argument extends to the acquisition of workforce skills, however, and workers themselves are likely to favour general skills (valuable on the external labour market) over those specific to an employer. More generally, the system may militate against the density of information flows which are the hallmark of geographically clustered development. However, the argument is dependent upon the importance of the probability of takeover which is less for unquoted companies. One notes, from the DTI's 'Innovations Scoreboard', that R & D expenditures in the UK are more highly concentrated among the larger firms than is the case in Germany or Japan (see Small and Swann 1993). Interestingly, in a comparison of British and German firms, Davis (1993) found some of the greatest differences in middle-sized companies. In the UK, these are much more likely to rely on equity finance than bank debt (the predominant form in Germany), and bank debt was shorter term. The high dividend pay-out rate found for these firms in the UK was consistent with the need to defend against takeover as outlined above.

The evolution of policy in the UK

Three broad areas of economic policy and one specific one bear directly on the development of knowledge-based industrial clusters—industry policy, science and technology policy, and regional policy are the broad areas. All three are intertwined in the specific social experiment and new process called Foresight, which falls most naturally under science and technology policy, but contains elements of the other two. This section briefly reviews the evolution of policy in the UK in these four areas.

During the post-war period two very distinct phases can be detected in all aspects of economic policy-making in the UK. First, there was a period in which primacy was given to the problem of market failure, combined with an optimistic belief in the efficacy of government action to correct such failures. This gave way in the 1970s to greater emphasis on the inherent efficiency of markets, and to scepticism about the ability of governments to correct market failure even where it could be shown to exist. This much Britain shares with many, if not all, other advanced economies. However, the context differs in each case, and in Britain the retreat from interventionist policies and the promotion of market incentives took a particularly acute form, although it would be wrong to suggest that the discontinuity was fundamental in all areas. The changes were most radical for the labour market, where the adjustments necessary in the face of supply-side shocks in the 1970s were demonstrably rather more costly in the case of the UK than other economies. The adversarial political system probably also contributed to the vehemence with which trade union reform and other labour market deregulation was approached. By comparison, reform in the areas of policy discussed here has been more modest.

Industry policy

Until the end of the 1970s, industry policy took, in the main, the form of support for fixed investment, often to aid restructuring in declining industries such as steel and shipbuilding. In the early 1980s this was partially replaced by support for technology and R & D in particular (Shepherd 1987), with the emphasis on new as opposed to declining industries. Notable initiatives included a new post of Minister for Information Technology as well as the Alvey programme referred to above. However, this situation changed considerably after the middle of the decade and a major review of support for technology: as a result government removed support for near market 'development' work, where it was believed that the market failure rationale was not strong, while initiating a new emphasis on collaborative research (perhaps on the grounds of the high initial barriers to such collaboration). At the same time, spending upon R & D programmes was largely subordinated to European programmes, not, according to

Sharp and Walker (1994), 'with any great enthusiasm, but more in the interest of gaining Britain's *juste retour* and avoiding responsibility for thinking strategically about the direction in which technologies and industries should develop'. A rather different strand of policy emphasis since this time was the targeting of assistance for smaller businesses. Among the more important schemes currently operating is the loan guarantee scheme for small firms lacking collateral. In addition there is a raft of measures introduced to support smaller business which take the form of advisory services and mechanisms for the encouragement of best practice (with therefore a greater emphasis on diffusion). Recently these services were brought under the umbrella of the Business Link programme (the 'one-stop shop'). It is important to note that although the Business Link mission specifically includes the encouragement of horizontal and vertical firm networks, it has been criticized for its failure to induce such relations, concentrating instead upon interactions between the agency and the firm.

However, it needs to be emphasized that the framework currently in place has evolved against a backdrop of very substantial *reductions* in resources for the support of industry. As Sharp and Walker (1994) point out, Britain must be alone among the OECD economies in actually reducing government support for R & D over this period. More generally, the UK has some of the lowest levels of state aid for industry in the EU.

Science policy

The development of science policy in the UK is also of direct relevance to the foundations of a competitiveness policy. It is at least one area where the question of government involvement has never been seriously questioned. Nevertheless, it too has undergone profound changes in the post-war period. A strong sense of continuity, however, can be found in the belief that Britain has a strong science and engineering base. The science and engineering base is defined in the 1993 White Paper *Realising our Potential* as the 'research and postgraduate training capacity based in the universities and colleges of higher education and in the Institutes, Units, and Centres operated by the Research Councils, together with the central facilities supported by the Councils and available for use by UK scientists and engineers'. Strong it may be, but the drawback is that it is too detached from industry to be channelled into innovation (Shohet 1996).

Various stages can be detected in the evolution of policy over the period, driven by the recognition that the rate of growth of resources devoted to science in the early post-war period was unsustainable, and that the contribution of science to technology and industry was much more complex than many simple formulations had allowed for, especially the so-called 'linear' or 'science push' conception of technological change. Policy involvement in the technology field was in a sense detached from science policy, and mostly concerned with defence or areas with strong defence connections such as nuclear power or aircraft.

Today, in the UK as elsewhere, science is regarded as presenting a 'strategic opportunity', so that it no longer makes sense to detach science policy from technology policy. This is exemplified by the 1993 White Paper, in which the importance of the international division of scientific labour is made explicit. The document noted 'a widely perceived contrast between our excellence in science and technology and our relative weakness in exploiting them to economic advantage' and 'the absence of a clear statement of government objectives'. It also recognized that decisions about 'strategic' research programmes were frequently taken 'without the benefit of any systematic, well informed assessment of the match between potential research outputs and the likelihood that they can be appropriated by firms and organisations'.

Foresight

The most interesting and promising recent policy initiative, and the one with the clearest potential relevance to clustering, is Foresight—the UK version of the Technology Foresight exercises that originated in Japan. Foresight is a natural extension of science and technology policy, following the new direction that was given by the 1993 White Paper. Foresight was launched in 1994 and closely shadowed the Japanese process already described. Sector panels were formed that brought research scientists and senior industrialists together, in common special fields of interest; to identify the drivers of long-term change and competitive opportunity, to survey their technological and market horizons for the imminent, the mid-term, and the distantly imaginable; and to turn both the wilder and the more familiar shores of possibility into sets of propositions, thrown to a pool of several thousand interested and more or less knowledgeable individuals for their structured responses, in a large-scale Delphi exercise. The panels then digested the answers and, at the end of the first fifteen months, published their conclusions on feasible opportunities and the scientific, industrial, commercial, and social conditions and desiderata in the way of their achievement. In early 1995, an overarching steering group drew these together, for all fifteen panels, into a set of generic priorities that crossed many of the separate disciplines, markets, and technologies. As a first consequence, the agenda of the cash-strapped funders of public sector research now take account of the competitive possibilities of academic science. By the middle of 1996, the Sector Panels continued to work, but in a more damped-down way, delivering their messages locally, in workshops, region by region, and drawing together a neighbourhood science base and the (mainly smaller) companies located near that base, and encouraging them to communicate and think ahead.

Foresight is not forecasting. It depends upon building a degree of confidence that the future is not predetermined, but that long-term national and regional competitive advantages can be created, by timely knowledge-sharing, strategic investment, and innovation. The prime condition for this to happen is for the research science community, entrepreneurs, and—to the extent that it is politic—government to envisage in concert (one dare not say 'plan') the entire translation process from initial science and engineering breakthrough into commercially successful innovation and into the creation of new markets, five, ten, or twenty years away.

What is envisaged, in this communicative process, is the antithesis of the old 'linear model' that supposed a vertical chain of separate and ordered events from hard science to an eventual market place, the market made inevitable by the technology. Instead, what is encouraged is a closely knit network of all those implicated in a potential innovation, meeting face to face, and interacting continuously. Foresight is another instance of the consensual approach which was tried, in a more corporatist form, in the days of the National Economic Development Council. But now the players are not the politically oriented industrial parties that have so often failed to agree, and resisted change and experimentation. They are individual scientists and entrepreneurs, looking for a new compatibility between their previously private incentive sets.

With sufficient energy behind it, and plenty of patience, Foresight should be capable of initiating both local and virtual clusters, and developing centres of technological and market excellence, that could determine future national competitive advantage. There are already promising signs of this within the research institutions involved in biotechnology. Between 1994 and 1997 the Biological Science and Biotechnology Research Council organized a Technology Interaction Board, with separate directorates for chemicals, food, and agriculture, involving key industrialists, university scientists, and research institutes in the implementation of the Foresight recommendations, within the overriding condition that the science that is supported is 'good' science. The inspiration of Foresight is very much in tune with the clustering principles. There is a strong sense of community involved, even when the community is—as in the case of the 10,000 professional physicists implicated through the Physics Institute— a *virtual* cluster based on a shared discipline. There is also a strong sense that the confidence and trust which distinguish a culture of innovation requires teamwork, the creation and sharing of tacit knowledge, and that degree of continuity for which a shared domain is a *sine qua non*. Foresight cannot create a clustering culture; but it can help to feed one. We have seen that Foresight works in Japan. It remains to discover whether the institutions and culture in the UK can also support that self-sustaining process (see Stout 1995).

Regional policy

The concept of the geographically bounded industrial cluster has profound implications for regional policy. Traditionally regional policy has been aimed at reducing regional inequalities: i.e. it has had an essentially redistributive element. In the UK, for example, its main purpose was to help areas with high levels of unemployment, and this was backed by the general principle of 'taking work to the worker'. Behind the latter principle lay the belief that once the question of the social and economic infrastructure had been solved, the bulk of manufacturing employment was actually 'footloose', so that there were negligible social costs handicapping the growth of chosen regions. Accordingly, infrastructure investment in the UK was skewed towards the problem regions. For example the motorway network in the UK developed faster in the north of England and Scotland than in the more capacity constrained south-east. Although questions were raised about whether policy instruments were biased towards capital or labour, there was little debate about the knowledge intensity of investments or about the role of agglomeration economies. Indeed, one common worry was that agglomerations might become *too large* with no market mechanism to ensure their optimum size was not exceeded. The basis for this argument was that, on the one hand, gross income per head would rise with population but at a diminishing rate, with these gains being privately appropriable; while on the other hand, agglomeration operating costs per head would eventually accelerate as the agglomeration grew.

By the 1980s, the more widespread recession and the shift toward more aggressively market-oriented policies put an end to the more redistributive measures. National policies were redirected toward the perceived urban problem. Local economic development has become an increasingly local matter, while there has been a substantial reduction in regional policy expenditure— to about one-quarter of its peak level in the 1960s. What assistance remains is targeted at fewer areas, and is channelled through independent organizations such as the Training and Enterprise Councils and their Scottish equivalent, the Local Enterprise Councils.

In tune with the changing economic policy perspective, many local efforts have aimed at stimulating entrepreneurship, especially in high-tech areas. Specific locational 'magnets' have been emphasized, including venture capital, transport, physical amenities, and the creation of science parks. The science park is a particularly interesting phenomenon in the context of clustering, for it can be seen to be a policy instrument specifically directed at the development of the knowledge resource, with implications for several of the processes vital for technological change which we identified earlier. Indeed a study by Monck et al. (1988) showed that firms located on science parks did have both the formal and informal links with universities which stimulated technology transfer. The growth rate of such firms was, however, found to be lower than New Technology Based Firms (NTBFs) elsewhere, but this finding may have been because of the higher numbers of NTBFs on science parks which were founded by academics, for whom growth was a lower priority, or who lacked entrepreneurial skills. More recent studies have not generally been favourable to science parks (e.g. Massey et al. 1992), although some research has indicated better survival rates (Keeble 1993).

The objectives of much local development policy have recently tended to coincide with those of technology policy, driving towards the goal of indigenous competitiveness. However, the agents of policy remain essentially fragmented and uncoordinated, with, in England at least, a lack of any strategic capacity or coordinating mechanism for the different agencies responsible for regional initiatives.

9.6 A WAY FORWARD

If the argument presented in this chapter is valid, competitiveness policy requires an assessment of the institutional framework that underpins Britain's industrial structure. In spite of three recent White Papers addressed to the competitiveness issue, we still do not have that assessment (Temple 1995). Nor have we provided one here. What we have set out to do is to show that the present framework, until the Foresight programme and currently in spite of it, is biasing investment behaviour—not simply against longer-term investments, but also against investments which depend upon standards of behaviour which encourage trust. In essence these are the investments which transform local agglomerations of activity into dynamic clusters in which the innovative entrepreneur is most likely to thrive and firm-specific technological capability be fostered. If this is indeed the case, and the development of knowledge-based specialization will decide the pattern of growth between the advanced economies, the need to address these sources of institutional failure is paramount. Policy, in such circumstances, can take one of two directions: radical reform of institutions which are believed to be responsible for the under-performance, or a more piecemeal development of institutions which can enhance the strengths, and correct the weaknesses, of the current system.

Consider the second approach. The first issue is the resources that the nation needs to devote to the creation and the diffusion of knowledge, as well as the development of the knowledge infra-structure. Whatever the strength of the emphasis on value for money, there is no evidence that the UK can buck an international trend and devote fewer public resources to the development of the knowledge base. On the other hand, dissatisfaction with the return to activities in the past may be legitimate, especially in the emphasis on defence-related R & D. This suggests that a switch of focus and emphasis, as well as additional resources, may be re-quired. A framework for this switch of emphasis and for channel-ling the additional resources could in fact be provided by a much higher profile and extended Foresight programme. Further it may well be that the creation of additional resources along the devel-opment path suggested by that programme is essential for its credibility.

Taken at face value, the theory lying behind the clustering phenomenon suggests that an appropriate objective for economic policy would be the exercise of direct influence over the location of industry in an attempt to create critical mass. However, for the various reasons discussed above, a more achievable, if indirect, objective would be to create highly visible 'magnets' for industrial location based upon Foresight criteria. The objective for policy here should be the promotion of differentiated excellence in the research base. Considerable credibility could be given to the Fore-sight process if specific additional funds were made available in those areas which were deemed to offer the greatest opportuni-ties. The analysis of this book suggests that the research base acts as a powerful attractor for private investment where critical mass has been achieved. This suggests that local *industrial* strength should be a factor in determining which bids for resources were successful. Moreover, this chapter has also suggested that a par-ticular failure in the UK is the difficulty of promulgating coopera-tive research. Although not always clear from its grounding in the theory of market failure, targeting cooperative bids has been an aspect of policy in recent years. The institutional analysis of the UK has, however, reinforced the desirability of using the consortium as the appropriate vehicle for providing support for R & D under this programme. Qualifying consortia might span industry and universities. Giving them a local dimension would help to ensure that such schemes were essentially complementary to existing European programmes promoting cooperative research. Consideration might also be given to the form of research supported. Emphasis might be given in this regard to programmes which had a defensive or 'tracking' objective—helping to mediate between the international orientation of university research and the highly specific technological competencies of the firm, and maximizing the probability of additionality by stimulating the development of firm-specific capabilities. This approach would therefore go beyond the rather vague wish for increased academic–industry interaction which permeates the current Foresight programme into some more definite support for local public goods.

However, policy needs to transcend these proposals to consider the case for two kinds of institutional reform. The first is of the institutions that affect technology transfer. Reform needs to embrace the objective of developing coherent *technological communities* which appear to be the true hallmark of the successful industrial cluster. One possibility would be to resurrect and develop the idea of the so-called Faraday Centre (CEST 1992) on a localized (possibly regional) basis as part of the institutional background for technology transfer and networking activities in the UK. One of the objections to the current Business Link scheme, it may be recalled, was that its basis is the bilateral transaction between the firm and the institution, despite the objective of developing networking among firms. The Faraday Centre by contrast, could serve as the basis for networking activities by:

1. deliberately fostering the movement of skilled personnel between industry and the science base;
2. pursuing, among its core activities, the tracking R & D which is most likely to generate complementarities with firm specific industrial R & D (other core activities might include the consultative service provided under Business Links);

3. undertaking specific R & D projects financed by a partnership between the Centre and industry consortia.

The second type of reform involves institutional innovation in the field of finance. The role of small firm start-ups in early stages of product cycles has already been stressed. In theory the diffused pattern of share ownership in the UK could, and perhaps should, be providing opportunities for higher-risk new technology-based start-ups by allowing investors the opportunities for the diversification of risk. It is of interest to ask why venture capital institutions have not filled the gap in the way that they appear to have done in the USA. It seems that the fixed costs attached to evaluating the risks and potential of newer technologies mean that new technology suffers in relation to, *inter alia*, the management buyout market. This is particularly important in relation to small-scale entrepreneurial start-ups where the finance required is actually too small. The absence of critical mass in the UK may exacerbate the problem in comparison with the USA. In this way the 'Macmillan Gap' of small firm finance of the 1930s is recreated today in the field of new technology start-ups. Current policy effectively recognizes the problem, but not perhaps its scale. Policy should consider the case for longer-term finance being made available within the Foresight framework and the proposed regional technology centres. As centres of excellence in these designated areas, they would provide in their own right powerful means for attracting other forms of external finance, for instance by creating 'packages' of investment in smaller firms in coherent forms. This special expertise may have other powerful spillovers, for example in the representation of small business interest in standards committees. It may also provide sufficient leverage for the City to devote additional resources to the evaluation of new technology.

It is doubtful whether powerful regional magnets can be created without the creation of *strategic capacity* at the regional level. The extent to which this would mark a departure from the way of thinking of current policy cannot be ignored. The role that regional economic councils have played in maintaining industrial and social cohesiveness in Germany has become clearer in recent years; to start with, however, such bodies might have much more limited objectives relating to education and training and the collective forms of R & D. The deep scepticism in Britain surrounding the role of government, and national government in particular, should not be underestimated, and remains an obstacle to policy reform. The extension of local democracy into the field of economic policy may be one way out of this impasse.

10

Conclusions

G. M. PETER SWANN AND MARTHA PREVEZER

The aim of this final chapter is to pull together the most important lessons from this study. We conclude by identifying some implications for policy to be drawn from the work.

10.1 FORCES THAT PROMOTE CLUSTERING

We have seen that, at least since the industrial revolution, there are many different forces causing clusters to emerge. While the initial location of a cluster may be a little arbitrary, when it has started to forge ahead it will tend to stay ahead, at least for a while. When clusters get large, saturation and congestion start to set in. At this stage the cluster may stop growing, and may even decline if it does not have and cannot attract new industries to replace the old. Some clusters never recover; others do. While some recovery may derive from the price mechanism, some through urban renewal, and some through the attractiveness of an old city's cultural capital, there is an important role here for convergence between old and new technologies in sustaining the resuscitation of a cluster.

The forces that can generate clustering could operate on the demand side or the supply side. In this book, our main focus has been on supply-side technological spillovers; such spillovers from company X (say) are most readily exploited by company Y when X and Y are located close together. We also recognized that there could be costs to clustering, and that when a cluster becomes very congested, indeed, the costs of locating there may exceed the benefits. While this could ultimately lead to the decline of a mature cluster, we argued that this decline will not always be terminal. When new technologies start to converge on well-established mature technologies, then the mature cluster can once again prove to be an attractive location for the new entrant.

We recognized in short a life cycle of the cluster, with strong positive feedback during the growth phase. Indeed, the empirical results of Chapter 4 identified a critical mass that has to be achieved before entry into the cluster will take off. We also identified a point of peak entry, at which the cluster is at its most attractive. As the cluster grows beyond that size, entry still continues, but at a reducing rate. Eventually net entry may stop. Some other authors have suggested that the life cycle of a high-technology cluster is probably of the order of fifty years from its start to maturity.

10.2 ENTRY ATTRACTORS AND GROWTH PROMOTERS

In computing, there are some sectors that seem to play an important role in attracting entrants to a particular location: communications, components, computers, systems, and computer services. Most of the entrants attracted are to the software and peripheral sectors, and few to the core manufacturing sectors. In biotechnology, the main entry attractor is the science base rather than other industry sectors.

A company located in a cluster with a strong representation of firms from the same industry subsector will tend to grow faster than average. But co-location with companies from different subsectors does not appear to be helpful—and indeed in some cases may have a detrimental effect on growth. This story seems to be the same in USA and UK computing and in US biotechnology.

Starting from scratch, the best way to grow a computer industry in a particular cluster seems to be to start with strong core manufacturing firms, or a mix of core manufacturing firms and some from the service, peripheral, or software sectors. It is harder to grow a strong computer industry in a particular cluster without that head start in core manufacturing. Moreover, if the size of the core manufacturing sector is constrained, the growth of the peripheral, service, and software sectors will be reduced, because entry will be limited. Conversely, the growth of core manufacturing sectors is little affected when other sectors decline, because the latter would in any case do little to attract entry to the core.

Generally speaking, though not invariably, if a cluster shows strength in one subsector of the computer industry, then that strength encourages the growth and entry of firms in other subsectors. This would imply that, instead of different computer industry clusters specializing in very different areas, the main clusters have strengths in all subsectors of the computer industry. If, for example, we break the computer industry into eight subsectors—communications, components, computer hardware, distributors, peripherals, services, software, and systems—we find that in any of these subsectors the state with the largest numbers of firms is California. The same applies to the biotechnology industry.

Finally, we found that diversified firms which operated in two or more of the subsectors of the computer industry grew at about the same rate, on average, as an equivalent collection of single-sector firms. While a greater degree of integration might in principle ensure that some of the synergies from different activities are captured within the single firm, our results suggest that on average this effect is not strong. This is consistent with the argument that, in the computer industry, the vertically non-integrated firm does not necessarily operate at a significant disadvantage compared to vertically integrated firms.

10.3 INTERPRETATION OF DIFFERENTIAL ENTRY ATTRACTOR AND GROWTH PROMOTION EFFECTS

This difference between the growth and entry models is consistent with the view that entrants and incumbents have different capacities to absorb the spillovers from incumbent firms in core manufacturing sectors, and that radical innovations in core manufacturing tend to provoke *entry* in the core and other sectors, rather than promoting rapid growth amongst incumbents.

One interpretation of these results which we find quite compelling is this: entrants and incumbents have different capacities to absorb the spillovers from incumbent firms in core hardware sectors, and radical innovations in core hardware sectors tend to provoke *entry* into the core and other sectors, more than promoting rapid growth amongst incumbents. This arises from the different organizational structures of large and small firms, and the implications of this for their ability to *absorb* knowledge.

Absorptive capacity, in the sense used by Cohen and Levinthal (1990), summarizes the ability of firms to assimilate knowledge from the external environment and to transfer knowledge across and between the subdivisions of the firm. Nelson and Winter (1982) point out that this depends less on individuals than on organizational structure, and that large complex organizations depend on tried and tested innovative routines. This reliance on routines makes large organizations poor at improvising responses to novel situations—or what Tushman and Anderson (1986) would call *competence destroying* technological change. Large firms cope better with technological change that is compatible with their technological vision, since, with a perceptive vision, firms can develop routines, and hence reduce the range of technological challenges that are *competence destroying*. Swann and Gill (1993) analysed five case studies of rapid technological change and found that, when change was consistent with what companies had imagined, the change did not disrupt existing market share patterns. Conversely, when rapid technological change was inconsistent with companies' technological vision, it often led to a significant redistribution of market share.

Hannan and Freeman (1977) have stressed that the internal political balance of the large organization can be severely disrupted by the sorts of organizational restructuring required to respond effectively to new challenges; and in the light of this, managers may choose to defer reorganization. This goes some way towards explaining why large incumbents do not absorb all the potential spillovers from other firms, why new entrants are better at absorption, and why, as a consequence, there was so much successful entry into these computer and biotechnology industry clusters.

In this analysis, entrants have played an important part in soaking up spillovers that might otherwise be lost, even if those entrants do not grow to be especially large. It is consistent with Simon's (1985) observation that it is learning from diverse knowledge bases which is most likely to yield innovation.

10.4 ROLE OF INITIAL CONDITIONS

From our models it was clear that the initial conditions prevailing in each location importantly influenced the development of clusters. A closer inspection of these conditions in individual US states revealed some key features. These included the presence of experienced venture capitalists and financing mechanisms on both the west and east coasts. But particularly important has been the ability to create and sustain fluid networks, using venture capitalists as intermediaries, whereby information about new opportunities and technologies has travelled swiftly within the community. This has been important in computing (Saxenian 1994), and particularly influential in helping biotechnology clusters to cross the scientific and industrial divide.

10.5 COMPARISON OF COMPUTING AND BIOTECHNOLOGY

The main differences between computing and biotechnology can be set out for the USA. It is impossible yet to be sure that the same set of differences pertain in the UK, because biotechnology there is still at such an early stage of development.

The first difference is that cross-sectoral effects on entry are strong in computing, but much weaker in biotechnology. In particular we found that strong, 'hard' sectors in US computing (notably computer hardware, systems, and semiconductor components) have a powerful attractive effect on entry into other sectors such as software and computer peripherals, and to a lesser extent on services. These strong effects are rarely found in biotechnology, and effectively only between therapeutics and diagnostics.

One possible reason for this is that technological developments in one area of computing can certainly create opportunities for other computer industry sectors, picked up by new entrants, as we have said. In contrast, firms in biotechnology tend to specialize in supplying particular user sectors. Technological developments here are therefore less likely to be helpful to those supplying other users. Another possible reason could be that computing is inherently a *network* technology, where the value of any component is as much to do with what it can connect to, as with what the component can do on its own. This means that while any one computer industry company may tend to specialize in the application of a relatively small subset of computer technologies, there are always potential synergies with other technologies. Biotechnology is not so obviously a network technology. Furthermore, any one company in biotechnology tends to apply the same set of generic technologies to generate solutions for particular end-user markets. That means that many of the consequent synergies are internal to a particular biotechnology sector. However, the role of incumbent firms as end-users and the networks of alliances between entrants within any one sector are important features of biotechnology clusters in the USA.

Second, the main attractor of new entry into biotechnology seems to be a strong science base. While the effects of this were not explored in the computing study, we argued that the science base is likely to have a much more potent effect on entry in the formative stages of a new industry than in the later stages. The science base had an important effect on the development of the computing industry in the 1950s and 1960s, but the effect is probably much weaker after that.

Third, there is some evidence of a growing interaction between computing and biotechnology especially in the field of bioinformatics. In particular, ever more of the important areas of biotechnology depend on state of the art developments in computing. These interactions appear to be significant as a force for geographical clustering in the early stages of new developments in the technologies, in particular where new computing technologies are significant for biotechnology. As the technologies become more generic and widespread, the need for clustering diminishes and the activities diffuse geographically. The reverse dependence of computing on biotechnology is much weaker, though there are some potential applications of biotechnology in computing.

10.6 A COMPARISON OF CLUSTERING IN THE USA AND UK

The unexpected conclusion from our comparison of clustering in the UK and the US computer industries is that clustering effects are *not* weaker in the UK. To be precise, the entry attractor effects in the UK and US computer entry models are of much the same size, even if not very closely correlated. This suggests that, although the pattern of entry attractor effects differs, the clustering forces are no weaker in the UK. This result is surprising, because it seems to contradict the widely held belief that a shortfall of entrepreneurial vigour in the UK means that important technological opportunities are not taken up. However, the sectoral composition of clusters in UK computing is significantly different from that in the USA, with very little core hardware and manufacturing of components, and greater emphasis on peripherals, software, distribution, and services. So whereas attractor effects appear to be as strong in the UK, they operate between different sectors. This may contribute to explaining why firms in all areas of the computer industry enjoy a higher trend growth rate in the USA than in the UK. We have not attempted to explore the full reasons for this, which may be the result of important structural differences in other sectors of the economy. And indeed, it may be the consequence of the fact that far more US clusters that UK clusters have progressed beyond the critical mass at which clusters start to grow more rapidly. But in terms of the coefficients of the entry model, the UK does not appear to start at a disadvantage.

In biotechnology, the nature of the attractor effects appears to be different in the UK from those in the USA. Firms are not attracted specifically by the bioscience base as they are in the USA; they are tending to locate nearer to general concentrations of university graduates and also near existing bioscience industry. This is due more to the tendency in the UK for new firms to locate close to their former employers. It may also be due to the greater difficulty in the UK in building local networks that span the scientific/industrial divide, making local links to the science base less easy to forge and hence less significant in the UK picture. Given that the strongest clusters in US biotechnology display precisely those characteristics of dense networks of collaborative relations between the local science base and industry, the absence of such networks in the UK may prove to be a significant drawback to the formation of such vibrant clusters.

10.7 DIVERSITY PROMOTES LONGEVITY OF CLUSTERS

The results of the simulations in Chapter 4 suggested that the performance of a particular subsector of the computing industry at a particular cluster depends on both the diversity of the cluster (single- or multi-technology) and the degree of convergence between the different computer technologies. When technologies have not converged, so that positive spillovers between different subsectors are limited, then the single-technology cluster outperforms the multi-technology cluster, essentially because in the latter (multi-technology), congestion starts to restrain growth in one subsector earlier that in the former (single-technology). When the technologies converge, on the other hand, the multi-technology cluster outperforms the single-technology cluster because the former exploits the inter-sectoral spillovers that the latter cannot have. There is, however, an optimum number of sectors: if a cluster starts with strengths in all subsectors of the industry, then congestion sets in too soon to allow full development of any one of these subsectors.

We can see a cycle in which single-technology clusters grow most rapidly when there is little or no convergence, but in which, when technologies start to converge and congestion emerges in early established clusters, the most successful clusters at a later stage may be multi-technology, and the single-technology cluster becomes less common.

We have not yet attempted to apply this simulation model to the case of biotechnology. Our conjecture is that because the cross-sectoral entry attractor effects are weaker in biotechnology than in computing, the single-technology cluster may be more competitive in that industry than in computing. But in the USA there has been considerable cross-fertilization of ideas between different parts of the science base relating to a number of sectors. Within strong US clusters, several sectors are represented. Moreover, regional specialization into particular biotechnology sectors in the UK does not seem to have helped clusters to form and may, indeed, be inhibiting that cross-fertilization of ideas between sectors which has helped clustering in the USA.

We have also found that congestion effects are not so far as important in biotechnology. But should the different parts of that industry start to converge in the same way as modelled here, then the multi-technology cluster may become the most competitive in biotechnology also.

10.8 POLICY LESSONS

We have argued that the industry cluster is an important means of the development of knowledge as a resource, and as a means to integrate different strands of economic policy—especially in science, regional, and industry policy, and through the Foresight programme. Policy needs to consider the creation of powerful and visible magnets for industrial location. The record of USA biotechnology suggests that the science base may act as a powerful attractor to new entry and entrepreneurship.

We suggest that a number of public institutions play an important role in the development of clusters. One of the most important is the research base, located in universities and other research laboratories. Given the potential of the science base to attract new entrants during the early stages of an industry's development— identified here as a potent force in USA biotechnology—there is a strong case for trying to establish highly visible magnets for industrial location. The Foresight process can play an important role here, because the combination of relevant science base and relevant industrial strength in the same region acts as a powerful enabler of technological change. But the UK government needs to make credible commitments to the trajectories suggested by the Foresight panels, a commitment which inescapably entails more resources for science and technology.

We also recognize the important role for institutions of technology transfer, for example, the Faraday centres proposed by CEST a few years ago. These institutions would be designed to promote and foster the positive feedback between industrial strength and the research base, on the one hand, and new firm entry and growth on the other. This would be achieved by promoting personnel mobility between industry and the science base, by promoting 'tracking' research in the science base that complements the firm-specific R & D conducted in companies, and by promoting joint R & D projects between industry consortia and Faraday centres.

Overall, the development of a cluster policy requires the creation of strategic capacity at a regional level, in the direction of the regional economic councils that operate in Germany. This represents a significant step ahead of economic policy in the UK as it stood at the end of 1996.

References

ACARD (1979), *Biotechnology: Report of a Joint Working Party*, London: HMSO.

Acs, Z., and AUDRETSCH, D. (1987), 'Innovation, Market Structure and Firm Size', *Review of Economics and Statistics*, 69: 567–75.

——— (1989), 'Small Firm Entry in US Manufacturing', *Economica*, 56: 255–65.

——— (1990), *Innovation in Small Firms*, Boston: MIT Press.

——— and FELDMAN, M. (1992), 'Real Effects of Academic Research: Comment', *American Economic Review Papers and Proceedings*, 82: 363–7.

——— ——— (1994), 'R & D Spillovers and Recipient Firm Size', *Review of Economics and Statistics*, 76: 336–40.

ALLEN, J. (1995), 'Science Parks and Regional Development'. Paper presented to the R & D Management Conference on Knowledge Technology and Innovative Organizations, Pisa, 1995.

ALLEN, R. (1983), 'Collective Invention', *Journal of Economic Behaviour and Organisation*, 4: 1–24.

AMIN, A., and GODDARD, J. (eds.) (1986), *Technological Change, Industrial Restructuring and Regional Development*, London: Allen and Unwin.

——— and ROBBINS, K. (1991), 'These are not Marshallian Times', in R. Camagni (ed.), *Innovation Networks: Spatial Perspectives*, London: Belhaven Press.

——— and THRIFT, N. (1991), 'Marshallian Nodes in Global Networks', paper presented at the European Science Foundation RURE meeting, Barcelona.

ANDERSON, P., and TUSHMAN, M. (1990), 'Technological Discontinuities and Dominant Designs: A Cyclical Model of Technological Change', *Administrative Science Quarterly*, 35: 604–33.

ARCHIBALD, G. C., and ROSENBLUTH, G. (1975), 'The "New" Theory of Consumer Demand and Monopolistic Competition', *Quarterly Journal of Economics*, 89: 569–90.

ARCHIBUGI, D., and PIANTA, M. (1992), *The Technological Specialisation of Advanced Countries*, Dordrecht: Kluwer.

ARORA, A., and GAMBARDELLA, A. (1993), 'The Division of Innovative Labour in Biotechnology', *H John Heinz III School of Public Policy and Management, Working Paper*, Pittsburgh: Carnegie Mellon.

ARROW, K. J. (1962a), 'The Economic Implications of Learning by Doing', *Review of Economic Studies*, 29: 155–73.

ARROW, K. J. (1962*b*), 'Economic Welfare and the Allocation of Resources for Inventions', in R. R. Nelson (ed.), *The Rate and Direction of Inventive Activity*, Princeton: Princeton University Press.

ARTHUR, W. B. (1989), 'Competing Technologies, Increasing Returns, and Lock-in by Historical Events', *Economic Journal*, 99 (394): 116–31.

——(1990), 'Silicon Valley Locational Clusters: Do Increasing Returns Imply Monopoly?', *Mathematical Social Sciences*, 19: 235–51.

——ERMOLIEV, Y., and KANIOVSKI, Y. (1987), 'Path-Dependent Processes and the Emergence of Macrostructure', *European Journal of Operational Research*, 30: 294–303.

AUDRETSCH, D. (1995), 'Innovation, growth and survival', *International Journal of Economic Organisation*, 13: 441–57.

——and FELDMAN, M. (1995), 'Innovative Clusters and the Industry Life-Cycle', *CEPR* Discussion Paper 1161.

————(1996), 'Knowledge Spillovers and the Geography of Innovation and Production', *American Economic Review*, 86 (3): 630–40.

——and STEPHAN, P. (1995), 'How Localized are Networks in Biotechnology', Wissenschaftszentrum Berlin fur Sozialforschung and Policy Research Center, Georgia State University, prepared for the IFS Conference on R & D, Innovation and Productivity, London.

AYDALOT, P., and KEEBLE, D. (eds.) (1988), *High-Technology Industry and Innovative Environments: The European Experience*, London: Routledge.

BAIROCH, P. (1988), *Cities and Economic Development from the Dawn of History to the Present*, Chicago: University of Chicago Press.

BALDWIN, J., and GORECKI, P. (1991*a*), 'Entry, Exit and Productivity Growth', in P. Geroski and J. Schwalbach (eds.), *Entry and Market Contestability: An International Comparison*, Oxford: Blackwell Pubs.

————(1991*b*), 'Firm Entry and Exit in the Canadian Manufacturing Sector', *Canadian Journal of Economics*, 24: 300–29.

BAPTISTA, R., and SWANN, G. M. P. (1996), 'The Dynamics of Firm Growth and Entry in Industrial Clusters: A Comparison of the US and UK Computer Industries', paper presented to International Schumpter Conference, Stockholm, June.

————(forthcoming), 'Do Firms in Clusters Innovate More?', *Research Policy*.

BARLEY, S., FREEMAN, J., and HYBELS, R. C. (1992), 'Strategic Alliances in Commercial Biotechnology', in N. Nohria and R. G. Eccles (eds.), *Networks and Organisations: Structure, Form and Action*, Boston, Mass: Harvard Business School Press, 311–47.

BEAUMONT, J. (1982), 'The Location, Mobility and Finance of New High-Technology Companies in the UK Electronics Industry', unpublished report, Department of Trade and Industry, South East Regional Office.

BECKMANN, M., and THISSE, J. (1986), 'The Location of Production Activities', in Nijkamp (ed.), *Handbook of Regional and Urban Economics*, vol. i, Elsevier Science Publishers.

BERNSTEIN, J. I. (1989), 'The Structure of Canadian Inter-industry R & D Spillovers and the Rates of Return to R & D', *Journal of Industrial Economics*, 37: 315–28.

——and NADIRI, M. I. (1988), 'Interindustry R & D Spillovers, Rates of Return and Production in High-Tech Industries', *American Economic Review, Papers and Proceedings*, 78 (2): 429–34.

————(1989), 'Research and Development and Intra-industry Spillovers: An Empirical Application of Dynamic Duality', *Review of Economic Studies*, 56: 249–69.

————(1991), 'Product Demand, Cost of Production, Spillovers and the Social Rate of Return to R & D', *NBER Working Paper 3625*.

BLOMSTRÖM, M. (1992), *Foreign Investment and Spillovers*, London: Routledge.

BLUME, S. (1985), *The Development of Dutch Science Policy in International Perspective, 1965–1985*, The Hague: Minitrie van Onderwijs en Wetenschappen.

BLUNDELL, R., GRIFFITH, R., and VAN REENAN, J. (1995a), 'Dynamic Count Data Models of Technological Innovation', *Economic Journal*, 105: 333–44.

————and WINDMEIJER, F. (1995b), 'Individual Effects and Dynamics in Count Data Models', *Mimeo*, University College London.

BREHENY, M., HART, D., and HOWELLS, J. (1992), 'Health and Wealth: The Development of the Pharmaceutical Industry in the South East of England Focusing on the Hertfordshire Sub-region', Reading: Spatial Economic Research Associates.

BRESCHI, S. (1995), 'Spatial Patterns of Innovation: Evidence from Patent Data', paper presented to the workshop on 'New Research Findings: The Economics of Scientific and Technological Research in Europe', Urbino.

BRESNAHAN, T. F., and TRAJTENBERG, M. (1992), 'General Purpose Technologies: Engines of Growth?', *CEPR Policy Paper* No. 300, Stanford, Calif.: Center for Economic Policy Research.

BREZIS, E. S., and KRUGMAN, P. (1993), 'Technology and the Life-Cycle of Cities', *NBER Working Paper, 4561*.

BRIGGS, A. (1968), *Victorian Cities*, London: Pelican Books.

BRUSCO, S. (1982), 'The Emilian Model: Productive Decentralisation and Social Integration', *Cambridge Journal of Economics*, 6: 167–84.

BULLOCK, W. O., and DIBNER, M. D. (1995), 'The state of the US biotechnology industry', *Trends in Biotechnology*, 13: 463–7.

CAMAGNI, R. (1991a), 'Local "Milieu", Uncertainty and Innovation Networks: Towards a Dynamic Theory of Economic Space', in Camagni 1991b.

CAMAGNI, R. (ed.) (1991b), *Innovation Networks: Spatial Perspectives*, London: Belhaven Press.

CARLSSON, B., and JACOBSSEN, S. (1994), 'Technological Systems and Economic Policy: The Diffusion of Factory Automation in Sweden', *Research Policy*, 23: 235–48.

Central Statistical Office (CSO) (1989), *Input–Output Tables for the UK, 1985*, London: HMSO.

——— (1993), *Regional Trends*, vol. xxviii, London: HMSO.

Centre for Exploitation of Science and Technology (CEST) (1992), 'Attitudes to Innovation in Germany and Britain: A Comparison', London: CEST.

CHAPPELL, W., KIMENYI, M., and MAYER, W. (1990), 'A Poisson Probability Model of Entry and Market Structure with an Application to U.S. Industries during 1972–77', *Southern Economic Journal*, Apr., 918–27.

CHARBIT, C., GAFFARD, J., LONGHI, C., PERRIN, J., QUERE, M., and RAVIX, J. (1991), *Coherence and Diversity of Systems of Innovation: The Study of Local Systems of Innovation in Europe*, Valbonne: LATAPSES.

CHRISTENSEN, C., and ROSENBLOOM, R. (1995), 'Explaining the Attacker's Advantage: Technological Paradigms, Organisational Dynamics and the Value Network', *Research Policy*, 24: 233–57.

CICCONE, A., and HALL, R. E. (1993), 'Productivity and the Density of Economic Activity', Working Paper in Economics E-93-6, The Hoover Institution, Stanford University.

CLOW A., and CLOW, N. L. (1958), 'The Chemical Industry: Interaction with the Industrial Revolution', ch. 8 (Part II) in C. Singer, E. J. Holmyard, A. R. Hall, and T. I. Williams (eds.), *A History of Technology*, vol. iv, Oxford: Oxford University Press.

COHEN, W. M., and LEVINTHAL, D. A. (1989), 'Innovation and Learning: The Two Faces of R & D', *Economic Journal*, 99: 569–96.

——————— (1990), 'Absorptive Capacity: A New Perspective on Learning and Innovation', *Administrative Science Quarterly*, 35 (1): 128–52.

COLLETIS, G. (1993), 'An Analysis of Technological Potential and Regional Development Processes in Rhône-Alpes', *European Planning Studies*, 1: 169–80.

Commission of the European Communities (CEC) (1994), 'An Industrial Competitiveness for the European Union', Brussels COM(94) 319.

CONTI, S., MALECKI, E., and OINAS, P. (1995), *The Industrial Enterprise and its Environment: Spatial Perspectives*, Aldershot: Avebury.

COOKE, P., and MORGAN, K. (1994), 'The Creative Milieu: A Regional Perspective on Innovation', in M. Dodgson and R. Rothwell (eds.), *The Handbook of Industrial Innovation*, London: Edward Elgar.

COOKSON, C. (1993), 'Lure of the City Lights: Smith and Nephew Defied Convention by Relocating R & D from Country Home to Science Park', *Financial Times*, 6 July.

COOMBS, J., and ALSTON, Y. R. (1993), *International Directory of Biotechnology*, New York: Macmillan.

DAVELAAR, E.-J., and NIJKAMP, P. (1990), 'Technological Innovation and Spatial Transformation', *Technology Forecasting and Social Change*, 37 (2): 181–202.

DAVID, P. A. (1985), 'Clio and the Economics of QWERTY', *American Economic Review Papers and Proceedings*, 75 (2): 332–6.

——(1987), 'Some New Standards for the Economics of Standardization in the Information Age', ch. 8 of P. Dasgupta and P. Stoneman (eds.), *Economic Policy and Technological Performance*, Cambridge: Cambridge University Press.

——and ROSENBLOOM, J. L. (1990), 'Marshallian Factor Market Externalities and the Dynamics of Industrial Localisation', *Journal of Urban Economics*, 28: 349–70.

DAVIS, E. P. (1993), 'Whither Corporate Relations?', in K. Hughes (ed.), *The Future of UK Competitiveness and the Role of Industrial Policy*, London: Policy Studies Institute.

DEBRESSON, C., and AMESSE, F. (1991), 'Networks of Innovators: A Review and an Introduction to the Issue', *Research Policy*, 20: 363–80.

DIBNER, M. D. (1991), *Biotechnology Guide USA, Companies, Data and Analysis*, 2nd edn., New York: Macmillan.

——(1995), *Biotechnology Guide USA*, 3rd edn., Institute for Biotechnology Information, New York: Macmillan.

DODGSON, M. (1990), 'Celltech: The First Ten Years of a Biotechnology Company', SPRU Discussion Paper Series, Brighton: University of Sussex.

——(1991a), *The Management of Technological Learning: Lessons from a Biotechnology Company*, New York: de Gruyter.

——(1991b), 'Strategic Alignment and Organisational Options in Biotechnology Firms', *Technology Analysis and Strategic Management*, 3 (2): 115–25.

——(1994), 'Technological Collaboration and Innovation', in M. Dodgson and R. Rothwell (eds.), *The Handbook of Industrial Innovation*, London: Edward Elgar.

DORFMAN, N. (1985), 'Route 128: The Development of a Regional High-Technology Economy', in D. Lampe (ed.), *The Massachusetts Miracle: High Technology and Economic Revitalisation*, Cambridge: MIT Press.

DOSI, G. (1982), 'Technological Paradigms and Technological Trajectories: A Suggested Interpretation of the Determinants and Directions of Technical Change', *Research Policy*, 11 (3): 147–62.

——(1988a), 'Sources, Procedures and Microeconomic Effects of Innovation', *Journal of Economic Literature*, 26: 1120–71.

——(1988b), 'The Nature of the Innovative Process', in G. Dosi, C.

Freeman, R. Nelson, G. Silverberg, and L. Soete (eds.), *Technical Change and Economic Theory*, London: Pinter Publishers.

DUNNILL, P., and RUDD, M. (1984), *Biotechnology and British Industry*, Swindon: Biotechnology Directorate of Science and Engineering Research Council.

DYERSON, R., and MUELLER, F. (1993), 'Intervention by Outsiders: A Strategic Management Perspective on the Government's Industrial Policy', *Journal of Public Policy*, 13 (1): 69–82.

Economist, The (1992), 'Computer Software', *The Economist*, 324 (7777), 19 Sept., 110.

——(1996), 'Single Market, Single Minded', 4 May, 79–80.

ELTIS, W. E., and HIGHAM, D. (1995), 'Closing the UK Competitiveness Gap', *National Institute Economic and Social Review* (Nov.), 71–85.

ERGAS, H. (1984), 'Why do some Countries Innovate more than Others?', Brussels: Centre for European Policy Studies, Paper No. 5.

——(1987), 'Does Technology Policy Matter?', in B. R. Guile and H. BROOKES (eds.), *Technology and Global Industry*, Washington, DC: National Academy Press.

ERNST & YOUNG (1993), *Biotech 93 Accelerating Commercialization*, San Francisco: Ernst & Young.

EVANS, A. W. (1985), *Urban Economics: An Introduction*, Oxford: Basil Blackwell.

FAGERBERG, J. (1995), 'User–Production Interaction, Learning and Comparative Advantage', *Cambridge Journal of Economics*, 19: 243–56.

FELDMAN, M. P. (1994), *The Geography of Innovation*, Dordrecht: Kluwer Academic Publishers.

——and AUDRETSCH, D. (1995), 'Science-Based Diversity, Specialisation, Localised Competition and Innovation', paper presented at the 22nd EARIE Conference, Sophia Antipolis, Sept. 1995.

FISHER, F. M., and TEMIN, P. (1974), 'Returns to Scale in Research and Development: What Does the Schumpeterian Hypothesis Imply?', *Journal of Political Economy*, 81: 56–70.

FLAHERTY, M. T. (1986), 'Coordinating International Manufacturing and Technology', in M. Porter (ed.), *Competition in Global Industries*, Cambridge, Mass.: Harvard Business School Press.

FLAMM, K. (1987), *Targeting the Computer: Government Support and International Competition*, Washington, DC: Brookings Institution.

——(1988), *Creating the Computer: Government, Industry and High Technology*, Washington, DC: Brookings Institution.

FORESTER, T. (1980), 'The Jelly Bean People of Silicon Valley', in T. Forester (ed.), *The Microelectronics Revolution*, Oxford: Basil Blackwell.

——(1987), *High-Tech Society*, Oxford: Basil Blackwell.

FREEMAN, C. (1982), *The Economics of Industrial Innovation*, 2nd edn., London: Pinter Publishers.

—— (1987), *Technology Policy and Economic Performance*, London: Pinter Publishers.

—— (1990), 'Schumpeter's Business Cycles Revisited', in A. Heertje and M. Perlman (eds.), *Evolving Technologies and Market Structure*, Cambridge: Cambridge University Press.

—— (1991), 'Networks of Innovators: A Synthesis of Research Issues', *Research Policy*, 20: 499–514.

FRÖBEL, F., HEINRICHS, J., and KREYE, O. (1980), *The New International Division of Labour*, Cambridge: Cambridge University Press.

GARNSEY, E. W., GALLOWAY, S. C., and MATHISEN, S. H. (1994), 'Flexibility and Specialisation in Question: Birth, Growth and Death Rates of Cambridge New Technology Based Firms 1988–92', *Entrepreneurship and Regional Development*, 6: 81–107.

GEROSKI, P. A. (1989), 'Entry, Innovation and Productivity Growth', *Review of Economics and Statistics*, 71: 572–8.

—— (1991*a*), 'Entry and the Rate of Innovation', *Economics of Innovation and New Technology*, 1 (3): 203–14.

—— (1991*b*), *Market Dynamics and Entry*, Oxford: Basil Blackwell Publishers.

—— (1995), 'What do we Know about Entry?', *International Journal of Industrial Organisation*, 13: 421–40.

GLAESER, E. L., KALLAL, H. D., SCHEINKMAN, J., and SHLEIFER, A. (1992), 'Growth in Cities', *Journal of Political Economy*, 100: 1126–52.

GLASMEIER, A. (1985), 'Innovative Manufacturing Industries: Spatial Incidence in the United States', in M. Castells (ed.), *High Technology, Space and Society*, Beverly Hills, Calif.: Sage.

GOLDSTEIN, G. S., and GRONENBERG, T. J. (1984), 'Economies of Scope and Economies of Agglomeration', *Journal of Urban Economics*, 16: 91–104.

GORDON, R. (1991), 'Innovation, Industrial Networks and High-Technology Regions', in Camagni, 1991*b*: 174–95.

GORT, M., and KLEPPER, S. (1982), 'Time Paths in the Diffusion of Product Innovations', *Economic Journal*, 92: 630–53.

GOURIROUX, C., MONFORT, A., and TROGNON, A. (1984), 'Pseudo-Maximum Likelihood Methods: An Application to Poisson Models', *Econometrica*, 52: 701–20.

GREEN, D. (1993), 'SmithKline to Move 1000 in Shake-up', *Financial Times*, 29 Oct.

GREENE, W. (1993), *Econometric Analysis*, 2nd edn., New York: Macmillan.

GRILICHES, Z. (1991), 'The Search for R & D Spillovers', *NBER Working Paper 3768*, Cambridge, Mass.: National Bureau of Economic Research, Scandinavian Journal of Economics.

GROSSMAN, G., and HELPMAN, E. (1992), *Innovation and Growth in the Global Economy*, Cambridge, Mass: MIT Press.

GUDGIN, G. (1995), 'Regional Problems and Policy in the UK', *Oxford Review of Economic Policy*, 11 (2): 18–63.

GUY, K., and ARNOLD, E. (1986), *Parallel Convergence*, London: Frances Pinter Publishers.

HACKING, A. J. (1986), *Economic Aspects of Biotechnology*, Cambridge Studies in Biotechnology 3, Cambridge: Cambridge University Press.

HAGEDOORN, J., and SCHAKENRAAD, J. (1990), 'Inter-firm Partnerships and Co-operative Strategies in Core Technologies' in C. Freeman and L. Soete (eds.), *New Explorations in the Economics of Technological Change*, London: Pinter Publishers.

——(1992), 'Leading Companies and Networks of Strategic Alliances in Information Technologies', *Research Policy*, 21 (2): 163–90.

HAGEN, J. VON, and HAMMOND, G. (1994), 'Industrial Localisation. An Empirical Test for Marshallian Localisation Economies', *CEPR* Discussion Paper 917.

HALL, P., MARKUSEN, A. R., OSBORN, R., and WACHSMAN, B. (1985), 'The American Computer Software Industry: Economics Development Prospects', in P. Hall and A. Markusen (eds.), *Silicon Landscapes*, Boston, Mass.: Allen and Unwin.

——(eds.) (1985), *Silicon Landscapes*, Boston: Allen and Unwin.

HALL, S. (1987), *Invisible Frontiers: The Race to Synthesize a Human Gene*, London: Sidgwick and Jackson.

HANNAN, M. T., and FREEMAN, J. (1977), 'The Population Ecology of Organisations', *American Journal of Sociology*, 83: 929–64.

HARRISON, B. (1992), 'Industrial Districts: Old Wine in New Bottles', *Regional Studies*, 26 (5): 469–83.

HAUSMAN, J., HALL, B., and GRILICHES, Z. (1984), 'Econometric Models for Count Data with an Application to the Patents-R & D Relationship', *Econometrica* 52: 909–38.

HAYTER, R., and PATCHELL, J. (1993), 'Different Trajectories in the Social Divisions of Labour: The Cutlery Industry in Sheffield, England and Tsubame, Japan', *Urban Studies*, 30 (8): 1427–45.

HECKMAN, J. (1979), 'Sample Selection Bias as a Specification Error', *Econometrica*, 47 (1): 153–61.

HELSLEY, R. W., and STRANGE, W. C. (1990), 'Matching and Agglomeration Economies in a System of Cities', *Regional Science and Urban Economics*, 20: 189–212.

HENDERSON, J. V. (1974), 'The Sizes and Types of Cities', *American Economic Review*, 64: 640–56.

——(1986), 'The Efficiency of Resource Usage and City Size', *Journal of Urban Economics*, 19: 47–70.

——(1994), 'Externalities and Industrial Development', *NBER Working Paper 4730*.

——(1993), 'Underinvestment and Incompetence as Responses to Radical Innovation: Evidence from the Photolithographic Alignment Equipment Industry', *RAND Journal of Economics*, 24: 248–70.

HERBIG, P., and GOLDEN, J. E. (1993*a*), 'How to Keep that Innovative Spirit Alive: An Examination of Evolving Innovative Hot-Spots', *Technology Forecasting and Social Change*, 44 (1): 75–90.

——(1993*b*), 'The Wheel of Innovation', *Technology Forecasting and Social Change*, 44 (3): 265–82.

HIPPEL, E. VON (1979), 'A Customer Active Paradigm for Industrial Product Idea Generation', in M. J. Baker (ed.), *Industrial Innovation*, London: Macmillan.

——(1980), 'The User's Role in Industrial Innovation', in B. Dean and J. Goldhar (eds.), *Management of Research and Innovation*, Amsterdam: North Holland.

——(1987), 'Cooperation between Rivals: Informal Know-how Trading', *Research Policy*, 16: 291–302.

——(1988), *The Sources of Innovation*, Oxford: Oxford University Press.

HOTELLING, H. (1929), 'The Stability of Competition', *Economic Journal*, 39: 41–57.

House of Lords (1985), *Report from the Select Committee on Overseas Trade*, vol. ii, London: HMSO.

——(1992), HL Paper 50, 1992–3 Session.

HOWELLS, J. (1984), 'The Location of Research and Development: Some Observations and Evidence from Britain', *Regional Studies*, 18: 13–29.

——(1990), 'The Location and Organisation of Research and Development: New Horizons', *Research Policy*, 19: 133–46.

——and WOOD, M. (1993), *The Globalisation of Production and Technology*, London: Belhaven Press.

HUDSON, R. (1992), 'Industrial Restructuring and Spatial Change: Myths and Realities in the Changing Geography of Production in the 1980's', Occasional Publication 27, Department of Geography, University of Durham.

HUGHES, A. (1994), 'The "Problems" of Finance for Smaller Businesses', in N. Dimsdale and M. Prevezer (eds.), *Capital Markets and Corporate Governance*, Oxford: Oxford University Press.

HYMER, S. H. (1979), 'The Multinational Corporation and the International Division of Labour', in S. Hymer and R. Cohen (eds.), *The Multinational Corporation: A Radical Approach*, Cambridge: Cambridge University Press.

ICI (1957), *Pharmaceutical Research at ICI 1936–1957*, Imperial Chemical Industries Ltd., Pharmaceuticals Research Division.

318   References

ISARD, W. (1956), *Location and Space-Economy*, Cambridge: MIT Press.
JACOBS, J. (1961), *The Death and Life of Great American Cities*, New York: Random House.
——(1969), *The Economy of Cities*, London: Penguin Books.
——(1984), *Cities and the Wealth of Nations: Principles of Economic Life*, New York: Vintage.
JAFFE, A. B. (1986), 'Technological Opportunity and Spillovers of R & D: Evidence from Firms' Patents, Profits and Market Value', *American Economic Review*, 76 (5): 984–1001.
——(1989), 'Real Effects of Academic Research', *American Economic Review*, 79: 957–70.
——TRAJTENBERG, M., and HENDERSON, R. (1993), 'Geographic Localization of Knowledge Spillovers as Evidenced by Patent Citations', *Quarterly Journal of Economics*, 108: 577–98.
JEPHCOTT, H. (1969), *Glaxo: The first 50 Years*, London: Glaxo.
JULIUSSEN, E., and JULIUSSEN, K. (1989), *Computer Industry Almanac 1989*, New York, NY: Brady.
KAMIEN, M., and SCHWARTZ, N. (1982), *Market Structure and Innovation*, Cambridge: Cambridge University Press.
KATZ, M. L., and SHAPIRO, C. (1985), 'Network Externalities, Competition and Compatibility: Innovation Product Preannouncements and Prediction', *American Economic Review*, 76: 940–55.
KEEBLE, D. (1988), 'High-Technology Industry and Local Environments in the United Kingdom', in P. Aydalot and D. Keeble (eds.), *High-Technology Industry and Innovative Environments: The European Experience*, London: Routledge.
——(1993), 'Regional Influences and Policy in New Technology Based Firm Creation and Growth', paper presented to the Conference on New Technology Based Firms in the 1990s, Manchester Business School 25–6 June.
KELLY, T. (1987), *The British Computer Industry: Crisis and Development*, London: Croom Helm.
——and KEEBLE, D. (1989), 'Locational Change and Corporate Organisation in High-Technology Industry: Computer Electronics in Great Britain', in M. Breheny and P. Hall (eds.), *The Growth and Development of High-Technology Industry: Anglo-American Perspectives*, New Jersey: Rowman and Littlefield.
KENNEDY, C. (1994), *ICI: The Company that Changed our Lives*, 2nd edn., London: Paul Chapman.
KENNEY, M. (1986), *Biotechnology: The University–Industry Complex*, New Haven: Yale University Press.
KLEPPER, S. (1996), 'Entry, Exit, Growth and Innovation over the Product Life-Cycle', *American Economic Review*, 86 (3): 562–83.
KLINE, S. J., and ROSENBERG, N. (1986), 'An Overview of Innovation', in

R. Landau and N. Rosenberg (eds.), *The Positive Sum Strategy*, Washington, DC: National Academy Press.

KODAMA, F. (1992), 'Technology Fusion and the New R & D', *Harvard Business Review* (July–Aug.), 70–8.

KOGUT, B., WALKER, G., and KIM, D. J. (1995), 'Cooperation and Entry Induction as an Extension of Technological Rivalry', *Research Policy*, 24: 77–95.

KRUGMAN, P. (1991*a*), *Geography and Trade*, Cambridge, Mass.: MIT Press.

——(1991*b*), 'Increasing Returns and Economic Geography', *Journal of Political Economy*, 99: 483–99.

LANGLOIS, R. N. (1992), 'External Economies and Economic Progress: The Case of the Microcomputer Industry', *Business History Review*, 66: 1–50.

——and ROBERTSON, P. L. (1995), *Firms, Markets, and Economic Change*, London: Routledge.

LARSEN, J. K., and ROGERS, E. M. (1984), *Silicon Valley Fever: Growth of High Technology Culture*, London: Allen and Unwin.

LAZONICK, W. (1993), 'Industry Clusters vs. Global Webs: Organisational Capabilities in the American Economy', *Industrial and Corporate Change*, 2 (1): 1–24.

LEE, K. B., and BURRILL, G. S. (1995), *Biotech 95: Reform Restructure and Renewal*, Ernst & Young Ninth Annual Report of the US Biotechnology Industry, Palo Alto: Ernst & Young.

LEIBENSTEIN, H. (1968), 'Entrepreneurship and Development', *American Economic Review* (May), 72–83.

LI, G. (1985), 'Robust Regression', in D. Hoaglin, F. Mosteller, and J. Tukey (eds.), *Exploring Data Tables, Trends and Shapes*, New York: John Wiley & Sons.

LICHTENBERG, R. (1960), *One-Tenth of a Nation*, Cambridge: Harvard University Press.

LIMPENS, I., VERSPAGEN, B., and BEELEN, E. (1992), 'Technology Policy in Eight European Countries: A Comparison', Maastricht: MERIT.

LOINGER, G., and PEYRACHE, V. (1988), 'Technological Clusters and Regional Economic Restructuring', in P. Aydalot and D. Keeble (eds.), *High-Technology Industry and Innovative Environments: The European Experience*, London: Routledge.

LÖSCH, A. (1954), *The Economics of Location*, New Haven: Yale University Press.

LOURI, H., and ANAGNOSTAKI, V. (1995), 'Entry in Greek Manufacturing Industry: Athens *vs.* the Rest of Greece', *Urban Studies*, 32 (7): 1127–33.

LUCAS, P., MULLER, A., and PIKE, W. (1994), *European Biotech 1994: A New Industry Emerges*, Brussels: Ernst & Young.

————(1995), *European Biotech 1995: Gathering Momentum*, Brussels: Ernst & Young.

Lucas, P., Muller, A., and Pike, W. (1996), *European Biotech 1996: Volatility and Value*, Brussels: Ernst & Young.

Lucas, R. (1988), 'On the Mechanics of Economic Development', *Journal of Monetary Economics*, 22: 3–42.

Lundvall, B. (1988), 'Innovation as an Interactive Process: From User–Producer Interaction to the National System of Innovation', in G. Dosi, C. Freeman, R. Nelson, G. Silverberg, and L. Soete (eds.), *Technical Change and Economic Theory*, London: Pinter Publishers.

McCrone, G. (1969), *Regional Policy in Britain*, London: Allen & Unwin.

Macdonald, S. (1987), 'British Science Parks: Reflections on the Politics of High Technology', *R & D Management*, 17 (1): 25–37.

McKelvey, M. (1994), *Evolutionary Innovation: Early Industrial Uses of Genetic Engineering*, Linköping: Department of Technology and Social Change, forthcoming Oxford University Press.

Maclean, M., and Rowland, T. (1985), *The Inmos Saga: A Triumph of National Enterprise?*, London: Francis Pinter Publishers.

Maillat, D., and Vasserot, J. (1988), 'Economic and Territorial Conditions for Indigenous Revival in Europe's Industrial Regions', in P. Aydalot and D. Keeble (eds.), *High-Technology Industry and Innovative Environments: The European Experience*, London: Routledge.

Malecki, E. J. (1980), 'Dimensions of R & D Location in the United States', *Research Policy*, 9: 2–22.

Malerba, F., and Orsenigo, L. (1990), 'Technological Regimes and Patterns of Innovation: A Theoretical and Empirical Investigation of the Italian Case', in A. Heertje and M. Perlman (eds.), *Evolving Technologies and Market Structure*, Cambridge: Cambridge University Press.

——— (1993), 'Technological Regimes and Firm Behaviour', *Industrial and Corporate Change*, 2 (1): 45–71.

Markusen, A. (1987), 'Government as Market: Industrial Location in the US Defence Industry', in H. W. Herzog and A. M. Schlottmann (eds.), *Industry Location and Public Policy*, Knoxville: University of Tennessee Press.

Marshall, A. (1920), *Principles of Economics*, 8th edn., London: Macmillan.

——— (1927), *Industry and Trade*, London: Macmillan.

Martin, P. J., and Rogers, C. A. (1994), 'Industrial Location and Public Infrastructure', *CEPR* Discussion Paper 909.

Massey, D. (1984), *Social Divisions of Labour: Social Structures and the Geography of Production*, London: Macmillan.

——— et al. (1992), *High Tech Fantasies: Science Parks in Society, Science and Space*, London: Routledge.

Mathias, P. (1983), *The First Industrial Nation: An Economic History of Britain 1700–1914*, 2nd edn., London: Routledge.

MAYER, W., and CHAPPELL, W. (1994), 'Determinants of Entry and Exit: An Application of the Compounded Bivariate Poisson Distribution to U.S. Industries, 1972–77', *Southern Economic Journal* (Apr.), 770–8.

MENSCH, G. (1979), *Stalemate in Technology: Innovations Overcome the Depression*, Cambridge, Mass.: Ballinger.

METCALFE, J. S., and BODEN, M. (1993), 'Paradigms, Strategies and the Evolutionary Basis of Technological Competition', ch. 4 of G. M. P. Swann (ed.), *New Technologies and the Firm*, London: Routledge.

MONCK, C. S. P., PORTER, R. B., QUINTAS, P. R., STOREY, D. J., and WYNARCZYK, P. (1988), *Science Parks and the Growth of High Technology Firms*, London: Croom Helm.

MORRIS, D. (1994), 'Problems of Corporate Control', in T. Buxton, P. Chapman, and P. Temple (eds.), *Britain's Economic Performance*, London: Routledge.

Mowery, D. C. (1995), 'The Practice of Technology Policy', in P. Stoneman (ed.), *Handbook of Economics and Technological Change*, Oxford: Blackwell.

——and ROSENBERG, N. (1989), *Technology and the Pursuit of Economic Growth*, Cambridge: Cambridge University Press.

MUMFORD, L. (1961), *The City in History*, London: Penguin Books.

MURRAY, G. C., and LOTT, J. (1995), 'Have UK Venture Capitalists a Bias against Investment in New Technology Firms?' *Research Policy*, 24: 283–99.

NADIRI, M. I., and MAMUNEAS, T. P. (1991), 'The Effects of Public Infrastructure and R & D Capital on the Cost Structure and Performance of US Manufacturing Industries', *NBER Working Paper* 3887.

————(1994), 'Infrastructure and Public R & D Investments, and the Growth of Factor Productivity in US Manufacturing Industries', *NBER Working Paper* 4845.

NELSON, R. R. (1984), *High Technology Policies: A Five Nation Comparison*, Washington, DC: American Enterprise Institute.

——(1993), *National Systems of Innovation*, Oxford: Oxford University Press.

——and Winter, S. G. (1982), *An Evolutionary Theory of Economic Change*, Cambridge, Mass.: Harvard University Press.

OAKEY, R. (1985), 'High Technology Industry and Agglomeration Economies', in P. Hall and A. Markusen (eds.), *Silicon Landscapes*, Boston: Allen and Unwin.

——FAULKNER, W., COOPER, S., and WALSH, V. (1990), *New Firms in the Biotechnology Industry*, London: Pinter.

ODAGIRI, H. (1992), *Growth through Competition and Competition through Growth*, Oxford: Oxford University Press.

OECD (1996), *Employment Outlook*, Paris: OECD.

ORR, D. (1974), 'The Determinants of Entry: A Study of the Canadian

322   *References*

Manufacturing Industries', *Review of Economics and Statistics*, 61: 58–66.

ORSENIGO, L. (1989), *The Emergence of Biotechnology*, London: Pinter Publishers.

OST (1995), *Technology Foresight Report 4: Health and Life Sciences*, Office of Science and Technology, London: HMSO.

OSTRY, S. (1991), 'Beyond the Border: The New International Policy Arena', in OECD, *Strategic Industries in a Global Economy*, Paris: OECD.

PATEL, P. (1995), 'Localised Production of Technology for Global Markets', *Cambridge Journal of Economics*, 19: 141–53.

PAVITT, K. (1987), *On the Nature of Technology*, Brighton: University of Sussex, Science Policy Research Unit.

——ROBSON, M., and TOWNSEND, J. (1987), 'The Size Distribution of Innovating Firms in the UK: 1945–1983', *Journal of Industrial Economics*, 35: 297–316.

PECK, S., and Temple, P. (1996), 'Understanding Competitiveness: The Determinants of Industrial Performance in the OECD Economies 1973–1992', presented to Economic History Society Conference, Lancaster, 30 Mar.

PERROUX, F. (1950), 'Economic Space: Theory and Applications', *Quarterly Journal of Economics*, 64 (1): 89–104.

PHILPOTT, J. C. (1989), 'Public Policy and Local Development: The Case of Stevenage New Town', in D. Gibbs (ed.), *Government Policy and Industrial Change*, London: Routledge, 266–85.

PIORE, M., and SABEL, C. (1984), *The Second Industrial Divide: Possibilities for Prosperity*, New York: Basic Books.

PORTER, M. E. (1990), *The Competitive Advantage of Nations*, London: Macmillan.

POWELL, W. W., and BRANTLEY, P. (1992), 'Competitive Cooperation in Biotechnology: Learning through Networks', in N. Nohria and R. G. Eccles (eds.), *Networks and Organisations: Structure Form and Action*, Boston, Mass.: Harvard Business School Press, 366–94.

PREVEZER, M. (1996), 'The Dynamics of Industrial Clustering in Biotechnology', *Small Business Economics*, 8: 1–17.

——and LOMI, A. (1995), 'Networks for Innovation in Biotechnology', *Centre for Business Strategy Working Paper No. 159*, London Business School, December, forthcoming in J. Butler and A. Piccaluga (eds.), *Knowledge, Technology and Innovation*, Milan: Guerini e Associati.

——and SHOHET, S. (1996), 'New Knowledge: Production versus Diffusion: The Case of UK Biotechnology', *Centre for Business Strategy Working Paper 162*, London Business School.

——and TEMPLE, P. (1994), 'Britain's Economic Performance: The Strategic Dimension', *Business Strategy Review*, Autumn 5 (3): 35–48.

——and TOKER, S. (1996), 'The Degree of Integration in Strategic Alliances in Biotechnology', *Technology Analysis and Strategic Management*, 8 (2): 117–33.

QUINTAS, P., and GUY, K. (1995), 'Collaborative Pre-competitive R & D and the Firm', *Research Policy*, 24: 325–48.

RAMON, S. (1988), *The Business of Science*, New York: Hill & Wang.

REICH, R. (1991), *The Work of Nations: Preparing Ourselves for 21st Century Capitalism*, New York: Knopf.

Research Centers USA (1991), *Research Centers Directory USA*, Detroit MI: Gale Research Inc.

ROBERTSON, P., and LANGLOIS, R. (1995), 'Innovation Networks and Vertical Integration', *Research Policy*, 24: 543–62.

ROMER, P. (1986), 'Increasing Returns and Long Run Growth', *Journal of Political Economy*, 94: 1002–37.

——(1990), 'Endogenous Technological Change', *Journal of Political Economy*, 98: S71–S102.

ROSENBERG, N. (1976), *Perspectives on Technology*, Cambridge: Cambridge University Press.

ROSENBLOOM, R., and CHRISTENSEN, C. (1994), 'Technological Discontinuities, Organisational Capabilities, and Strategic Commitments', *Industrial and Corporate Change*, 3 (3): 655–85.

ROUSSEOUW, P., and LEROY, A. (1987), *Robust Regression and Outlier Detection*, New York: John Wiley & Sons.

RUBINSTEIN, J. M. (1992), *The Changing US Auto Industry: A Geographical Analysis*, London: Routledge.

SABEL, C. (1989), 'Flexible Specialisation and the Re-emergence of Regional Economies', in P. Hirst and J. Zeitlin (eds.), *Reversing Industrial Decline? Industrial Structure and Policy in Britain and Her Competitors*, Oxford: Berg Publishers.

SAKO, M. (1995), 'Suppliers Associations in the Japanese Automobile Industry: Collective Action for Technology Diffusion', *Centre for Economic Policy Research*, DP series no. 1147.

SAXENIAN, A. (1985a), 'The Genesis of Silicon Valley', in P. Hall and A. Markusen (eds.), *Silicon Landscapes*, Boston: Allen & Unwin.

——(1985b), 'Silicon Valley and Route 128: Regional Prototypes or Historical Exceptions?', in M. Castells (ed.), *High Technology, Space and Society*, Beverly Hills, Calif.: Sage.

——(1990), 'Regional Networks and the Resurgence of Silicon Valley', *California Management Review*, 33: 89–111.

——(1994), *Regional Advantage: Culture and Competition in Silicon Valley and Route 128*, Cambridge, Mass.: Harvard University Press.

SCHERER, F. M. (1982), 'Inter-industry Technology Flows and Productivity Growth', *Review of Economics and Statistics*, 64: 627–34.

SCHERER, F. M. (1984), 'Using Linked Patent and R & D Data to Measure Inter-industry Technology Flows', in Z. Griliches (ed.), *R & D, Patents and Productivity*, Chicago: University of Chicago Press.

——and Ross, D. (1990), *Industrial Market Structure and Economic Performance*, Boston: Houghton Mifflin.

SCHUMPETER, J. A. (1928), 'The Instability of Capitalism', *Economic Journal*, 38: 361–86.

——(1934), *The Theory of Economic Development*, Cambridge: Harvard University Press.

——(1939), *Business Cycles: A Theoretical, Historical and Statistical Analysis*, vols. i, ii, New York: McGraw Hill.

——(1943), *Capitalism, Socialism and Democracy*, London: Allen and Unwin.

SCITOVSKY, T. (1963), 'Two Concepts of External Economies', repr. in A. N. Agrawala and S. P. Singh (eds.), *The Economics of Underdevelopment*, Oxford: Oxford University Press.

SCOTT, A. J. (1988), *New Industrial Spaces: Flexible Production Organisation and Regional Development in North America and Western Europe*, London: Pion.

——(1994), 'The Geographic Foundations of Industrial Performance', presented at the Prince Bertil Symposium, Stockholm.

SCOTT, M. (1994), *Technopolis*, Berkeley and Los Angeles: University of California Press.

SEGAL, N., and QUINCE, R. (1985), 'The Cambridge Phenomenon: The Growth of High Technology Industry in a University Town', Segal Quince and Partners.

SHARP, M. (1994), 'Innovation in the Chemicals Industry', in M. Dodgson and R. Rothwell (eds.), *The Handbook of Industrial Innovation*, London, Edward Elgar, 169–81.

——and Walker, W. (1994), 'Thatcherism and Technical Advance: Reform without Progress?', in T. Buxton, P. Chapman, and P. Temple (eds.), *Britain's Economic Performance*, London: Routledge.

SHEPHERD, J. (1987), 'Industrial Support Policies', *National Economic and Social Review*, 122: 59–71.

SHOHET, S. (1994), 'Painting UK Biotech by Numbers', *Bio/Technology*, 12 (10) European Supplement, 5–7.

——(1996), 'Industry and UK Science Policy', London Business School mimeo.

——and PREVEZER, M. (1996), 'UK Biotechnology: Institutional Linkages, Technology Transfer and the Role of Intermediaries', *R & D Management*, 26 (3): 283–98.

SILVER, M. (1984), *Enterprise and the Scope of the Firm*, London: Martin Robertson.

SIMON, H. (1985), 'What do we Know about the Creative Process?', in

R. L. Kuhn (ed.), *Frontiers in Creative and Innovative Management*, 3–20, Cambridge, Mass.: Ballinger.

SLAUGHTER, S. (1993), 'Innovation and Learning during Implementation: A Comparison of User and Manufacturer Innovations', *Research Policy*, 22: 81–95.

SMALL, I., and SWANN, P. (1993), 'R & D Performance of UK Companies', *Business Strategy Review* 4 (3) (Autumn), 41–51.

SMITH, D. (1971), *Industrial Location: An Economic Geographical Analysis*, New York: Wiley.

SPENCE, M. (1984), 'Cost Reduction, Competition and Industry Performance', *Econometrica*, 52: 101–21.

STAHL, K. (1987), 'Theories of Urban Business Location', in E. Mills (ed.), *Handbook of Regional and Urban Economics*, vol. ii, Elsevier Science Publishers.

STEADMAN, A. (1993), 'Survey of Hertfordshire: Mutual Encouragement—Employment in Stevenage is Moving to the Services Sector', *Financial Times*, 28 Apr.

STEIN, J. (1989), 'Efficient Capital Markets, Inefficient Firms: A Model of Myopic Corporate Behaviour', *Quarterly Journal of Economics*, 104: 655–70.

STEPHAN, P. (1994), 'Differences in the Post-Entry Value of Biotech Firms: The Role of Human Capital', presented to the Conference on the Post Entry Performance of Firms, Lisbon, 22–8 May.

STONE, R. (1971), *Mathematical Models of the Economy and Other Essays*, London: Chapman and Hall.

STORPER, M., and HARRISON, B. (1991), 'Flexibility, Hierarchy and Regional Development: The Changing Structure of Industrial Production Systems and their Forms of Governance in the 1990s', *Research Policy*, 20: 407–22.

STOUT, D. K. (1995), 'The Foresight Process', *Science, Technology and Innovation* (Science Policy), 8 (5): 22–5.

SWANN, G. M. P. (1990), 'Product Competition and the Dimensions of Product Space', *International Journal of Industrial Organisation*, 8 (2): 281–95.

——(1992a), 'Rapid Technology Change, "Technological Visions", Corporate Organisation and Market Structure', *Economics of Innovation and New Technology*, 2 (2): 3–25.

——(1992b), 'Standards, Beneficial Competition and Market Failure', *Proceedings of the International Conference on the Value of Competition*, Milan, 28–39.

——(1993a), 'Identifying Asymmetric Competitor Networks from Characteristics Data: Application to the Spreadsheet Software Market', *Economic Journal*, 103: 468–73.

——(1993b), 'Can High Technology Services Prosper if High Technology

Manufacturing Doesn't?', *Centre for Business Strategy Working Paper* 143, London Business School.

SWANN, G. M. P. (1993c), 'Clusters in High Technology Industries', *Business Economist*, 25 (1): 27–36.

—— (1996), 'Technology Evolution and the Rise and Fall of Industrial Clusters', *Revue internationale de systémique*, 10 (3): 285–302.

—— (forthcoming 1998), 'Innovation and the Rise, Fall and Renaissance of Industrial Clusters in Europe', in F. Malerba and A. Gambardella (eds.), *The Organisation of Innovative Activities in Europe*, Cambridge: Cambridge University Press.

—— and GILL, J. (1993), *Corporate Vision and Rapid Technological Change: The Evolution of Market Structure*, London: Routledge.

—— and PREVEZER, M. J. (1996), 'A Comparison of the Dynamics of Industrial Clustering in Computing and Biotechnology', *Research Policy*, 25: 1139–57.

—— TEMPLE, P., and SHURMER, M. (1996), 'Standards and Trade Performance: The UK Experience', *Economic Journal*, 106 (438): 1297–313.

TASSEY, G. (1991), 'The Functions of Technology Infrastructure in a Competitive Economy', *Research Policy*, 20: 329–43.

TAYLOR, T. (1985), 'High Technology Industry and the Development of Science Parks', in P. Hall and A. Markusen (eds.), *Silicon Landscapes*, Boston: Allen & Unwin.

TEECE, D. (1986a), 'Transaction Cost Economics and the Multinational Enterprise: An Assessment', *Journal of Economic Behaviour and Organisation*, 7: 21–45.

—— (1986b), 'Profiting from Technological Innovation: Implications for Integration, Collaboration, Licensing and Public Policy', *Research Policy*, 15: 285–305.

TEITELMAN, R. (1989), *Gene Dreams: Wall Street, Academia and the Rise of Biotechnology*, New York, Basic Books Inc.

TEMPLE, P. (1995), 'The Competitiveness White Papers: What Lessons for Industrial Policy', *Centre for Industrial Policy and Performance Bulletin*, no. 8 (Summer).

—— and URGA, G. (1996), 'The Competitivness of UK Imports: Evidence from Manufacturing', *Centre for Business Strategy Working Paper*, London Business School.

TERLECKYJ, N. (1980), 'Direct and Indirect Effects of Industrial Research and Development on the Productivity Growth of Industries', in J. N. Kendrick and B. N. Vaccara (eds.), *New Developments in Productivity Measurement and Analysis*, Chicago: University of Chicago Press.

THOMPSON, W. R. (1962), 'Locational Differences in Inventive Effort and their Determinants', in R. R. Nelson (ed.), *The Rate and Direction of Inventive Activity*, Princeton University Press.

THWAITES, A. T. (1982), 'Some Evidence of Regional Variation in the

Introduction and Diffusion of Industrial Processes within British Manufacturing Industry', *Regional Studies*, 16: 371–81.

TIEBOUT, C. M. (1956), 'A Pure Theory of Local Expenditures', *Journal of Political Economy* 64: 416–24.

TUSHMAN, M. L., and ANDERSON, P. (1986), 'Technological Discontinuities and Organisational Environments', *Administrative Science Quarterly*, 31 (3): 439–65.

University Funding Council (UFC) (1992), 'Research Assessment Exercise 1992: The Outcome', Circular 26/92, Bristol.

WATKINS, T. A. (1991), 'A Model of R & D Consortia as Public Policy', *Research Policy*, 20: 87–107.

WEBB, J., and CLEARY, D. (1993), 'Supplier–User Relationships and the Management of Expertise in Computer Systems Development', ch. 5 of P. Swann (ed.), *New Technologies and the Firm*, London: Routledge.

WEBER, A. (1928), *Theory of the Location of Industries*, trans. C. J. Friedrich, Chicago: Chicago University Press (originally published in German in 1909).

WEBSTER, A. (1989), 'Privatisation of Public Research: The Case of a Plant Breeding Institute', *Science and Public Policy*, 16 (4): 224–32.

Wellcome (1980), *One Hundred Years of Wellcome 1880–1980*, Wellcome Foundation.

WHITE, H. (1980), 'A Heteroskedasticity-Consistent Covariance Matrix Estimator and a Direct Test for Heteroskedasticity', *Econometrica*, 48 (4): 817–38.

WILLIAMSON, O. (1985), *The Economic Institutions of Capitalism*, New York: Free Press.

——(1993), 'Transaction Cost Economics and Organisation Theory', *Industrial and Corporate Change*, 2 (2): 107–56.

ZANDER, I., and SÖLVELL, O. (1995), 'Determinants of Local Technological Activity: Implications for Innovation in the Multinational Firm', paper presented at the EMOT Workshop on Technology and the Theory of the Firm, University of Reading, May.

ZUCKER, L., and DARBY, M. (1995), 'Virtuous Circles of Productivity: Star Bioscientists and the Institutional Transformation of Industry', *National Bureau of Economic Research Working Paper 5342*, Cambridge, Mass.

————and BREWER, M. (1994), 'Intellectual Capital and the Birth of US Biotechnology Enterprises', *National Bureau of Economic Research Working Paper 4653*, Cambridge, Mass.

Index

Note: **emboldened** page numbers show major chapter entries

Index